Down Country Roads

Home Cooking

Copyright © 2007 High Plains Publishers, Inc.
Contents previously published in 2004

HIGH PLAINS/MIDWEST AG
JOURNAL ™

Home Cookin' is a collection of tried and true recipes. Some of the recipes have been made for generations while others are new creations that have quickly become family favorites.

The recipes in *Home Cookin'* were entered in the *Journal's* third recipe contest. While many of them are sure to become winners in your home, you'll find the contest-winning dishes featured on the dividers of this book.

This third book of *High Plains/Midwest Ag Journal's Down Country Roads* cookbook collection holds recipes that are sure to stand the test of time with your family!

TABLE OF CONTENTS

FAVORITE RECIPES
FROM MY COOKBOOK

Recipe Name	Page Number

Published and Printed By
Cookbook Publishers, Inc.
P.O. Box 15920
Lenexa, Kansas 66285-5920

Appetizers & Snacks

Appetizers & Snacks Recipe Contest Winners

First
Hot Rueben Dip
Brandi Jecha, Timken, Kansas
Page 17

Second
Macadamia Popcorn
Iola Egle, Bella Vista, Arkansas
Page 19

Third
Mocha Punch
Mabel Penner, Whitewater, Kansas
Page 20

APPETIZERS AND SNACKS

ALMOND BARK TREAT

Flo M. Burtnett
Gage, OK

2 lb. vanilla almond bark	1 c. peanut butter
3 c. Rice Krispies cereal	2 c. mini-marshmallows

Place almond bark and peanut butter in microwave safe bowl. Microwave on high for 30 seconds. Stir and return to microwave oven for 30 more seconds. Continue this procedure until almond bark and peanut butter are well mixed and smooth. Add Rice Krispies and put them in the refrigerator if you want them firm more quickly.

ANTIPASTO SPREAD

Jean Lorenz
Sanford, CO

2 (4 oz.) cans mushroom stems and pieces, drained and finely chopped	½ c. celery, finely chopped
	¾ c. red wine vinegar
	¾ c. olive oil
1 (14 oz.) can artichoke hearts, drained and finely chopped	2 Tbsp. instant minced onions
	2½ tsp. dried oregano leaves
1 (10 oz.) jar pimento stuffed olives, drained and finely chopped	1 tsp. onion salt
	1 tsp. salt
	1 tsp. seasoned salt
1 (6 oz.) can black olives, drained and finely chopped	1 tsp. garlic salt
	1 tsp. sugar
¼ c. green pepper, finely chopped	1 tsp. cracked black pepper

Combine mushrooms, artichoke hearts, pimento stuffed olives, black olives, green pepper, and celery; mix well. Set aside. Combine vinegar, olive oil, instant onions, dried oregano leaves, onion salt, seasoned salt, garlic salt, sugar, and black pepper in a saucepan; bring to a boil. Pour dressing over vegetables; place in a large jar with a tight-fitting lid. Shake jar to stir ingredients. Refrigerate overnight. Serve spread with assorted crackers. Yields 7 cups.

APRICOT CHEWS

Carol F. Mandrell
Olton, TX

1 c. dried apricots,
  chopped
1 c. sweetened condensed
  milk

1 tsp. sugar
2 Tbsp. lemon juice
1 Tbsp. flour
2 c. pecans, chopped

Mix all together. Drop on well greased cookie sheet in bite-size servings. Bake 20 minutes at 300°F and remove immediately from pan to cooling racks.

BEAN DIP SUPREME

Bobbi Higgs
Ulysses, KS

1 can refried beans
1 (small) container sour
  cream

1 (small) can green chiles
1 c. Cheddar-Monterey
  Jack cheese

Mix refried beans with ½ can of water. Warm on stove. Puree the can of green chiles until smooth. Place warm beans in serving bowl; add green chiles, sour cream, and shredded cheeses. Mix at table and serve with warm tortilla chips.

BEST EGG SPREAD

Amber Uhlenhake
Ossian, IA

6 hard boiled eggs, diced
1 (8 oz.) pkg. cream
  cheese
2 c. cheese, shredded
1 pkg. dry Ranch salad
  dressing mix

1 c. pecans or other nut,
  chopped
½ c. peppers, diced

In a large bowl, mix together the cream cheese, shredded cheese, dressing mix, and eggs. Form into a log or ball. Mix the nuts with the pepper and roll the cheese mix into it. Chill for at least 2 hours and serve with crackers.

CAPPUCCINO MIX

Flo M. Burtnett
Gage, OK

1 c. instant coffee creamer (non-dairy)	½ c. sugar
1 c. instant chocolate drink mix	½ tsp. cinnamon
⅔ c. instant coffee crystals	¼ tsp. nutmeg

Combine and mix all ingredients well. Store in an airtight container. To prepare one serving, add 3 tablespoons mix to a cup. Add 6 ounces hot water. Stir. Makes 3 cups dry mix.

CARAMEL CHEWS

Gwenda Batterman
Amarillo, TX

2 c. Rice Krispies cereal	1 c. pecans, chopped
1 c. Corn Flakes cereal	36 caramels
1 c. coconut (do not pack)	3 Tbsp. evaporated milk

Mix Rice Krispies, Corn Flakes, coconut, and pecans together. Melt caramels and milk in microwave. Pour over mix. Stir until coated. Wet hands with water and form loosely into balls. Forming too tightly will cause them to dry out and become hard more quickly.

CARROT DIP

Margaret Trojan
Beaver Crossing, NE

½ (of an 8 oz.) container sour cream	¼ tsp. salt
½ (of an 8 oz.) pkg. cream cheese, softened	¼ tsp. black pepper
¼ c. mayonnaise or salad dressing	1½ c. carrots, finely chopped
2 tsp. soy sauce	⅓ c. green onions, chopped
1½ tsp. prepared horseradish, optional	

In medium bowl, beat together sour cream, cream cheese, mayonnaise, soy sauce, horseradish if using, salt, pepper and mix until smooth. Stir in shredded carrots and onions until combined. Cover and chill 4 to 24 hours. Stir the dip before serving. Makes 2 servings.

Do not prepare more than 24 hours in advance as the dip will become too thin.

CHEESE BALL

Julie Haverland
Deepwater, MO

2 (8 oz.) pkg. cream cheese, soften to room temperature
1 (small) container small curd cottage cheese

1 pkg. dry buttermilk Ranch salad dressing mix
1 lb. ham, diced small

In a large bowl, mix cream cheese, cottage cheese, and dressing mix together. (Use heavy duty mixer or mix with hands.) Add ham. Form into a ball and cover with plastic wrap or put into a serving bowl.

CHEESE BALL

Kim Oborny
Durham, KS

2 (8 oz.) pkg. cream cheese (regular-no substitutions)
1 c. crushed pineapple, well drained
½ c. green pepper, chopped fine

2 tsp. minced onion
1 tsp. garlic salt
1 tsp. seasoned salt
½ c. pecans, chopped

In a bowl, combine cream cheese (let soften a little to make it easier to mix), pineapple, green pepper, minced onion, garlic salt, seasoned salt, and 1 to 2 tablespoons of the pecans. Mix well. Should form a nice ball. Place remaining pecans in a shallow bowl or shallow tray. Roll the cream cheese ball in pecans to coat the outside. Place on serving dish and serve with cheese or club crackers.

CHEESE BALL

Diane Meisinger
Hillsboro, KS

2 (8 oz.) pkg. cream cheese
10 to 12 oz. Cheddar cheese, shredded
1 (small) can crushed pineapple, drained well
3 Tbsp. green onion, chopped
1 Tbsp. Worcestershire sauce
Pecans

In large bowl, soften cream cheese in microwave until you can stir it. Add Cheddar cheese, crushed pineapple, onions, and Worcestershire sauce and stir until well blended. Refrigerate for an hour and then divide into 2 balls. Roll each section into finely chopped pecans. Serve with crackers.

This will keep in the refrigerator for up to 7 days.

CHEESE KRISPS

Carol F. Mandrell
Olton, TX

2 sticks margarine
1 (10 oz.) pkg. sharp Cheddar cheese
½ c. Parmesan cheese
1½ tsp. salt
1 tsp. paprika
½ tsp. cayenne pepper
2 c. flour
2 c. Rice Krispies cereal

Grate the Cheddar cheese and melt the margarine. Mix together and add the Parmesan cheese. Mix. Sift the dry ingredients and mix into the first mixture. Add Rice Krispies; mix well. Roll in small balls, place on greased cookie sheet, and flatten with a fork. Bake at 350°F. for 10 to 12 minutes. Makes about 75 krispies.

CHEESE LOG

Kelly Moore
Topeka, KS

1 lb. processed American cheese
1 (8 oz.) pkg. cream cheese
1 (small) jar pimento, chopped
1 (small) can green chilies, chopped
1 to 2 green onions, chopped
1 c. pecans, chopped

Soften cheeses to room temperature. Put wax paper on top and bottom then roll processed cheese out into a rectangle, not too thin, with a rolling pin. Spread cream cheese, pimento, green chilies, and green onions. Roll with wax paper as in a jellyroll. Press pecans on outside of roll. Chill and serve with crackers.

CHEX MIX

Donna Evans
Turpin, OK

1 (12 oz.) can mixed nuts
1 (8 oz.) bag plain M&M candies
1 (8 oz.) bag peanut M&M candies
1 (98 oz.) bag small pretzels

5 c. Cheerios cereal
5 c. Rice Chex cereal
1 (22 to 24 oz.) pkg. vanilla almond bark
3 Tbsp. vegetable oil

Using a large container (the top of a heavy plastic angel food carrier works well), mix all ingredients except almond bark and oil. Place almond bark and vegetable oil in glass container, microwave on medium high until melted. Stir occasionally. Pour melted almond bark over dry ingredients and stir until coated. After the mixture has cooled, break in pieces. Store in zip lock bags.

Instead of using mixed nuts and M&M candies, I sometimes use purchased trail mix which includes raisins. Sometimes I substitute small butter crackers. This recipe makes nice gifts.

CHILI CHEX MIX

Merrill Powers
Spearville, KS

4 c. Corn Chex cereal
4 c. Cheerios cereal
4 c. pretzel sticks
4 c. cheese-flavored snack crackers
1 c. margarine, melted
½ c. vegetable oil

3 Tbsp. Worcestershire sauce
1 Tbsp. garlic powder
1 Tbsp. seasoned salt
1 Tbsp. chili powder
1 tsp. cayenne pepper

In a large roasting pan, combine the cereals, pretzels, and crackers. Combine the margarine, oil, Worcestershire sauce, and seasonings; stir. Pour over cereal mixture and toss to coat. Bake at 225°F. for 2 to 2½ hours, stirring every 30 minutes. Store in airtight containers; freezes well. Yield: 16 cups.

This is a spicy twist for chex mix.

CHOCOLATE CARAMEL FONDUE

Amber Jeans
Tonkawa, OK

1 (14 oz.) can sweetened
  condensed milk
1 (12 oz.) jar caramel ice
  cream topping

3 (1 oz.) sq. unsweetened
  chocolate
Assorted fresh fruit
Pretzels

In saucepan, combine milk, caramel topping, and chocolate. Cook over low heat until chocolate is melted. Serve with fruit or pretzels. This is wonderful with strawberries, orange slices, apple slices, and bananas.

CHRISTMAS MEATBALLS

Mabel Penner
Whitewater, KS

2 eggs
1 pkg. onion soup mix
½ c. seasoned bread
  crumbs
¼ c. dried cranberries,
  chopped
2 Tbsp. fresh parsley,
  minced
1½ lb. ground beef

1 (16 oz.) can whole-berry
  cranberry sauce
¾ c. ketchup
½ c. beef broth
3 Tbsp. brown sugar
3 Tbsp. onion, finely
  chopped
2 tsp. cider vinegar

In a bowl, combine eggs, soup mix, bread crumbs, cranberries, and parsley. Crumble beef over mixture and mix well. Shape into 1 inch balls; place 12 to 14 balls on a microwave safe plate. Cover with waxed paper, microwave on high 3 to 4 minutes or until no longer pink. Remove to paper towels to drain. Repeat with remaining meatballs. In a 2 quart microwave safe dish, combine ketchup, beef broth, brown sugar, onion, and vinegar to make sauce. Cover and microwave on high for 3 to 4 minutes or until heated through, rotating once. Gently stir in meatballs. Cover and cook on high for 1 to 2 minutes or until heated through. Yields about 3 dozen.

CINNAMON QUICK BITES

Tammy Bell
Osawatomie, KS

1 loaf (thin sliced) sandwich bread	Margarine, softened
	Cinnamon
1 (8 oz.) pkg. cream cheese, softened	Sugar

Cut crusts off bread. Flatten each slice with a rolling pin. Spread each piece with a layer of cream cheese. Roll slices of bread tightly; cut rolls into bite-size pieces. Dip each roll into melted butter and then roll in cinnamon and sugar. Bake on cookie sheet at 350°F. until rolls are bubbly and puffy.

Bites can be frozen and baked later. This is a great finger food for showers, brunches, or an after school snack. This is a snack the kids can help make.

CORN DIP

Roxie Berning
Marienthal, KS

2 cans Mexican style corn, drained	1 c. Cheddar cheese, shredded
1 c. mayonnaise	¼ tsp. garlic salt
1 c. sour cream	1 Tbsp. onion, chopped

Mix all together and serve with crackers or chips.

CRAB DIP

Tammy Bell
Osawatomie, KS

2 (8 oz.) pkg. cream cheese, softened	⅛ tsp. garlic salt
¼ c. onion, chopped	1 c. Ranch salad dressing
1 c. imitation crabmeat, chopped	

Mix all ingredients and chill. Serve with crackers.

I usually halve the recipe as it makes quite a bit.

8

CRANBERRY DIP

Diane Denny
Jacksonville, FL

2 c. sour cream
1 can whole berry
   cranberries

1 Tbsp. lemon juice
½ c. nuts, chopped
   (optional)

Mix the ingredients together and chill until ready to serve. Surround the bowl with a choice of crackers for dipping.

A refreshing difference to your normal "chip and dip".

CREAM CHEESE CORN DIP

Pat Habiger
Spearville, KS

2 (8 oz.) pkg. cream
   cheese, softened
1 (4 oz.) pkg. dry Ranch
   salad dressing mix
1 (16 oz.) can whole
   kernel corn, drained

1 (8 oz.) can black olives
1 sweet red pepper, finely
   chopped
2 jalapeno peppers,
   chopped

Mix cream cheese with dry dressing mix. Drain corn; add to cream cheese. Add olives, pepper, and jalapeno peppers; mix well. Serve with crackers, chips, or raw veggies. Yield: 20 servings.

I like to use carrot sticks and celery as this is cool with the hot peppers.

CREAM CHEESE ROLL-UPS

Danielle Crouch
Estancia, NM

4 (large) whole flour
   tortillas
1 (8 oz.) pkg. cream
   cheese
12 to 15 thinly sliced
   turkey, ham, roast beef
   (meat of your choice)

Taco seasoning or
   seasoned salt (flavoring
   of your choice)
6 to 8 slices American
   cheese (sandwich slices)

Bring cream cheese to room temperature; spread evenly and generously over tortilla, leaving fingernail length space from all edges except one small part. Dash seasoning of your choice lightly over cream cheese, then arrange thinly sliced meat, overlapping in the center to leave edge on the outside of tortilla. Top meat with sandwich cheese only across the center going left to right on the tortilla, keeping edge with cream cheese at the 12 o'clock position. Warm tortilla in microwave just long enough to make tortilla soft. Place edge of tortilla covered with cream cheese away from you and begin to roll tight enough that tortilla doesn't crack. Keep in mind that the cream cheese will spread when you begin to roll. Rolled up tortilla should be about the size of a half dollar. Use the cream cheese edge to seal up wrap. Place seam side down onto a plate and continue making the other rolls. Cover with plastic wrap and chill for 1 to 2 hours, until firm. Remove from cold and slice ends off of the rolls, then slice into ¼ inch slices. Arrange onto a serving platter, alternating meat varieties for a nice presentation. Cover with plastic wrap and keep cool until time to serve.

You can use a variety of meats, sliced cheeses, and spices to suit you and your guest's tastes.

CREAMY CRAB DIP

Joan Stegman
Offerle, KS

¼ c. mayonnaise
¼ c. sour cream
1 tsp. Old Bay seasoning
1 tsp. fresh lemon juice
1 (6 oz.) can white
   crabmeat, drained and
   picked over

2 green onions, finely
   chopped
2 Tbsp. red bell pepper,
   chopped
Salt, freshly ground
   pepper

In a medium bowl, mix mayonnaise, sour cream, seasoning, and lemon juice until smooth. Add crab, green onions, and pepper stir until ingredients are well combined. Season to taste with salt and pepper.

DIPPEY DO

Juanita Gross
Clearwater, KS

1 c. salad dressing
½ c. ketchup

2 tsp. bottled horseradish
   (or to taste)

Mix all ingredients thoroughly.

Great dip with shrimp or fried fish.

DOUBLE NUTTY BISCOTTI

Iola Egle
Bella Vista, AR

1½ c. blanched whole almonds
½ c. hazelnuts
4 c. all-purpose flour
2 tsp. baking powder
1 tsp. cinnamon
5 eggs
½ c. unsalted butter, melted and cooled
2 c. sugar

Lay almonds in single layer on cookie sheet and toast in 375°F. oven until golden color, about 10 minutes. Cool. Grind ½ cup of the almonds fine. Toast hazelnuts until the skins crack. Remove the skins by placing in a towel and rubbing off the skins as much as possible. Chop coarsely. Reduce oven temperature to 350°F. Butter cookie sheets lightly. Combine and sift together flour, baking powder, and cinnamon. Add all the almonds and hazelnuts. In a large bowl, whisk eggs until frothy. Add butter and sugar; mix until combined. Add flour-nut mixture. The dough will be rather sticky, but shape into four 12 x 2½ inch logs. Place four inches apart on parchment paper on cookie sheet. Smooth tops. Bake 25 minutes or until firm when pressed in the center. Gently slide logs off the pans and cut them diagonally into ½ inch slices. Stand the pieces up right on the cookie sheets. Return to oven and bake 20 minutes longer until crisp and lightly browned. Cool on wire rack. Melt chocolate or almond bark and dip ends of baked biscotti in chocolate; lay dipped cookie on wax paper until chocolate is firm.

I turn the oven down to 300°F. because I don't like the biscotti to be so brown.

DRIED BEEF DIP

Kelly Larson
Marquette, KS

1 (8 oz.) pkg. cream cheese
1 pkg. dried beef, chopped
2 Tbsp. onion flakes
½ c. sour cream
2 Tbsp. milk
½ tsp. garlic salt
½ tsp. pepper
¼ c. green pepper (optional)
½ c. pecans, chopped
2 Tbsp. butter

Mix all ingredients together and top with chopped pecans and butter. Bake at 350°F. for 30 minutes. Serve hot with chips or crackers.

My family loves this dip anytime.

FANTASTIC CRAB DIP

Beverly Long
Lowry City, MO

1 (8 oz.) pkg. cream
  cheese
1 tsp. lemon juice
1 tsp. Worcestershire
  sauce

2 cloves garlic, minced
2 green onions, chopped
6 oz. crabmeat

Mix cream cheese and lemon juice until smooth; add Worcestershire sauce, garlic, onions, and crabmeat. Cover and store in refrigerator.

FAST CARAMEL CORN

Janet Rauch
Deep River, IA

4 qt. popped corn (1 bag
  microwave)
2 c. brown sugar

4 c. miniature
  marshmallows
1 stick margarine

Melt ingredients and pour over popped corn.

FINALS WEEK SURVIVAL MIX

Amy Edwards
Tulsa, OK

1 c. brown sugar
1 stick butter
¼ c. white corn syrup

½ tsp. baking soda
1 (12 oz.) box Crispix
  cereal

Melt all ingredients, except baking soda, and Crispix in a glass bowl in the microwave. Boil for 2 minutes. Add soda and pour over Crispix in a large clean paper grocery bag. Stir; fold sack over and microwave for 1½ minutes. Shake and microwave for 1½ minutes more. Spread out on a tray to cool. Eat up!

My younger sister used to make this to snack on when studying for finals at Oklahoma State University, but it is a great snack for anytime!

12

FINGER SANDWICHES

Gwenda Batterman
Amarillo, TX

2 lb. cooked ham, ground
3 Tbsp. sweet pickle relish
Salad dressing to taste

Salt and pepper to taste
1 loaf white or wheat
bread

Mix ham, sweet pickle relish, salad dressing, salt, and pepper. Spread 2 to 3 tablespoons on approximately ½ loaf of bread slices. Top with remaining bread slices. Cut each sandwich from corner to corner; make 4 triangles. May want to trim off crust.

FLAKY DELI SLICES

Pat Stutz
Utica, KS

Pie crusts
¼ c. Parmesan cheese,
  grated
¾ lb. ham, thinly sliced

¼ lb. pepperoni, thinly
  sliced
1 (4 oz.) c. Cheddar
  cheese, shredded

Unfold crusts. Press out fold lines. Sprinkle each crust with Parmesan cheese. Top each crust with ham, pepperoni, and Cheddar cheese to within 1 inch of edges. Loosely roll up each crust. Place roll, seam side down, on ungreased cookie sheet. Fold under ends. Bake at 450°F. for 12 to 17 minutes until golden brown. Cool 5 minutes. Cut each roll into 16 slices. Best served warm. Makes 32 servings.

FLUFFY ANGEL FROST

Jean Lorenz
Sanford, CO

1 (6 oz.) can frozen pink
  lemonade
1 c. milk
1 (10 oz.) pkg. frozen
  strawberries in syrup,
  partially thawed

1 pt. strawberry or vanilla
  ice cream

In a blender, place frozen lemonade concentrate, milk, strawberries, and ice cream in order given. Blend until smooth. Pour into glasses; serve immediately. Makes about 1 quart.

FRESH SALSA

Amy Edwards
Tulsa, OK

½ tsp. fresh ground black
  pepper
1 tsp. ground cumin
1 tsp. salt
1 clove crushed garlic
1 (28 oz.) can diced
  tomatoes, drained

1 can Ro-Tel diced
  tomatoes and chilies
½ (small) onion, diced
2 fresh jalapenos, seed
  and chop
1 Tbsp. vinegar
2 Tbsp. fresh lime juice

Combine black pepper, cumin, salt, and garlic in small bowl and microwave 20 to 30 seconds. Combine all ingredients in food processor for a few seconds until the salsa reaches the consistency you want. Store in refrigerator for up to 2 weeks.

This is a very easy and inexpensive recipe to make. You won't want to buy canned salsa again!

GO GO TOMATO COCKTAIL

Uarda Koll
Marysville, KS

3 c. tomato juice
3 Tbsp. vinegar
2 Tbsp. lemon juice
2 Tbsp. sugar

1 bay leaf
3 Tbsp. onion, minced
¾ c. dried celery

Mix all ingredients together. Heat to boiling, then simmer 10 minutes. Chill overnight, then strain.

GUACAMOLE DIP

Tammy Bell
Osawatomie, KS

3 medium (or 4 small) ripe
  avocados
1 Tbsp. lemon juice
¼ tsp. salt

½ tsp. garlic salt
3 to 5 dashes hot sauce
1 tomato, chopped
1 small onion, chopped

Mash avocados with lemon juice, salt, garlic salt, and hot sauce. Add tomato and onion; stir. Chill. Serve with chips.

The way my family eats it, I have to double the recipe.

HAM AND CREAM CHEESE SPREAD

Maudie Burden
Centerview, MO

1 (8 oz.) pkg. cream
  cheese, softened
1 (8 oz.) c. sour cream
¼ tsp. garlic powder
2 (2½ oz.) pkg. deli ham,
  chopped

2 to 3 green onions, thinly
  sliced
Miniature bagels, split

In a small mixing bowl, combine the cream cheese, sour cream, and garlic powder until smooth. Stir in ham and onions. Serve with bagels. Yields about 2½ cups.

HOLIDAY DIP

Rita Schiefelbein
Clear Lake, SD

2 (8 oz.) containers cream
  cheese, softened
½ c. salad dressing
⅓ c. Parmesan cheese,
  grated

½ bottle real bacon bits
½ c. green onion and tops

Mix well the cream cheese and salad dressing. Add Parmesan cheese, bacon bits, and green onion and mix well. Serve with crackers.

HOLIDAY GREETINGS PUNCH

Diane Meisinger
Hillsboro, KS

¾ c. sugar
2 c. lemon juice
1 (46 oz.) can red fruit
  punch

1 two liter bottle ginger
  ale
Ice

Stir and dissolve sugar in the lemon juice. Add fruit punch. Before serving, add chilled ginger ale and ice. This looks nice in a punch bowl, garnished with orange slices and maraschino cherries or an ice ring with cranberries and mint leaves.

HOME-STYLE CROCKPOT TOMATO JUICE

Joyce Sievers
Slater, IA

10 to 12 (large) tomatoes
1 tsp. salt
1 tsp. seasoned salt
¼ tsp. pepper
1 Tbsp. sugar

Wash tomatoes. Remove core and blossom ends. Place in crockpot. Cook on low for 4 to 6 hours or until tomatoes are done. Press through a sieve or food mill. Pour in a pitcher. Add seasonings. Chill. Makes about 4 cups of juice.

HOT BACON

Brendon Powers
Spearville, KS

3 eggs, beaten
2 tsp. dry mustard
3 tsp. cayenne pepper
1 Tbsp. vinegar
1 lb. bacon, regular slice
3 sleeves saltine crackers, crushed

Slice pound of bacon into thirds. Mix egg, mustard, cayenne, and vinegar together. Dip each piece of bacon into egg mixture and roll in cracker crumbs. Place on foil lined shallow baking sheet. Bake at 350°F. for 20 minutes. Yield: 60 appetizers.

HOT BITES

Teresa Zimmerman
Plevna, KS

2 lb. jalapeno peppers
1 (8 oz.) pkg. cream cheese, softened
½ c. Cheddar cheese, shredded
½ c. Monterey Jack cheese, shredded
6 slices bacon, fried, crumbled
½ tsp. salt
1 tsp. chili powder
2 c. dry bread crumbs

Wash peppers and slice in half lengthwise. Carefully clean all seeds from peppers (wear rubber gloves). Cream all cheeses, bacon, and spices together until smooth. Stir in bacon. Stuff pepper shells with cheese mixture. Roll each pepper in crumbs and place on sprayed baking sheet, cheese side up. Bake at 350°F. for 25 to 30 minutes.

HOT CHOCOLATE MIX

Donna J. Walker
Kismet, KS

1 (8 qt.) box powdered
  milk
1 (No. 16) can (3 c.)
  Nesquick

1 (6 oz.) jar (1 c.) non-
  dairy creamer
2 c. powdered sugar
½ tsp. salt

Mix al ingredients; store in airtight container. Use ⅓ cup to ½ cup per cup of boiling water.

HOT CRACKERS

Carol F. Mandrell
Olton, TX

1 box crackers
1 c. vegetable oil
1 Tbsp. garlic powder,
  more or less to taste

1 Tbsp. red pepper flakes,
  more or less to taste
1 pkg. Ranch salad
  dressing mix

Mix all ingredients, except crackers. Pour over crackers in a container with a lid that can be turned. Turn container several times and do it every so often for a while.

HOT REUBEN DIP

Brandi Jecha
Timken, KS

1 lb. corned beef
1 can sauerkraut
1½ c. sour cream
1 (8 oz.) pkg. cream
  cheese

1 (12 oz.) pkg. Swiss
  cheese

Chop meat. Drain kraut. Put all ingredients into a crockpot and heat. Serve with thin crackers.

HOT SPINACH AND ARTICHOKE DIP

Amy Edwards
Tulsa, OK

1 (14 oz.) can artichoke hearts
1 c. real mayonnaise
1 c. grated Parmesan cheese
¼ tsp. lemon juice
¼ tsp. Tabasco sauce
½ pkg. frozen chopped spinach, thaw
Paprika

Rinse, drain, and chop artichoke hearts. Combine all ingredients. Spoon into lightly greased small casserole dish. Sprinkle with paprika and bake at 350°F. for 20 minutes. Serve hot with crackers, tortilla chips, or vegetables.

This dip is great to make for an appetizer or anytime snack.

JIM'S BARBECUE SAUCE

Jim Reed
Parkville, MO

2 Tbsp. butter
1 (small) onion
1 clove garlic, minced
¾ c. water
1 c. ketchup
1 Tbsp. vinegar
2 Tbsp. Worcestershire sauce
2 heaping Tbsp. brown sugar
1 tsp. dried mustard, ground
¼ tsp. black pepper
1 tsp. seasoning salt (optional)

Saute onion and garlic in butter until clear. Stir in ketchup and water. Add vinegar, Worcestershire sauce, brown sugar, dried mustard, pepper, and seasoning salt. Cover with a lid jar or screen. Simmer ½ hour. Stir frequently. Use as a side sauce or to baste grilled meat during last 10 minutes of cooking.

JUMBLEBERRY TRIFLE

Madeline Fangman
Hereford, TX

1 (18 oz.) jar blueberry
   jam
4 bananas, sliced
1 (10 oz.) pkg. frozen
   sweetened
   strawberries, thawed
1 frozen pound cake,
   thawed

1½ c. whipping cream
1 (8 oz.) box vanilla
   pudding
Squirt of lemon (on
   bananas)

Stir together strawberries and 1 cup jam. Cover sauce and chill 20 minutes. Cut pound cake into ¼ inch thick slices. Spread remaining jam on one side of half of slices; top with remaining slices. Cut sandwiches into ½ inch cubes; set aside. Spoon 1 tablespoon berry sauce into 8 large wine glasses; top with about ¼ cup each of cake cubes, vanilla pudding, and whipping cream. Repeat layers once, ending with berry sauce. Serve immediately, or chill until ready to serve. Garnish if desired. Makes 8 servings. Preparation time: 45 minutes, chill 50 minutes.

This trifle can also be put together in a 2 quart bowl or trifle bowl.

MACADAMIA POPCORN

Iola Egle
Bella Vista, AR

1 (12 oz.) pkg. white
   chocolate morsels or
   almond bark
1 bag buttered microwave
   popcorn, popped

1 (4 oz.) jar macadamia
   nuts, crushed (optional)

Mix nuts and popcorn. Pour melted white bark over them. Spread out on waxed paper on jelly roll pan to dry. Break apart.

MOCHA PUNCH

Mabel Penner
Whitewater, KS

1½ qt. water
½ c. instant chocolate
  drink mix
½ c. sugar
¼ c. instant coffee
  granules

½ gal. vanilla ice cream
½ gal. chocolate ice
  cream
1 c. whipped topping
Chocolate curls (optional)

In a large saucepan, bring water to a boil. Remove from the heat. Add drink mix, sugar, and coffee; stir until dissolved. Cover and refrigerate for 4 hours or overnight. About 30 minutes before serving, pour into a punch bowl. Add ice cream by scoopfuls; stir until partially melted. Garnish with dollops of whipped cream and chocolate curls if desired. Yields 20 to 25 servings.

ONION-SESAME SNACK MIX

Teresa Zimmerman
Plevna, KS

3 c. oyster crackers
2 c. dry-roasted peanuts
½ c. margarine

1 pkg. dry onion soup mix
¼ c. sesame seeds

In a large bowl, combine crackers and peanuts. In a small saucepan, melt margarine; add remaining ingredients, except crackers. Pour over cracker mixture; toss until well coated. Spread evenly on a baking sheet. Bake 10 to 12 minutes or until light brown at 350°F. Cool completely in pan. Store in an airtight container. Yields 5 cups.

PATIO BREAD

Rita Schiefelbein
Clear Lake, SD

½ c. butter
½ c. mayonnaise
½ c. Mozzarella cheese,
  shredded
1 (4 oz.) can black olives,
  chopped
1 (4 oz.) jar pimento,
  chopped

¼ c. green onions and
  tops
½ tsp. garlic salt
¼ tsp. dill weed
1 loaf French bread, sliced
  about 1½ inches thick

Mix together well the butter, mayonnaise, and cheese, then add olives, pimento, onions, garlic salt, and dill weed. Spread on bread slices, place on baking sheet, and bake 12 to 15 minutes in 325°F. oven.

You won't be able to eat just one.

PEPPERED CHEESE BALL

Donna L. Thorp
Kismet, KS

2 (8 oz.) pkg. cream
cheese
1 pkg. Ranch salad
dressing and seasoning
mix

1 c. Cheddar cheese,
shredded
2 Tbsp. seasoned pepper
1 Tbsp. Parmesan cheese,
shredded

Mix cream cheese, Ranch mix, and Cheddar cheese until well blended. Pour pepper and Parmesan cheese on wax paper and mix together. Divide cream cheese mixture in 2 parts. Roll each part separately over the pepper and cheese into a ball until covered. Wrap in wax paper and refrigerate until time to eat. Serve with your favorite crackers.

The pepper seasoning keeps your guests wanting more. If it is too spicy, use less pepper and more Parmesan cheese.

PFEFFERNUESSE

Iola Egle
Bella Vista, AR

3 c. sugar
1 c. whole milk
4 c. white syrup
1 c. lard (or shortening)
1 Tbsp. cinnamon
2 Tbsp. baking powder

1 Tbsp. mace
1 Tbsp. cloves
1 Tbsp. salt
Flour to make a stiff
dough
2 to 3 Tbsp. anise oil

Boil sugar and milk together. Set aside to cool. Heat together syrup and lard just until lard is melted. When mixtures are cool, mix with sifted dry ingredients, first in electric mixer, then by kneading like bread. It takes lots of flour. Let stand in the refrigerator overnight. Take about ½ cup dough and roll into a long string about the size and shape of your little finger. Cut off small squares and place on greased and floured cookie sheet. Be sure the squares do not touch. Bake at 350°F. about 6 to 8 minutes, only until they are lightly browned.

You can also roll the peppernuts in powdered sugar. Anise oil can be purchased at a pharmacy counter.

PICKER-UPPER-SNACK

Sarah Sawyer
McCook, NE

1 Heath candy bar
¼ c. whole milk

2½ c. vanilla ice cream
1 tsp. hot fudge topping

Freeze the Heath candy bar. Before unwrapping it, break it into tiny pieces with a knife handle. Combine al ingredients in blender and blend for about 30 seconds on medium speed. Stop the blender to stir the mixture with a spoon if necessary and repeat until well mixed. Pour into a 16 ounce glass or two 8 ounce stemmed glasses.

In the hot summertime, this gives me new energy to finish the duties of the afternoon. I like to share with a friend as we relax.

POPCORN CAKE

Annilee Kniffen
Lorena, TX

½ c. butter
½ c. cooking oil
1 lb. marshmallows
4 qt. popped corn

1 lb. peanuts, parched or salted
1 (large) pkg. M&M's chocolate candies

In large container, mix together the popped corn, peanuts, and M&M's. In saucepan, melt together the butter, oil, and marshmallows. Pour over the popcorn mixture until blended. Pack in a buttered angel food cake pan. When cool, remove to a cake plate, slice and serve.

REFRIED BEAN AND TACO DIP

Martha Ritter
Marquette, KS

1 large can refried beans
1 can evaporated milk
1½ lb. ground beef, cooked and drained
1 (8 oz.) jar picante sauce

1 pkg. taco seasoning mix
1 lb. processed American cheese
10 oz. Cheddar cheese

Mix all ingredients in crockpot. Cook until all cheeses are melted, then cook for one hour longer on low. Keep hot in crockpot.

RHUBARB JAM

Dorothy M. Brown
Monett, MO

4 c. rhubarb
4 c. sugar
1 (small) can crushed
   pineapple

1 pkg. red colored gelatin

Chop rhubarb finely. Combine rhubarb and sugar and let stand a few hours. Stir occasionally. Boil rhubarb and sugar 10 minutes. Add pineapple and boil an additional 5 to 7 minutes. Remove from heat; add gelatin and seal in jars.

SALSA

Linda Pauls
Buhler, KS

3 cloves garlic, chopped
   fine
2 large onions, chopped
4 green peppers, chopped
9 c. tomatoes, chopped
   (use blender for part of
   them)
7 jalapeno peppers,
   seeded and diced (use
   rubber gloves)

¼ c. cilantro, chopped
¾ c. vinegar
3 tsp. salt
½ tsp. basil leaves
½ tsp. all-purpose
   seasoning
½ c. sugar
1 Tbsp. lime juice

Combine all ingredients in a large saucepan; simmer for 30 minutes. Put into clean jars and process in a water bath for 15 minutes. Makes 6 pints.

This salsa is good with any variety of chips.

SANDWICH CHEESE SPREAD

Thelma Maxwell
Dodge City, KS

1 lb. American cheese
1 jar pimentos

4 sweet pickles
⅛ tsp. celery seed

Grind the cheese, pickles, and pimentos; add celery seed. Mix with salad dressing to make into dainty sandwiches, or use mayonnaise of your choice.

SAUSAGE BALLS

Coleen Koch
Summerfield, KS

1 lb. ground sausage   1 c. Bisquick
1 c. Cheddar cheese

Mix together by hand. Roll into walnut sized balls. Bake at 350°F. for 10 to 15 minutes. Place on paper towels to drain. May be kept warm in a crockpot set on low.

SPICED PECANS

Donna L. Thorp
Kismet, KS

4 c. pecans   1 to 2 tsp. cinnamon
2 egg whites   1/8 tsp. salt
1 c. sugar   1/2 lb. butter

Toast pecans in a jelly roll pan at 325°F. until golden brown, about 10 minutes. Beat egg whites until stiff. Fold in sugar, cinnamon, and salt. Stir in pecans. Melt butter in jelly roll pan. Spread pecan mixture over butter and bake 30 minutes, gently turning every 10 minutes until they absorb all the butter.

Put some spiced pecans in a decorative dish with a bow. It makes a special gift given from the heart.

SPICY CHEESE BALL

Marilyn Barner
Belle Plaine, KS

1 (8 oz.) pkg. cream   8 drops hot sauce
  cheese, softened   1 Tbsp. garlic salt
1 c. pecans, finely   1/8 tsp. chili powder
  chopped
1 Tbsp. Worcestershire
  sauce

Mix all ingredients, except chili powder, together. You will need to use your hands. Form into a ball and roll in a liberal amount of chili powder. Ball should look mostly red with chili powder. Wrap in plastic wrap and keep refrigerated. Serve with your choice of crackers.

SPINACH BALLS

Thelma Maxwell
Dodge City, KS

2 (8 oz.) pkg. frozen
  spinach, chopped
½ c. margarine
6 eggs

1 (6 oz.) pkg. prepared
  stuffing, chicken flavor
1 c. Parmesan cheese,
  grated

Cook spinach as package instructs. Mix with margarine, stuffing (including flavor packet), eggs, and Parmesan cheese. Let cool to shape into walnut-size balls. Bake at 350°F. for 15 minutes. Makes 36 balls.

Can make ahead and freeze. If frozen, bake longer than the 15 minutes.

SPINACH CHEESE DIP

Tammy Bell
Osawatomie, KS

1½ lb. white American
  cheese
½ (small) box frozen
  spinach, thawed and
  chopped

1 (small) jar pimentos
2 Tbsp. minced onions
1 pt. half & half
1 (small) can green chilies,
  chopped

Mix all ingredients in crockpot until melted. It can be made in the microwave; place in a microwave-safe dish and stir until melted. Serve with chips.

This is a dip that is best when hot.

SPINGERLE

Iola Egle
Bella Vista, AR

4 eggs
2 c. sugar
2 tsp. aniseed, crushed
3½ c. sifted all-purpose
  flour

½ tsp. baking powder
3 to 4 Tbsp. whole
  aniseed

Beat eggs until very light. Gradually stir in sugar, beating well after each addition. Stir in crushed aniseed. Sift flour with baking powder; add 3 cups of flour to mixture to make a stiff dough. If dough is too soft, add more flour, a little at a time. Dough should be stiff enough to roll out to ⅓ inch thickness. Flour Springerle rolling pin or molds. Press hard upon dough to get a good picture. Cut cookies apart; these cookies are usually stamped with quaint wooden molds or rollers to make a picture. If you do not have a mold, cut the dough into ¾ inch by 2½ inch bars. Grease cookie sheets and sprinkle each sheet with 1 tablespoon whole aniseed. Place cookies, picture side up, on cookie sheets. Let stand overnight in cool place to dry out. Bake at 300°F. for about 15 minutes or until lower part of cookie is pale yellow. Makes about 5 dozen.

Anise oil is not an everyday used spice; you can purchase it at a pharmacy counter.

STRAWBERRY SPARKLE PUNCH
Lois Mills
Lake City, KS

4 c. fresh or frozen strawberries
1 (3 oz.) pkg. strawberry flavored gelatin
1 c. boiling water
1 (6 oz.) can frozen lemonade concentrate

1 (32 oz.) bottle cranberry juice cocktail, chilled
2 c. cold water
1 (28 oz.) bottle ginger ale
Chilled strawberries for garnish if desired

Puree strawberries in blender; place puree in large punch bowl. Strain if desired to remove seeds. Dissolve gelatin in boiling water; stir in lemonade concentrate. Add mixture to punch bowl; add cranberry cocktail and cold water. Slowly add ginger ale. If desired, serve with fresh strawberry garnish or crushed ice.

SUPER NACHOS
Thelma Baldock
Delphos, KS

1 (16 oz.) pkg. tortilla chips
1 c. salsa
1 (4 oz.) can jalapenos, diced
1 (4 oz.) can green chilies, diced

1½ c. Cheddar cheese, shredded
1½ c. Monterey Jack cheese, shredded
½ c. tomatoes, diced

Spread chips out on an oven proof platter. Sprinkle cheeses on top. Microwave 1 to 2 minutes or heat in 350°F. oven until cheese melts. Spoon on salsa. Top with remaining ingredients. Garnish as desired with salsa, sour cream, sliced green onions, or guacamole. Makes 4 to 6 servings.

TASTY SNACKS

Neva Jones
O'Neill, NE

6 c. hexagon shaped
cereal
1 (10 or 12 oz.) can mixed
nuts

1 (10 oz.) pkg. pretzels,
broken
¾ c. margarine
¾ c. brown sugar, packed

In a large bowl, combine cereal, nuts, and pretzels. In a saucepan over low heat, melt margarine; add brown sugar. Cook and stir until sugar is dissolved (about two minutes). Pour over cereal mixture. Stir to coat and place half of the mixture into a sprayed large 15 x 10½ inch baking pan. Bake at 325°F. for 8 minutes; stir and bake another 5 minutes. Spread onto waxed paper to cool. Repeat with remaining mixture.

TEXAS CAVIAR

Vicki Thompson
Pauls Valley, OK

2 (15.5 oz.) cans black-
eyed peas with jalapeno
peppers, rinsed and
drained
1 (10 oz.) can tomatoes
with green chiles, diced
2 avocados, diced

1 (small) green bell
pepper, diced
½ purple onion, diced
¾ c. Zesty Italian dressing
½ tsp. salt
1 Tbsp. fresh lime juice

Mix all the ingredients together; cover and keep in refrigerator. Serve with tortilla chips.

TIGER BUTTER

Aron Fangman
Hereford, TX

½ c. crunchy peanut
butter
½ c. chocolate chips

1 lb. almond bark or
white chocolate

Melt almond bark or white chocolate and peanut butter in microwave 3 to 4 minutes on 50 percent power, stirring after 2 minutes. Spread mixture onto a foil-lined cookie sheet. Melt chocolate 1 to 2 minutes at 50 percent power in microwave. Drizzle chocolate over peanut butter mixture and swirl together. Chill. Break into pieces to serve.

TORTILLA PINWHEELS

Shelley Fangman
Hereford, TX

1 (8 oz.) pkg. dairy sour
  cream
1 (8 oz.) pkg. cream
  cheese, softened
1 (4 oz.) can diced green
  chiles, well drained
1 (4 oz.) can chopped
  black olives, well
  drained

1 c. Cheddar cheese,
  grated
½ c. green onion,
  chopped
Garlic powder to taste
Seasoned salt to taste
5 (10 inch) flour tortillas

Mix all of the filling ingredients together thoroughly. Divide the filling and spread evenly over the tortillas; roll up tortillas. Cover tightly with plastic wrap, twisting ends; refrigerate for several hours. Unwrap; cut in slices ½ to ¾ inch thick. Makes about 65 servings.

An electric knife works best to cut pinwheels. You can garnish with parsley and serve with salsa.

TORTILLA ROLL-UPS

Julie Haverland
Deepwater, MO

1 (8 oz.) pkg. cream
  cheese, softened

1 (16 oz.) jar chunky salsa
10 (10 inch) flour tortillas

In a medium bowl, use a mixer to smooth the cream cheese. Pour in salsa, 1 tablespoon at a time, while continuing to mix. Continue adding salsa and mixing until the ingredients have attained a spreadable consistency. Spread the mixture on the flour tortillas. Roll the tortillas and slice them into bite-sized pieces. Refrigerate until serving.

Variation: Mix cream cheese and salsa as instructed above; place in bowl and serve with tortilla chips.

TORTILLA ROLLUPS

Pauline Riley
Dodge City, KS

6 (large or small) flour
  tortillas
1 pkg. cream cheese at
  room temperature
1 pkg. dried beef, cut thin

1 can green chiles,
  chopped
2 Tbsp. onion, finely
  chopped

Mix all ingredients and spread over the tortillas evenly. Roll up and place on cookie sheet and place in freezer for about 20 to 30 minutes. Remove and slice about ½ to ¼ inch. Ready to serve.

TUNA CHEESE SOUP

Elizabeth Brattin Keever
Pierce City, MO

1 can cream of Cheddar
  cheese soup

1 can tuna (in spring
  water)

Mix soup according to directions on the can and heat. Drain the tuna well; add to soup and reheat. Ready to serve.

VI'S SPICED DILL PICKLES

Lucile Fuller
Wichita, KS

1 (48 oz.) jar dill pickles
2 c. sugar

⅔ c. cider vinegar
1 Tbsp. pickling spices

Drain liquid from pickles and rinse well. Refrigerate overnight. In small saucepan, bring sugar, vinegar, and pickling spices to a boil for a minute. While still hot, pour mixture over pickles in the jar. Seal and refrigerate until cool. Turn occasionally for first two days.

WARM CRAB DIP

Donna L. Thorp
Kismet, KS

2 (8 oz.) pkg. cream
  cheese
1 (small) can crabmeat
4 Tbsp. milk or crab liquid

4 Tbsp. dehydrated
  onions
⅓ c. pecans, chopped

Mix all ingredients, except pecans, with a mixer until well blended. Put in small casserole dish. Top with chopped pecans. Bake at 375°F. for 20 minutes.

This crab dip is great with wheat crackers.

WHITE CHOCOLATE PARTY MIX

Iola Egle
Bella Vista, AR

1 lb. white chocolate bark or white chocolate chips
3 c. Rice Chex cereal
3 c. Corn Chex cereal
2 c. Cheerios
3 c. stick pretzels
2 c. dry roasted peanuts
1 lb. plain or peanut M&M's chocolate candies

Melt white chocolate in double boiler on low heat or in microwave. Stir to melt completely. Combine dry ingredients in large bowl. Pour white chocolate over cereal mix and stir to coat. Spread evenly on waxed paper to cool. Break into bite-sized pieces.

Makes perfect TV snack.

Breads

Breads
Recipe Contest Winners

First
Cranberry Ripple Cake
Barb Kasel, Adams, Minnesota
Page 38

Second
Citrus Nut Scones with Orange Butter
Jean Lorenz, Sanford, Colorado
Page 37

Third
Good Morning Cranberry Biscotti
Jeanette Pearson, Plymouth, Nebraska
Page 42

BREADS

APPLE MUFFINS

Debbie Hinman
Carter, SD

1 egg
½ c. milk
¼ c. oil
1 c. apples, raw and
    grated
1½ c. sifted flour
½ c. sugar

2 tsp. baking powder
½ tsp. salt
½ tsp. cinnamon
⅓ c. brown sugar
⅓ c. nuts, chopped
½ tsp. cinnamon

Beat egg with a fork. Stir in milk, oil, and apples. Sift the dry ingredients together and add to the first mixture, stirring just until moistened. Fill 12 paper lined regular muffin cups. Top with the nut crunch topping prepared with brown sugar, nuts, and cinnamon. Bake 25 to 30 minutes at 400°F.

APPLE MUFFINS

Margaret Trojan
Beaver Crossing, NE

2 (large) apples, peeled
    and finely diced
1 c. sugar
2 c. flour
2 tsp. cinnamon

½ c. vegetable oil
1 egg
2 tsp. vanilla
1 c. raisins
1 c. pecans, chopped

Mix apples and sugar, then set aside. Stir flour, soda, cinnamon, and salt with a fork. Mix together vegetable oil, egg, and vanilla in a bowl. Stir oil mixture into apples. Stir in flour mixture. Stir in raisins and nuts. Drop into well greased muffin tins, filling ¾ full. Bake in 350°F. oven for 20 minutes. Makes 24 muffins.

AUNT ELNA'S LEMON BREAD

Coleen Koch
Summerfield, KS

6 Tbsp. shortening
2 beaten eggs
1½ c. sifted flour
½ tsp. salt
1 c. sugar

1 Tbsp. grated lemon peel
1 tsp. baking powder
½ c. milk
⅓ c. sugar
3 Tbsp. lemon juice

Cream shortening and 1 cup sugar. Add beaten eggs and lemon peel. Sift flour, baking powder, and salt. Add alternately with milk. Pour in greased and floured loaf pan. Bake at 350°F. for 1 hour. Cool in pan 15 minutes. Dissolve ⅓ cup sugar in the lemon juice. Pour over bread; let set 10 minutes. Remove from pan.

BANANA BREAD

Charlotte Schmidt
Clintonville, WI

1½ c. (3 large) ripe
    bananas
1 egg
2 Tbsp. canola oil
¼ c. milk
¼ to ½ c. sugar

1 tsp. salt
1 tsp. baking soda
½ tsp. baking powder
1½ c. flour (1 c. white and
    ½ c. whole wheat,
    optional)

Mash bananas and add the egg, oil, milk, and sugar; beat well. Add the flour, salt, baking soda, and baking powder. Gently fold the flour mixture. Don't overbeat. Bake in 9x5 inch greased loaf pan. Bake at 350°F. oven 30 to 35 minutes.

This is a healthy recipe, as it calls for a small amount of oil and sugar.

BANANA NUT BREAD

Ann Kane
Wichita, KS

½ c. liquid shortening
1 c. sugar
2 eggs
2 large very ripe bananas
1 tsp. lemon juice

2 c. sifted flour
1 tsp. soda
½ tsp. salt
½ c. walnut pieces

Preheat oven to 350°F. Grease two 8½ x 4½ x 2⅝ inch loaf pans or a 9⅝ x 5½ inch loaf pan. In food processor or large mixer bowl, beat shortening, sugar, eggs, bananas, and lemon juice. Add flour, soda, and salt, sifted together. Mix well, then add nut pieces. Pour into pan or pans. Bake 1 hour or longer until golden brown and firm in the middle. Cool 10 minutes and then remove from pans.

The bread stores very well in foil or plastic bag. Freezes well.

BEST EVER MUFFINS

Julie Haverland
Deepwater, MO

2 c. all-purpose flour	**1 egg**
3 tsp. baking powder	**1 c. milk**
½ tsp. salt	**¼ c. vegetable oil**
¾ c. white sugar	

Stir together the flour, baking powder, salt, and sugar in large bowl. Make a well in the center. In a small bowl, beat egg with a fork; stir in milk and oil. Pour all at once into the well in the flour mixture. Mix quickly and lightly with a fork until moistened, but do not over beat. The batter will be lumpy. Pour batter into paper lined muffin pan cups. Bake at 400°F. for 25 to 30 minutes.

Variations: For Blueberry Muffins, add 1 cup blueberries. Raisin Muffins, add 1 cup raisins, finely chopped. Orange-Cranberry Muffins, add 2 tablespoons grated orange zest and ¾ cup cranberries, chopped.

BOSTON MARKET CORNBREAD

Kim Due
Friend, NE

1 box cornbread mix (optional, 2 boxes cornbread mix)	**1 box yellow cake mix**

Mix both boxes according to directions and combine the batter. You can use a large mixing bowl and add both boxes together. If you have boxes of only cornbread mix, use a brownie-sized baking pan, 8x8 inch. If you are going to use a box of regular cake mix, use a 9x13 inch pan. Bake at 350°F. for 30 minutes or until done.

Our kids love helping in the kitchen and this is a fun recipe the kids enjoy making.

BRAN BREAD OR ROLLS

Thelma Maxwell
Dodge City, KS

1 c. bran cereal
½ c. sugar
⅔ c. shortening
1 c. warm milk
1 c. boiling water
2 pkg. yeast, dissolved in
 ¼ c. warm water

2 eggs
2 tsp. salt
1 c. whole wheat flour
5 or 6 c. white flour

Pour boiling water over bran, sugar, salt, and shortening. Cool. Dissolve yeast in warm water. Add bran mixture. Add warm milk and eggs. Mix well. Add wheat flour, then white flour until mixture is not too sticky. Do not add too much flour. Needs to be just past the sticky stage to knead for about 10 minutes. Let rise overnight in refrigerator or may let rise at room temperature until doubled in bulk. Punch down and make into bread loaves or into rolls. Works well for either rolls or loaves of bread. Use 7½ x 3¾ x 2 inch bread pans, which makes 5 loaves that size. Bake 20 to 30 minutes in 350°F oven after letting rise until light, an hour or two. Bake rolls 15 minutes at 350°F, after letting rise until double.

Grandkids really enjoy eating these rolls!

BRUNCH BUBBLE BREAD

Lucile Fuller
Wichita, KS

1 pkg. frozen dinner rolls
1 pkg. butterscotch
 pudding mix (not
 instant)
½ c. brown sugar

½ c. pecan halves
½ (8 oz.) jar maraschino
 cherries
1 stick margarine

Melt ½ stick of margarine and ½ cup brown sugar and pour into bottom of Bundt pan. Arrange the pecans and cherries in bottom of pan. Melt ½ stick margarine in a cup. Place dry pudding mix in another cup. Dip a frozen dinner roll in the margarine, roll it in the pudding mix, and place in the pan. Continue until all rolls have been used. Usually there are 24 rolls in a package. Place the Bundt pan in a cold oven to rise overnight. In the morning, preheat the oven to 350°F. and bake the rolls 30 to 40 minutes. Turn pan upside down onto a large cake dish. Time the baking to serve the rolls while still warm.

BUTTERHORNS

Thelma Baldock
Delphos, KS

1 c. milk, scalded
½ c. shortening
½ c. sugar
1 tsp. salt

1 pkg. granular yeast
3 eggs, beaten
4½ c. flour

Combine milk, shortening, sugar, and salt; cool to lukewarm. Add crumbled yeast and stir well. Add eggs and flour; mix to smooth soft dough. Knead lightly on floured surface. Place dough in greased bowl; turn over so top is greased. Cover and let rise until at least doubled in bulk. Divide dough in thirds; roll each third on lightly floured surface to 9 inch circle. Brush with melted margarine. Cut each circle in 12 wedge-shaped pieces; roll each wedge, starting with wide end, rolling to point. Arrange in greased baking pan and brush with salad oil. Cover and let rise until very light. Bake at 400° to 450°F. for 15 minutes. For crescents, shape in curve on baking pan. Makes 3 dozen.

BUTTERMILK PANCAKES

Vickie Gassman
Clayton, KS

1 lb. sausage, ground
2 eggs
2 c. buttermilk
2 c. whole wheat flour
2 Tbsp. sugar

4 Tbsp. vegetable oil
2 tsp. baking powder
1 tsp. salt
1 tsp. baking soda

Brown and drain sausage well. Beat eggs until fluffy. Beat in buttermilk, flour, sugar, vegetable oil, baking powder, salt, and baking soda until smooth. Add sausage. Grease heated griddle. Makes (16) 4 inch pancakes.

Any leftovers can be frozen and then zapped in microwave. Sour milk can be used instead of buttermilk.

CINNAMON ROLLS

Barbara Long
Montezuma, IA

2 pkg. active dry yeast
½ c. granulated sugar
½ c. warm water
1½ c. whole milk

½ c. canola oil
2 eggs
1½ tsp. salt
6 to 7 c. flour

Mix sugar with yeast. Add to warm water (120°). Stir to dissolve. Let sit 5 minutes for the yeast to begin to work. Warm milk to 120°F. in the microwave and add the milk, oil, salt, eggs, and three cups of the flour to the yeast mixture. Beat at medium speed using a dough hook for 2 to 3 minutes until thick and elastic. Beat in the remaining flour, one cup at a time, to make a soft dough which leaves the sides of the bowl. Turn out on a floured pastry cloth and knead. Add only enough flour to prevent it from sticking. If you have a heavy-duty mixer and can mix the dough until all the flour is mixed, you don't have to knead very long, just until the dough springs back when pressed. Cover and let rest 20 to 30 minutes; when the dough keeps the indentation, it has raised enough. Punch down and roll out into a rectangle. Spread with ½ cup butter and ½ cup white sugar with 2 tablespoons cinnamon. Roll as for a jellyroll. Cut 1 inch slices with a string or dental floss by wrapping the roll, crossing the string, and pulling tight. Let raise at room temperature about 30 minutes and bake at 375°F. for 20 minutes. Makes 12 large cinnamon rolls. Drizzle a powdered sugar glaze over the hot rolls.

1 lb. powdered sugar
½ c. butter
1 Tbsp. vanilla

Enough hot water to give the desired consistency (like pudding)

If you prefer to bake these rolls later, instead of letting them raise at room temperature, put in the refrigerator, covered with plastic wrap, for up to 24 hours. Remove from refrigerator and let come to room temperature for at least 15 minutes and then bake as directed.

I also use the ends of the rolls to make miniature loaves of bread for the grandchildren. They love those small loaves of bread.

CINNAMON ROLLS

Mabel Penner
Whitewater, KS

1 c. water
1 c. milk
½ c. oil
2 tsp. salt
2 eggs
2 Tbsp. yeast
½ c. sugar
6 c. flour

½ c. margarine, softened
1½ c. sugar
2 Tbsp. cinnamon
⅓ c. margarine
2 c. powdered sugar
1 tsp. vanilla
2 Tbsp. hot water

Mix water and milk; heat to lukewarm. Add oil, salt, eggs, yeast, sugar, and flour. Mix together and knead until soft dough forms that can be rolled out. Let rise ½ hour. Punch down and rise 1 hour. Roll out; spread with filling consisting of margarine, sugar, and cinnamon. Roll up and cut into about 1 inch size; put into pan. Rise for 15 minutes, then bake at 350°F. for 20 minutes. To prepare glaze, mix together margarine, powdered sugar, vanilla, and hot water. Spread on warm rolls.

A delicious family favorite.

CINNAMON ROLLS IN A SNAP
Cynthia A. Haynes
Holyoke, CO

4½ c. prepared biscuit mix
1⅓ c. milk
2 Tbsp. margarine, softened
¼ c. sugar
1 tsp. cinnamon (I add more)

⅓ c. raisins (optional)
2 c. powdered sugar
2 Tbsp. milk
2 Tbsp. butter, melted
1 tsp. vanilla

In a bowl, combine biscuit mix and milk. Turn onto a floured surface and knead 8 to 10 times. Roll dough into a 12x10 inch rectangle. Spread with butter. Combine sugar, cinnamon, and raisins; sprinkle over butter. Roll up from a long side; pinch seam to seal. Cut into 12 slices. Place with cut side down onto a large greased cookie sheet. Bake in 450°F oven for 10 to 12 minutes or until golden brown. Mix icing and spread over rolls. Serve immediately. Makes 1 dozen.

When my daughter was a new bride, she received this recipe from her mother-in-law. It soon became a favorite of our families for its easy preparation, resulting in such a delicious breakfast treat. Leftovers reheat just like fresh baked when warmed up.

CITRUS NUT SCONES WITH ORANGE BUTTER
Jean Lorenz
Sanford, CO

2 c. flour
3 Tbsp. sugar
½ tsp. salt
2½ tsp. baking powder
⅓ c. butter
2 tsp. orange peel, grated
2 tsp. lemon peel, grated

½ c. walnuts, finely chopped
¼ c. milk
1 large egg, beaten
½ c. butter, softened
2 Tbsp. orange marmalade

Lightly grease cookie sheet. In large bowl, combine flour, sugar, salt, and baking powder. With pastry blender, cut in butter until mixture resembles coarse crumbs. Add walnuts and orange and lemon peel; mix well. With fork, stir in milk and egg just until mixture leaves sides of bowl and soft dough forms. Turn dough out on floured surface and knead lightly a few times. Divide dough in half. On cookie sheet pat out each into a 6 to 8 inch circle. Sprinkle with sugar. Cut into 6 wedges and separate slightly. Bake at 400°F. for 15 to 18 minutes until golden brown. To prepare orange butter, in a small bowl, beat butter until light and fluffy. Stir in marmalade. Serve with warm scones.

CRANBERRY RIPPLE CAKE

Barb Kasel
Adams, MN

2 c. all-purpose flour
1 tsp. baking powder
1 tsp. baking soda
¼ tsp. salt
½ c. butter or margarine, softened
1 c. sugar

½ tsp. almond extract
2 eggs
1 c. dairy sour cream
1 (16 oz.) can whole cranberry sauce
½ c. pecans, chopped

Stir together flour, baking powder, baking soda, and salt. In a large bowl, beat butter or margarine 30 seconds. Add sugar and extract; beat until fluffy. Add eggs; beat well. Add flour mixture and sour cream alternately to creamed mixture, beating after each addition until smooth. Spread half the batter in a greased and floured 10 inch tube pan. Spoon 1 cup of cranberry sauce over batter. Spoon remaining batter over sauce, spreading as much as possible. Top with remaining cranberry sauce. Sprinkle pecans over top. Bake in a 350°F. oven 40 to 50 minutes. Cool 10 minutes. Remove from pan; cool on wire rack.

This fancy coffee cake is fun to make and serve for brunches.

DILLY ROLLS

Julie Schmidt
Smith Center, KS

2 c. (16 oz.) small curd
cottage cheese
2 Tbsp. butter or
margarine
2 (¼ oz.) pkg. active dry
yeast
½ c. warm water (100° to
115°F.)
2 eggs

¼ c. sugar
2 Tbsp. dried minced
onion
1 to 2 Tbsp. dill weed or
seed
1 Tbsp. salt
½ tsp. baking soda
4½ to 5 c. all-purpose
flour

In a large saucepan over medium heat, cook cottage cheese and butter until butter is melted. Cook to 110° to 115°F. In a large mixing bowl, dissolve yeast in water. Add eggs, sugar, onion, dill, salt, baking soda, and cottage cheese mixture. Add 3 cups of flour; beat until smooth. Add enough remaining flour to form a soft dough. Turn onto a floured board; knead until smooth and elastic, about 6 to 8 minutes. Place in a greased bowl, turning once to grease top. Cover and let rise in a warm place until doubled, about 1 hour. Punch dough down. Form into 24 balls; place in a greased 13x9x2 inch baking pan that has been sprayed with nonstick cooking spray. Cover and let rise until doubled, about 45 minutes. Bake at 350°F. for 20 to 25 minutes. Yield: 2 dozen.

They are so light and fluffy and the dill and onion combination you just have to taste to appreciate!

EASY POPPY SEED BREAD

Clara Hinman
Flagler, CO

1 box lemon cake mix
1 box instant lemon
pudding
½ c. oil
1 c. hot water
4 eggs

2 Tbsp. poppy seed
½ c. orange juice
¾ c. powdered sugar
½ tsp. butter flavoring
½ tsp. vanilla
½ tsp. almond flavoring

Combine cake mix, lemon pudding, cooking oil, and water. Mix these ingredients well. Add the eggs, one at a time, beating after each one. Mix in the poppy seed. Bake in 2 greased loaf pans at 350°F. for 45 minutes. While it is baking, make a glaze. Mix together orange juice, powdered sugar, butter flavoring, vanilla, and almond flavoring; pour over breads while still warm.

This freezes well and is delicious. Great for the afternoon coffee break.

EASY ZUCCHINI BREAD

Theresa Fangman
Hereford, TX

3 eggs
2 c. sugar
1 c. oil
2 c. zucchini, grated
3 tsp. vanilla

3 c. flour
½ tsp. baking powder
1 tsp. baking soda
1 tsp. salt
3 tsp. cinnamon

Beat eggs and add oil, sugar, zucchini, and vanilla. Mix well. Add dry ingredients. Turn into 2 greased and floured bread pans. Chopped nuts may be added if desired. Bake at 350°F. for 1 hour.

FANTASTIC POPPY SEED BREAD

Euda Switzer
Oklahoma City, OK

3 c. flour
½ tsp. salt
1½ tsp. baking powder
2 Tbsp. poppy seed
1½ tsp. almond extract
2 c. sugar
1½ c. vegetable oil

3 eggs
1½ tsp. vanilla
1½ c. milk
¾ c. sugar
¼ c. orange juice
½ tsp. almond extract

Combine flour, salt, baking powder, and poppy seed; set aside. Cream sugar, oil, eggs, vanilla, and almond extract. Add dry ingredients while slowly adding milk. Bake in greased and floured Bundt pan or 5 mini pans for 40 to 60 minutes at 350°F. To prepare glaze, put sugar, orange juice, and almond extract in saucepan and heat until sugar is dissolved. Do not boil. Drizzle glaze over top of bread after you take from oven.

I was visiting in Minnesota and was served this bread. I ate so much I just couldn't leave it alone.

FLUFFY APPLE WALNUT MUFFINS

Amber Uhlenhake
Ossian, IA

½ c. margarine
1¼ c. sugar
1 tsp. vanilla
½ tsp. salt
2 eggs
1¾ c. flour
2 tsp. baking powder
½ tsp. cinnamon

½ c. milk
2 c. tart apples, peeled, sliced, and cored
½ c. walnuts, chopped
¼ c. sugar
½ tsp. cinnamon
3 Tbsp. flour
2 Tbsp. margarine, cubed

Cream together margarine, sugar, vanilla, salt, eggs, flour, baking powder, cinnamon, and milk. Fold in the walnuts and apples. Fill greased jumbo muffin cups ¾ full with batter. Combine the remaining sugar, cinnamon, flour, and margarine. Sprinkle the cinnamon crumble over the muffin tops. Bake at 375°F. for 30 minutes or until golden brown.

GARLIC CHEESE BREAD

Nanette Conger
Fairfield, IA

3½ c. all-purpose flour
1 pkg. active dry yeast
½ c. milk
½ c. water
½ c. vegetable oil
¼ c. white sugar

1 tsp. salt
2 tsp. garlic powder
2 large eggs, beaten
1 c. Cheddar cheese, finely shredded

Combine 1½ cups flour and yeast. Heat milk, water, oil, sugar, salt, and garlic powder (120° to 130°F.), stirring to blend. Add to flour mixture along with eggs and cheese. Beat by hand until batter is smooth. Using a spoon, mix in remaining flour (batter will be stiff). Pour batter into well greased 9x5x3 inch loaf pan. Let rise in a warm place until it is just to the top of the pan (about 1 hour). Bake at 375°F. for 30 to 35 minutes. Cool slightly in pan before removing. Makes 1 loaf.

This bread is great toasted in the toaster or on the grill.

GOOD MORNING CRANBERRY BISCOTTI

Jeanette Pearson
Plymouth, NE

2 (large) eggs
1 c. sugar
1 tsp. orange flavoring
1 tsp. real vanilla flavoring
1 (large) orange, grated
  peel

2 c. flour
1 tsp. baking soda
¼ tsp. sea salt or table
  salt
¾ c. dried cranberries
Raw sugar crystals

Lightly beat eggs. Beat in sugar, orange peel, and flavorings. Stir together flour, baking soda, and salt. Add to wet ingredients and beat well. Stir in cranberries. On a floured surface, shape dough into a log. Transfer to a paper lined baking tray. Sprinkle with raw sugar crystals and flatten to ½ to ¾ inch thickness. Sprinkle with additional sugar. Bake at 350°F. for about 20 minutes or until it has a nice golden crust. Do not underbake. Lower oven temperature to 325°F. Remove from oven and cut in diagonal slices. Return to oven and bake an additional 5 to 7 minutes on each side. If you prefer, you can turn off the heat and let them dry in the warm oven. Watch so they do not brown too much. After completely cooled, store in an airtight container to keep fresh and crisp.

My husband enjoys these in the morning with a good cup of coffee.

GRANDMA PATTERSON'S BANANA NUT BREAD

Debbie Hunt
Anthony, KS

½ c. margarine
1½ c. sugar
2 eggs, well beaten
1⅓ c. bananas, mashed
6 Tbsp. sour milk

4 c. sifted flour
½ tsp. salt
1 tsp. baking soda
1 tsp. baking powder
1 c. nuts, chopped

Cream together margarine and sugar; add beaten eggs, bananas, and milk. Combine flour, salt, baking soda, and baking powder. Add to liquid ingredients slowly; mix well. Add nuts last. Bake in two 8x4x2 inch pans for 45 minutes at 350°F.

42

GRANOLA

LaDonna Miller
Wichita, KS

4½ c. quick oats
1 c. sunflower seeds
1 c. chopped hazelnuts
  (pecans are good, too)
½ c. grapeseed oil

1 c. honey
1 Tbsp. brown sugar
¼ tsp. salt
1 c. water
1 c. raisins

Preheat oven to 350°F. Combine oats, sunflower seeds, and hazelnuts in large bowl. Combine oil, honey, brown sugar, salt, and water in small pan and simmer. Stir to mix and turn off heat. Slowly pour this mixture over oats and nuts, mixing and moistening thoroughly as you go. Spread the granola out in a large tray. Bake for 15 minutes. Toss well. Turn heat down to 275°F. and bake another 45 minutes, tossing every 15 minutes. Turn heat down to 250°F. and bake for another 30 minutes, tossing every 15 minutes. Now turn heat down to 225°F; add the raisins. Mix well. Bake for another 20 to 30 minutes, tossing every 10 to 15 minutes, until the mixture appears dry. Remove the tray from oven. Toss granola every now and then until it has cooled thoroughly. Store in tightly closed container. Makes 9 cups.

Top with fresh fruit and eat as cereal with milk. Bananas, blueberries, or blackberries are especially good.

HERBAL BREAD

Margaret Trojan
Beaver Crossing, NE

1 pkg. active dry yeast
¼ c. lukewarm water
1 (8 oz.) ctn. sour cream
1 egg
1 Tbsp. vegetable oil
2 tsp. honey
¼ tsp. baking soda

1 tsp. salt
¼ c. onion, minced
½ tsp. thyme, dried
4 to 4½ c. all-purpose
  unbleached flour,
  divided
Margarine, melted

Dissolve yeast in warm water in small bowl. Let stand 10 minutes or until foamy. Heat sour cream to about 120°F. Pour warm sour cream into medium bowl. Add egg, oil, honey, baking soda, salt, onion, and thyme. Stir; add yeast mixture. Stir to mix. Add 4 cups flour, 1 cup at a time, mixing thoroughly. Turn out dough onto a lightly floured surface. Knead gently for 1 minute; let rest 10 minutes. Knead 4 minutes, adding small amounts of remaining flour as needed to keep dough manageable. The dough will be elastic, but slightly sticky. Rinse and dry bowl, then oil surface of dough; place into bowl. Cover with a cloth and let rise in warm, draft free area about 1 hour or until doubled. Punch down dough; knead briefly to expel air bubbles. Divide into three equal pieces. Roll each into 18 inch rope. Braid ropes to form loaf; tuck ends underneath. Place loaf on greased baking sheet, cover, and let rise about 30 minutes or until doubled. Bake at 350°F. for 25 to 30 minutes or until golden brown and bread sounds hollow when tapped. Cool on rack 15 minutes; brush with melted margarine.

HOMEMADE QUICK MIX

Annilee Kniffen
Lorena, TX

8½ c. all-purpose flour
1 Tbsp. salt
1 tsp. baking soda
2 Tbsp. baking powder

2 tsp. cream of tartar
1½ c. instant powdered
  milk
1½ c. shortening

Combine flour, salt, baking soda, baking powder, cream of tartar, and dry milk. Blend well. With pastry blender, cut in shortening until mixture resembles cornmeal in texture. Store in airtight container. Makes about 13 cups. Use as you would any commercial mix.

As a variation, you may use ½ all-purpose flour and ½ whole wheat flour.

KOLACHES

Alice P. Boehme
Mullinville, KS

2 pkg. yeast
½ c. water
½ c. warm milk
½ c. sugar
1 tsp. salt

2 eggs
⅔ c. margarine (soft)
4½ to 5 c. flour
1 can cherry pie filling

Dissolve yeast in warm water. Stir in milk, sugar, salt, egg, butter, and 2 cups of the flour. Beat until smooth. Stir in enough remaining flour to make dough easy to handle. Turn dough onto lightly floured surface; knead until smooth and elastic, about 5 minutes. Place in greased bowl; cover and let rise in warm place until double, about 1½ hours. Punch down dough, divide into 24 equal pieces, and place about 3 inches apart on greased baking sheets. Make depression in center of each and fill with 1½ tablespoons filling, leaving ¼ inch ridge around outside of circle. I use cherry pie filling for the filling. Let rise until double, about 30 minutes. Heat oven to 350°F. and bake 15 minutes.

LEMONY BERRY MUFFINS

Margaret Trojan
Beaver Crossing, NE

1 (18.25 oz.) box lemon
  cake mix
4 eggs
1 c. milk (non-fat or
  regular)

½ c. margarine, softened
1 c. blueberries (fresh or
  frozen)

In large bowl, beat together all ingredients, except blueberries. Evenly coat 24 muffin cups lightly with cooking spray or line cups with paper liners. Spoon mixture into cups, filling each about ⅔ full. Evenly sprinkle blueberries on top of each muffin. Bake at 350°F. for 18 to 23 minutes or until a toothpick inserted in the center comes out clean.

MAPLE NUT TWIST

Julie Schmidt
Smith Center, KS

¾ c. milk
¼ c. margarine
2¾ to 3 c. all-purpose
  flour
3 Tbsp. sugar
½ tsp. salt

1 pkg. yeast
1 tsp. maple flavoring
1 egg
⅓ c. margarine (to spread
  on layers)

Filling:

½ c. sugar
⅓ c. chopped nuts
  (optional)

1 tsp. cinnamon
1 tsp. maple flavoring
1 c. powdered sugar

Glaze:

1 to 2 Tbsp. margarine
1 to 2 Tbsp. milk

½ tsp. maple flavoring

Heat milk and margarine until very warm (120° to 130°F.). In large bowl, blend warm liquids, 1 cup flour, sugar, salt, yeast, flavoring, and egg; mix. Beat 2 minutes at medium speed. Stir in remaining flour to form a soft dough. Knead until smooth and elastic. Place dough in greased bowl and let rise until doubled. Combine filling ingredients. Grease 12 inch pizza pan. Punch down dough and divide into 3 balls. Roll or press 1 ball to cover bottom of pan. Brush dough with melted margarine. Sprinkle with ⅓ filling. Repeat layers of dough, melted margarine, and filling with 2 other balls of dough. To shape, place a glass about 2 inches in diameter in center of dough. With scissors, cut from outside edge to the glass, forming 16 pie shaped wedges. Twist each wedge 4 or 5 times. Remove glass. Cover; let rise until light, 30 to 45 minutes. Heat oven to 375°F. Bake 18 to 22 minutes, until light brown. In small bowl, blend glaze. Drizzle over warm coffee cake.

I have made these as gifts for teachers and friends and they are such a pretty gift to give.

MORNING GLORY MUFFINS

Iola Egle
Bella Vista, AR

1½ c. sugar
½ c. oil
3 eggs
2 tsp. vanilla
2 c. flour
2 tsp. baking powder
¼ tsp. salt

1 tsp. cinnamon
2 c. carrots, grated
½ c. raisins
½ c. coconut
½ c. raw apple, diced
½ c. nuts

Combine sugar, oil, eggs, and vanilla in a large bowl; set aside. Sift together flour, baking powder, salt, and cinnamon. Add dry ingredients to liquid ingredients and stir until just moistened. Gently fold in carrots, raisins, coconut, apple, and nutmeats. Spoon into greased muffin tins to about ⅔ full. Bake at 350°F. for 20 to 25 minutes. Serve immediately with butter.

This muffin is good for breakfast or served with a dinner meal.

NO KNEAD COMPANY ROLLS

Clara Ough
Hebron, NE

½ c. lukewarm water
3 Tbsp. sugar
¼ c. dry yeast
5 c. milk, scalded
1 c. sugar

2 tsp. salt
½ c. butter
4 eggs, beaten
14 c. sifted flour

Dissolve yeast in lukewarm water in which the sugar has been added. Scald milk with sugar, salt, and butter. Cool; add beaten eggs. Add this to the yeast mixture. Gradually add flour until you have a dough stiff enough to pull away from the bowl. Cover and let rise until doubled. Shape into tea rolls or cinnamon rolls. Let rise again and bake at 375°F. for about 20 minutes or until a golden brown.

NUT FILLED DINNER ROLLS

Beverly Feit
Eaton, CO

Filling:

⅔ c. butter
2 c. sifted powdered
  sugar

1¾ c. walnuts, finely
  chopped
1 box hot roll mix

Cream together butter, powdered sugar, and add walnuts for filling. Follow steps on roll mix. Roll dough to 22x12 inch rectangle on a floured surface. Starting in the middle, going down, spread dough with filling. Fold top half over filling. Press dough together around rectangle to seal filling. Cut into 1 inch strips from the top to the bottom. Twist dough by starting at folded end and continue twisting to form a circle. Tuck end of dough under. Bake on greased cookie sheet at 350°F. for 18 to 20 minutes. Drizzle any kind of bottled orange juice on top of rolls. Bake an additional 3 to 5 minutes longer or until golden brown.

The rolls look very nice and are great for special get togethers.

OVERNIGHT CINNAMON-CARAMEL ROLLS

Juanita K. Parker
Ness City, KS

2 pkg. dry yeast
½ c. warm water
2 c. milk, scalded
⅓ c. sugar
1 egg
⅓ c. oil or shortening
2 tsp. salt
6½ to 7 c. flour

3 tsp. baking powder
4 Tbsp. butter
2 tsp. cinnamon
½ c. sugar
1 c. brown sugar
½ c. butter
2 Tbsp. corn syrup
½ c. nuts

Dissolve yeast in warm water. Cool milk to lukewarm and stir into yeast with ⅓ cup sugar, shortening, baking powder, salt, egg, and 3 cups flour. Beat until smooth. Stir in enough flour to make dough easy to handle. Knead for 10 minutes. Let rise until double, 1 to 1½ hours. Punch down dough and roll out into two rectangles, 9x14 inches. Spread with 4 tablespoons butter, melted. Mix 2 teaspoons cinnamon and ½ cup sugar. Sprinkle over rectangles. Roll up dough, pinching edges to seal. Cut each roll into 12 pieces. Before placing in pans, prepare caramel mixture by heating 1 cup brown sugar and ½ cup butter until melted. Add 2 tablespoons corn syrup. Divide mixture between baking pans and sprinkle ½ cup chopped nuts in each pan. (Either pecans or walnuts can be used.) Wrap pans in foil and put into refrigerator up to 48 hours.

When you want the rolls baked, take from refrigerator, remove foil, and bake in 350°F. oven for 30 to 35 minutes.

This is a very versatile recipe for those who need a morning pastry. Everything can be prepared one to two days ahead of time. The caramel part can be increased to 1½ recipes for a roll with more caramel topping.

OVERNIGHT COFFEE CAKE

Juanita K. Parker
Ness City, KS

2 c. flour
1 c. sugar
½ c. brown sugar
⅔ c. shortening
1 c. buttermilk
1 tsp. baking soda
1 tsp. baking powder

1 tsp. cinnamon
½ tsp. salt
2 eggs
½ c. brown sugar
½ c. nuts, chopped
1 tsp. cinnamon

Grease a 9x13 inch pan. On low speed, blend flour, sugar, shortening, buttermilk, baking soda, baking powder, cinnamon, salt, and eggs. Beat 3 minutes at medium speed. Spread in pan. For topping, mix brown sugar, cinnamon, and nuts. Pour over batter. Cover and refrigerate overnight. Bake 30 to 40 minutes at 350°F.

PANCAKES

Pauline Riley
Dodge City, KS

2 Tbsp. bacon drippings
1 egg
1 c. milk
1 c. flour

½ tsp. salt
2 Tbsp. sugar
2 Tbsp. baking powder

Mix all ingredients together. Do not beat. Pour pancakes, desired size, into hot greased skillet. Turn when tops are bubbly.

PLUM-CRAZY BREAD

Flo M. Burtnett
Gage, OK

2 (14 oz.) cans purple
  plums
1 stick margarine
2 tsp. baking soda
2 c. flour

1 c. sugar
½ tsp. salt
½ tsp. cinnamon
½ tsp. cloves
½ c. raisins

Grease and flour 9x5 inch loaf pan. Drain plums, remove the seeds, and puree the fruit in food processor. You should have 1 cup of pureed fruit. Heat pulp with margarine, stirring until melted. Remove from heat and place in a large mixing bowl. Stir in the baking soda. The mixture will foam and take on an ugly brown color. Let mixture cool to lukewarm. Add flour, cinnamon, cloves, and raisins. Mix well and pour into prepared pan. Bake at 350°F. for 70 to 80 minutes, until center is firm. Test with a toothpick.

If batter seems dry, add a little plum juice.

POPOVERS

Flo M. Burtnett
Gage, OK

2 eggs
1 c. milk

½ tsp. salt
1 c. flour

Beat eggs until creamy. Add milk, salt, and flour. Follow recipe exactly. Never add baking powder or more flour. The batter must be thin. Fill greased and floured muffin tins halfway with the batter and bake at 375°F. for 35 minutes. These popovers will swell to 5 times their original bulk and will be hollow. Serve warm with butter. Makes 12 popovers.

POTATO BREAD IN A BREAD MACHINE

Julie Schmidt
Smith Center, KS

1½ c. water
2 Tbsp. butter
3 Tbsp. sugar
1 tsp. salt

4¼ c. all-purpose flour
⅔ c. instant potato flakes
1½ tsp. dry yeast

Measure the water and butter and add to the bread machine baking pan. Add the sugar, salt, flour, and potato flakes in the order listed and tap firmly. Make a well in the dry ingredients and add the yeast. Place in the bread machine and close the lid. Select "Basic Bread" and set crust control as desired. Press start. Cool before slicing. Yield: 1 loaf.

PRIZE ROLLS

Velma Hockett
Santanta, KS

½ c. shortening
½ c. sugar
2 eggs
1 tsp. salt

1 pkg. yeast
4 c. flour
1 c. warm water
3 tsp. warm water

Combine shortening, sugar, and salt. Add the beaten eggs. Dissolve yeast in 3 teaspoons of water; add to the shortening mix. Add 1 cup warm water and 2 cups of the flour and mix well. Add rest of the flour and knead until smooth. Place in a clean bowl and cover and let rise 2 hours. Put the dough in the refrigerator. When ready to use, take out the rolls and let rise 3 hours. Bake in 400°F. oven for 10 minutes.

It's very important to let dough rise 3 hours.

QUICK AND EASY BISCUITS

Janet Rauch
Deep River, IA

2 c. flour
1 c. half & half
1 Tbsp. sugar

⅓ c. mayonnaise
2 tsp. baking powder
1 tsp. baking soda

Mix ingredients together and drop with cookie dipper. Bake at 400° to 450°F. for 12 minutes or until golden brown.

These are good with gravy on top and easy to make for someone who can't make biscuits.

RANCH, BACON, CHEESE BREAD

Bobbi Higgs
Ulysses, KS

1 pkg. frozen bread rolls
1 lb. bacon
1 pkg. dry Ranch salad
   dressing mix

1 c. shredded Cheddar
   cheese

Place rolls in greased pan, cover, let rise. Pre-cook and crumble bacon. Heat oven to 400°F. Sprinkle raised rolls with Ranch dressing mix, bacon bits, and cheese. Bake in oven approximately 20 minutes or until done.

SAVORY BUTTERHORNS

Linda Pauls
Buhler, KS

1 c. plus 2 Tbsp. water (110°F. to 115°F.)	1 large egg, beaten
1 pkg. active dry yeast	2 Tbsp. wheat bran
1/3 c. non-fat dry milk powder	1 2/3 c. whole wheat flour
2 Tbsp. sugar	1 1/2 c. bread flour, several Tbsp. more if needed
1/4 c. shortening, melted	1/4 c. margarine, melted
1 tsp. salt	1 Tbsp. dried parsley, crushed
1 tsp. all-purpose seasoning	1/2 tsp. garlic salt
	1/4 c. Parmesan cheese

In a large mixing bowl, dissolve yeast in warm water. Add powdered milk, sugar, shortening, salt, seasoning, beaten egg, and bran. Add whole wheat flour and beat well. Add enough of bread flour to form a soft dough. Knead 6 to 8 minutes by hand or with a dough hook. Place in lightly greased bowl, turning once to grease the top. Cover, let rise until double. Punch down and let rest 10 minutes. In a small bowl, combine margarine, parsley, and garlic salt. Set aside. Roll 1/2 of dough into a 12 inch circle, spread with 1/2 of margarine mixture and sprinkle with 1/2 of Parmesan cheese. Cut into 12 pieces, roll up each pie-wedge, starting at the wide end and roll up; place seam side down on lightly greased baking sheet. Continue with rest of dough the same way. Let rise until almost doubled. Bake in 375°F. oven for 13 to 15 minutes or nicely browned. Remove from baking sheet; cool on wire rack. Yield: 24 rolls.

SHELIA'S WONDERFUL STRAWBERRY BREAD

Euda Switzer
Oklahoma City, OK

4 eggs, slightly beaten	1 tsp. baking soda
1 1/3 c. vegetable oil	1 tsp. baking powder
2 (10 oz.) pkg. frozen strawberries, mashed	3 c. flour
2 c. sugar	1 Tbsp. cinnamon
	1 tsp. salt

Mix together eggs, oil, and strawberries. Mix together flour, cinnamon, salt, sugar, baking soda, and baking powder. Add to strawberry mixture. Stir together well. Put in 2 loaf pans and bake 1 hour at 350°F. Test with knife for doneness.

SOUR CREAM BANANA MUFFINS

Barb Kasel
Adams, MN

1 c. sugar	½ c. sour cream
½ c. butter or margarine	1 tsp. vanilla
1 egg	4 bananas, very ripe and
2 c. flour	mashed
1 tsp. baking soda	½ c. nuts, chopped

Preheat oven to 350°F. Cream sugar and butter until light and beat in egg until smooth. Add flour and baking soda alternately with sour cream. Add vanilla, bananas, and nuts. Divide batter among 12 medium greased muffin cups. Bake 25 to 30 minutes.

SPOON BREAD

Ellen Olivier
Harper, KS

¾ c. corn meal	1 c. milk
1 Tbsp. flour	1 c. sour cream
3 Tbsp. sugar	1 (14 oz.) can cream corn
¼ tsp. salt	¾ c. cheese, shredded
1 egg, beaten	

Mix cornmeal, flour, sugar, and salt together. Add beaten egg, milk, sour cream, and cream corn. Stir well and pour into an 8x10 inch baking dish. Top with the cheese and bake at 350°F. for 35 to 40 minutes.

I have also browned one pound of ground beef and added the spoon bread on top, baking it in a 9x12 inch baking dish.

TOASTED OATMEAL RAISIN BREAD

Alice P. Boehme
Mullinville, KS

3 to 3½ c. flour
2 c. whole wheat flour
½ tsp. salt
2 pkg. yeast
1 c. milk
¼ c. honey
½ c. water

1 tsp. cinnamon
¼ c. margarine
2 eggs
1½ c. old-fashioned oats, slightly toasted
2 c. raisins
½ c. walnuts, chopped

In a large bowl, mix 1½ cups flour, salt, and undissolved yeast. Combine water, milk, honey, and margarine in a saucepan. Heat until very warm (120°F. to 130°F.). Gradually add to the dry ingredients and beat for 2 minutes. Add eggs, toasted oatmeal, and 1 cup of flour. Beat for 2 more minutes on high speed setting. Stir in raisins, walnuts, cinnamon, and additional flour to make a stiff dough. Knead for 8 to 10 minutes. Place in greased bowl, cover, and let rise for 1½ hours. Punch down dough and divide in ½. Shape into 2 loaves and place in greased loaf pans. Cover and let rise 1 more hour. Bake in a preheated 350°F. oven for 30 minutes. Take out of pans and brush with margarine.

TOFFEE COFFEE CAKE

Pat Stutz
Utica, KS

1 c. brown sugar, firmly packed
1 c. white sugar
2 c. sifted flour
1 tsp. baking soda
½ tsp. salt
½ c. (1 stick) butter

1 c. buttermilk
1 egg
½ tsp. vanilla
1 (12 oz.) pkg. toffee bites
½ c. pecans, chopped (optional)

Grease or spray 9x13 inch pan. Mix white sugar and brown sugar in a bowl. Sift flour, baking soda, and salt; mix well. Cut in butter. Set aside ½ of mixture. To the remaining mixture, add buttermilk, egg, and vanilla. Beat well and turn into pan. Combine the reserved mix with candy and nuts. Sprinkle over the batter. Bake at 350°F. for 30 to 35 minutes.

Out of this world.

TORTILLAS

Thelma Maxwell
Dodge City, KS

2 c. flour
2 tsp. baking powder
2 Tbsp. oil

⅛ tsp. salt
¾ c. cold water

Mix ingredients together. Make approximately 1 inch balls. Roll out flat with pastry cloth and rolling pin. Brown very lightly in thin layer of oil in skillet on both sides. Make 12 tortillas. Fill with favorite taco mix.

WALNUT RAISIN WHEAT BREAD

Alice P. Boehme
Mullinville, KS

1 pkg. yeast
1 c. warm milk
1 c. warm water
½ tsp. pepper
2½ to 3 c. flour

2 c. raisins
2 Tbsp. sugar
1 tsp. salt
2 c. whole wheat flour
1 c. walnuts, chopped

Combine warm water, warm milk, and yeast in a large bowl or mixer bowl if using a mixer. Let sit until yeast foams, about 5 minutes. Add raisins, pepper, flour, sugar, salt, whole wheat flour, and walnuts and mix for 2 to 3 minutes. Knead dough for 8 to 10 minutes, adding extra flour as needed. Place in greased bowl, cover and let rise until doubled in bulk, about 1½ hours. Punch dough down and divide in half. Shape into 2 loaves and place in greased loaf pans. Let rise 30 to 45 minutes. Preheat oven to 350°F. and bake for 30 minutes. Take out of pan and brush with margarine.

WHOLE WHEAT BREAD

Shelley Fangman
Hereford, TX

2 c. scalded milk
1½ tsp. salt
¼ c. lukewarm water
3 c. whole wheat flour

¼ c. brown sugar
2 Tbsp. oil
1 pkg. yeast
3 c. white flour

Add salt, shortening, and sugar to scalded milk and cool to lukewarm. Add yeast to lukewarm water and 1 teaspoon white sugar. Let stand 5 minutes. Combine yeast and milk in a large bowl. Add all whole wheat flour and enough white flour to make a soft dough. Place remaining flour on board and knead the dough till smooth and elastic. Place in greased bowl; turn over so that greased side is on top. Cover with cloth. Let rise until doubled in bulk, about 1 hour. Punch down and let rise a second time if desired. Divide dough in ½ and place in loaf pans. Let rise about 30 minutes. Bake for 10 minutes at 400°F; reduce temperature to 375°F. and bake 35 to 40 minutes longer. Makes 2 loaves.

YUMMY MORNING ROLLS
Margaret Trojan
Beaver Crossing, NE

1 bag (24 count) frozen
    dinner rolls
1 (3¾ oz.) pkg.
    butterscotch pudding
    (not instant)

½ c. butter
¾ c. brown sugar
¾ tsp. cinnamon
½ c. nuts, chopped
    (pecans or walnuts)

Arrange rolls in lightly greased Bundt pan. Sprinkle dry ingredients over rolls. Cook remaining ingredients over low heat until sugar is dissolved and mixture bubbles, stirring constantly. Pour over rolls. Cover tightly with foil and let stand on counter overnight. Next morning, bake at 350°F. for 30 minutes.

Notes

Main Dishes

Main Dishes
Recipe Contest Winners

First
Chicken Salad Crescent Bake
Deb Smith, Fowler, Colorado
Page 72

Second
Basil Cream Chicken
Arlene Bontrager, Hutchinson, Kansas
Page 60

Third
Black Bean Soup, Marilyn Barner
Belle Plaine, Kansas
Page 64

MAIN DISHES

1-2-3 MACARONI BAKE

Vivian J. Tank
Fremont, NE

1½ c. chicken, cooked and diced
½ tsp. garlic salt
1 tsp. salt
4 Tbsp. dehydrated onions
4 Tbsp. dehydrated garlic, sliced

1½ c. broccoli flowerets
1 (1 lb.) jar double Cheddar cheese sauce
½ c. Cheddar cheese, shredded
2 c. macaroni, cooked
Pepper to taste

Heat diced chicken with garlic salt, ½ teaspoon salt, 3 tablespoons onions, and 3 tablespoons garlic and mix with cooked macaroni. In the microwave, blanch for 2 to 3 minutes broccoli in a few drops of water with ½ teaspoon salt, 1 tablespoon onion, and 1 tablespoon garlic. Drain off the water. Mix all ingredients together and add the Cheddar cheese sauce. Bake in the oven at 350°F. for 20 minutes or on high in the microwave for 12 to 15 minutes. Top with shredded cheese; return to oven or microwave to melt cheese. Serves 6 to 8 people.

Our family thinks this recipe is great, and asks for it often.

7 LAYER MAGIC

Diane Meisinger
Hillsboro, KS

Potatoes, peeled and sliced
½ carrot, finely sliced
Onions, chopped
Celery, chopped

1 can peas
1 lb. ground beef, browned
1 can mushroom soup

Layer in 13x9 inch glass pan potatoes, carrots, onions, celery, peas, ground beef, and mushroom soup (mixed with a little water or milk). Cover and bake for 70 to 80 minutes at 350°F. Uncover and bake 15 minutes longer.

Increase or decrease the vegetables according to your family's tastes. Salt and pepper to your liking.

BAKED POTATO SOUP

Evelyn Brownlee
Liberal, KS

5 lb. potatoes
1 c. butter
1 c. flour
3 c. milk
2 cans chicken broth

Salt and pepper
Cheese, grated
Sour cream
Green onions
Bacon, crumbled

Rub oil on potatoes and bake one hour. Cool in refrigerator. Cut in ½ and scoop out the chunks of potatoes. Brown butter and add flour; stir until smooth. Add milk until it becomes roux. Add chicken broth to desired consistency. Cook all ingredients until warmed. Garnish with the cheese, sour cream, green onions, and bacon.

While warming, if you desire a thicker soup, mash some of the potatoes.

BAKED SANDWICH

Kimberly Chambers
Norcatur, KS

12 slices buttered bread
6 slices Cheddar cheese
1 can chunked ham
4 eggs

2½ c. milk
Mustard to taste
Onion salt to taste
Pepper to taste

In a buttered 9x13 inch pan, place six slices of the bread (buttered side down). Top with a cheese slice and spread with a little mustard. Add the crumbled ham, then top with the other slices of bread. Beat eggs; add milk and seasonings. Pour mixture over the sandwiches. Let stand at least 1 hour or overnight. Bake 50 minutes at 325°F. (or until golden brown).

BAKED STEAK

Diane Meisinger
Hillsboro, KS

2 lb. round steak
1 c. flour
1 Tbsp. salt
1 Tbsp. black pepper
Cooking oil

2 cans cream of
   mushroom soup
1 (large) onion
2 c. sour cream
1 c. milk

Cut round steak into serving size pieces. Roll each side raw steak in flour, salt, and pepper. Cook in hot skillet with cooking oil (⅛ inch deep) until browned on each side, about 10 minutes per side. Place browned pieces in roaster. When finished frying steaks, reserve drippings and add onion. Cook till transparent. Add milk and stir to make light gravy. Add cream of mushroom soup and sour cream; pour this mixture over browned steaks. Bake in 300°F. oven for 4 to 5 hours until tender. Serve with mashed potatoes and use the gravy from the steaks.

This is a nice meal for cold winter nights.

BAR-Q-BRISKET

Lois Mills
Lake City, KS

Brisket
2 Tbsp. vinegar
2 Tbsp. sugar
2 Tbsp. salt
2 garlic cloves
½ tsp. pepper
2 bay leaves

1 stalk celery
1 onion, chopped
4 cloves
1 Tbsp. horseradish
1 Tbsp. mustard
BBQ sauce (to taste)

Place brisket in water to cover. If brisket is too large, cut in ½. Put all the ingredients in the brisket; cook 3 to 4 hours on low heat. Cool overnight. Slice with electric knife. Line pan in foil and layer with sliced brisket. Save 1 cup broth, celery, onion, and spices. Add horseradish, mustard, and BBQ sauce. Put this over sliced brisket and cover. Bake in 250°F. oven for 2 hours.

BARBECUED MEATBALLS

Janell Papke
Cortland, NE

1 lb. ground beef
½ c. onion
½ c. green pepper
1 c. cracker crumbs
½ c. milk
1 egg

Salt and pepper to taste
1½ Tbsp. Worcestershire
   sauce
¼ c. vinegar
½ c. ketchup
¼ c. barbecue sauce

Combine ground beef, onion, green pepper, cracker crumbs, milk, egg, and salt and pepper; shape into balls and place in 9x9 inch pan. Combine Worcestershire sauce, vinegar, ketchup, and barbecue sauce and pour over meatballs. Bake at 350°F. for 1 hour.

BASIL CREAM CHICKEN

Arlene Bontrager
Hutchinson, KS

4 boneless, skinless
  chicken breasts, cubed
½ c. onions, chopped
2 (4 oz.) cans sliced
  mushrooms, drained
⅓ c. margarine
⅓ c. flour
1 Tbsp. chicken soup base
  flavoring

4 c. milk
1 (8 oz.) pkg. cream
  cheese, cubed
½ tsp. salt
1 (8 oz.) pkg. spaghetti or
  fettuccine
½ c. Parmesan cheese,
  grated
1 tsp. basil

In a skillet, saute chicken breasts until done. I usually marinate breasts before cooking with Italian dressing for several hours or overnight. Set aside. In a large saucepan, melt margarine; add onions and saute a couple of minutes. Stir in flour and salt until smooth. Add soup base flavoring and milk, stirring and cooking until thickened. Add cream cheese and Parmesan cheese, stirring until melted and smooth. Add basil and mushrooms. In another large saucepan, cook spaghetti until done; drain. In a 9x13x2 inch baking dish, spray with nonstick cooking spray. Pour in spaghetti, layering over the cooked chicken. Pour cream sauce over all. Cover and bake.

BEAN SOUP

LaDonna Miller
Wichita, KS

1 lb. ground turkey
1 can pork and beans
1 can hot chili beans
1 can butter beans
½ chopped onion (or
  more)

1 tsp. mustard
¼ c. ketchup
½ c. brown sugar
1 can tomato soup

Brown turkey and onion. Fill crockpot and add water to your liking. Can sizes can be enlarged to increase quantity. Stir every ½ hour or so. Takes about 3 hours on high to complete.

BEEF BRISKET

Lori Zimmerman
Ulysses, KS

3 to 5 lb. brisket
1 tsp. celery salt
1 tsp. onion salt
1 tsp. garlic salt
½ tsp. hickory smoked
   salt
1 tsp. pepper
½ Tbsp. Worcestershire
   sauce
½ Tbsp. liquid smoke
1 can beer
½ to ¾ c. beef broth

Combine all spices, Worcestershire sauce, and liquid smoke, making a paste-like consistency. Rub on brisket. Place in slow cooker. Add beer. Cook on low for 8 to 10 hours. Remove to plate or cutting board and discard juice. After meat has cooled a bit, slice and return to slow cooker. Add just enough beef broth to cover bottom of cooker to keep the meat moist. Top with barbecue sauce. Return to low until warmed through.

The meat cooks so nicely, no knife needed here.

BEEF CHOW MEIN SKILLET

Grace Bernasek
Axtell, KS

1 lb. ground beef
1 large onion
4 c. hot water
3 c. celery, chopped
1 (8 oz.) pkg. fresh
   mushrooms, quartered
1½ c. water
1 (8 oz.) can water
   chestnuts, sliced
3 Tbsp. reduced sodium
   soy sauce
1 Tbsp. brown sugar
2 tsp. beef bouillon
   granules
1 tsp. garlic powder
⅛ tsp. pepper
2 Tbsp. cornstarch
1 Tbsp. water
3 c. hot cooked rice
1 c. chow mein noodles

In a large nonstick skillet cook beef and onions; drain. Stir celery, mushrooms, water chestnuts, soy sauce, brown sugar, bouillon granules, garlic, and pepper. Bring to a boil. Reduce heat and simmer for 15 to 20 minutes or until vegetables are tender. Combine cornstarch and cold water and blend until smooth. Stir into meat mixture and stir for 2 minutes or until thickened. Serve over rice if desired; top with chow mein noodles.

BEEF ENCHILADA CASSEROLE

Cindy Woody
Blooming Grove, TX

1 lb. ground beef
½ c. onion, chopped
1 can green chili enchilada sauce
1 can cream of chicken soup

10 regular flour tortillas, torn into bite-sized pieces
2 c. cheese, grated

Brown ground beef and onion in a large skillet. Add salt, pepper, garlic, cumin, or chili powder if you like. Add the soup and enchilada sauce, then stir in tortilla pieces. Put in a 9x13 inch casserole dish and bake at 375°F. until cheese is melted. Can be made ahead and stored in refrigerator. Freezes and reheats well.

To make a lower fat version, use lean ground beef, reduced fat soup, and a low fat cheese. If you want to reduce the carbs, use fewer tortillas. This dish is always a crowd pleaser and goes fast at covered dish luncheons.

BEEF ENCHILADAS

Kim Oborny
Durham, KS

2 lb. ground beef
1 (10 oz.) can enchilada sauce (mild)
2 (1.25 oz.) pkg. taco seasoning
½ c. water

1 (10 count) pkg. medium size flour tortillas
1 (2 lb.) pkg. Colby and Monterey Jack cheese mix, finely shredded

Brown ground beef and drain. Add taco seasoning and water. Mix well and let simmer 5 minutes. Take one tortilla and sprinkle a tiny bit of the cheese toward one side, then place 1 to 2 spoonfuls of meat mixture on top of cheese and roll up. Repeat with remaining tortillas. Place all in a 9x13 inch pan, lightly greased with a nonstick cooking spray. Pour the can of enchilada sauce over all, coating evenly. Top with remaining cheese. Bake at 350°F. until heated and cheese is melted and bubbly.

Top with picante sauce and sour cream if desired.

BEEF GREEN CHILI ENCHILADAS

Kim Robinson
Dexter, NM

4 to 6 c. roast beef
1 (15 oz.) green enchilada
   sauce
1 can cream of chicken
   soup

½ c. broth from roast
¼ c. milk
¼ c. sour cream
Shredded Cheddar cheese
1 pkg. flour tortillas

Shred roast beef and set aside. Mix together enchilada sauce, cream of chicken soup, and roast broth in a small bowl. Spread ½ cup of sauce mixture in a 9x13 inch pan. Using 1 flour tortilla at a time, place ⅓ cup of roast and sprinkle with a little grated cheese at one end and roll up. Cut in half and put in pan. Repeat until entire pan is filled. Cover tortillas with remaining sauce and 1½ cups of grated cheese. Cover and bake at 350°F. for 30 to 40 minutes. Serve with additional sour cream and/or guacamole.

Makes great use of leftover pot roast.

BEEF STEW

Ivy Maltbie
Amorita, OK

1½ lb. ground beef
4 potatoes, peeled and
   diced
4 stalks celery, diced

4 carrots, diced
1 (46 oz.) can tomato juice
1 pkg. beef stew mix

Brown ground beef and drain grease. Add diced potatoes, carrots, celery, tomato juice, and beef stew mix. Bring stew to a boil and then let simmer until vegetables are soft.

BEEF TIPS AND GRAVY

Julie Schmidt
Smith Center, KS

1½ lb. stew meat
1 can cream of celery
   soup
1 can cream of mushroom
   soup

1 pkg. dry onion soup mix
⅓ c. water

Place stew meat into baking dish or crockpot. Sprinkle dry onion soup over meat. Add soups diluted with water. Bake in oven at 275°F. for 4 hours or in a crockpot on low for 8 hours. Fifteen minutes before serving, stir in ½ cup sour cream. Serve over cooked noodles or rice.

BEEFY PARMESAN PASTA
Freedom, OK

1½ lb. ground beef
1 can beef broth
1 (14.5 oz.) can Italian
   style diced tomatoes

2 c. pasta
¾ c. Parmesan cheese

In a large skillet over medium or high heat, brown the ground beef. Remove the beef and drain. In the skillet, add the beef broth, tomatoes, and pasta. Stir to coat all of the pasta, then bring to a boil and then reduce the heat. Cook, uncovered, for 15 to 20 minutes, stirring frequently. Return beef to the skillet and stir in ½ cup of the cheese. Sprinkle with remaining cheese over each serving.

BLACK BEAN SOUP
Marilyn Barner
Belle Plaine, KS

1 (small) pkg. black beans
½ lb. ground beef
½ lb. sausage
½ bunch celery, chopped
2 c. onions, chopped

2 c. beef broth
1½ tsp. dry basil, chopped
2 Tbsp. Cajun seasoning
1 tsp. black pepper
⅛ tsp. cayenne pepper

Cook black beans according to package directions. Brown ground beef and sausage. Drain. Saute celery and onions in small amount of meat grease. Add meats, celery, onions, broth, basil, Cajun seasoning, pepper, and cayenne pepper to the bean mixture. Simmer on top of stove at least 30 minutes. Some water or more beef broth may be added if needed. Serve with your choice of crackers.

I have made this soup with all ground beef instead of sausage, and it is very good that way, too.

BOURBON KICK STEAK

Diane Meisinger
Hillsboro, KS

2 Tbsp. onion, finely
  chopped
½ c. bourbon
½ c. soy sauce
⅓ c. brown sugar

⅓ c. lemon juice
2 tsp. garlic, chopped
4 (10 oz.) strip steaks
  (using an equiv. cut of
  meat is fine)

Mix onion, bourbon, soy sauce, brown sugar, lemon juice, and garlic in a small bowl. Stir until well blended. Place steaks in a 13x9 inch glass baking dish. Pour marinade over steaks. Cover and refrigerate for 4 to 8 hours, turning over once about halfway through marinating. Grill on very hot grill for 2 minutes on each side, then over medium heat until desired doneness.

BROCCOLI SOUP

Judy Hall
McCook, NE

Broccoli (a whole head or
  to your taste)
2 c. celery, diced
1 can cream of chicken
  soup

1 c. low fat cottage
  cheese
2 c. low fat milk
Salt and pepper to taste

Cook broccoli and celery in water until tender. Drain. Blend chicken soup, cottage cheese, and milk in blender until smooth. Pour over broccoli and heat until hot.

You may add about a cup of Cheddar cheese or until the color is as you like it. My husband says this soup is a "keeper".

BRUNCH CASSEROLE

Annilee Kniffen
Lorena, TX

1½ lb. sausage, regular
1 (8 oz.) can crescent rolls
2 c. Mozzarella cheese,
  shredded

4 eggs, beaten
¾ c. milk
¼ tsp. salt
⅛ tsp. pepper

Crumble sausage and cook. Drain well. Line a buttered 13x9 inch dish with crescent rolls. Firmly press to seal seams. Sprinkle with sausage and cheese. Mix eggs, milk, salt, and pepper. Beat well and pour over sausage and cheese. Bake at 375°F. for 20 to 25 minutes. Let stand 5 minutes; cut and serve.

CASHEW CHICKEN
Karen Sysel
Dorchester, NE

2 cubes chicken bouillon
1¾ c. boiling water
2 Tbsp. soy sauce
5 tsp. cornstarch
2 tsp. light brown sugar
2 chicken breasts, diced
1 tsp. ground ginger
2 Tbsp. vegetable oil

2 c. mushrooms, chopped
½ c. green onion, chopped
1 (small) onion, chopped
1 (8 oz.) can water chestnuts
½ c. cashews
Cooked rice

Chop vegetables; set aside. In small saucepan, dissolve bouillon cubes in hot water. Add soy sauce, cornstarch, sugar, and ginger. In large skillet, brown chicken in oil. Add bouillon mixture. Cook until slightly thickened. Watch as sauce can burn quickly. Put in vegetables. Simmer, uncovered, 5 to 8 minutes, stirring occasionally. Add cashews. Serve over hot cooked rice. Serves 4 to 6.

CHARLIE'S GARLIC CHICKEN
Charles E. Dobbs
Medford, NY

1 bulb garlic
2 c. basil
1 c. mint
1 can black olives
4 c. extra-virgin olive oil
1 (medium) tomato
2 tsp. hot sauce
Sea salt to taste
Pepper to taste

3 to 4 lb. chicken, cut up
1 pkg. string beans (fresh or frozen)
1 c. rice (brown or white)
2¼ c. chicken stock
1 bottle white wine
1 loaf Italian bread
¼ to ½ c. cheese, grated

Add bulb of garlic, basil leaves, mint leaves, black confirmed pitted olives, extra-virgin olive oil, hot sauce, tomato, sea salt, and black pepper into a blender. Blend until you have what looks like a green pea soup. Place the chicken in a large bowl; pour half of the garlic sauce on the chicken. Make sure to add white wine to cover the chicken; 1 bottle should be good. If more liquid is needed, add water. Marinate for at least 24 to 36 hours. Keep some of the sauce for basting and for garlic bread (see below). Bake the chicken in the oven at 350°F. for about 1 hour. The last 15 minutes, increase the temperature to 450°F. to get it crispy. Coat the chicken pieces with the leftover sauce; check every 15 minutes and keep adding more. Serve with white rice and Italian string bean combo. Add rice to chicken stock and Italian frozen or fresh string beans; cook, covered, until all of the liquid has been absorbed. Take 1 loaf of Italian bread, slice about ¾ inch thick, brush with garlic sauce, and sprinkle with your favorite grated cheese. Place in oven at 375°F. for about 10 to 15 minutes; bake until golden brown.

CHEDDAR HAM ROLL

Amber Uhlenhake
Ossian, IA

1 tube crusty French bread
2 c. shredded Cheddar cheese
¼ lb. thin sliced deli ham
1 Tbsp. butter, melted
1 Tbsp. grated Parmesan cheese

Unroll dough into a 14x12 inch rectangle. Sprinkle with cheese to within ½ inch of the edges. Top with a single layer of ham. Roll up tightly, jellyroll style. Place seam side down on a baking sheet coated with nonstick spray. Brush top with butter and sprinkle with Parmesan cheese. Bake at 375°F. for 20 to 25 minutes. Cool 5 minutes and serve. Any type of shredded cheese should do.

CHEESY MEATLOAF

Jacalyn Nichols
Copeland, KS

2 lb. ground beef
½ c. onion, chopped
¼ c. green pepper, chopped
½ c. oatmeal (dry)
2 eggs, beaten
1½ tsp. seasoned salt
¼ tsp. pepper
1 (16 oz.) can tomato sauce
Cheese

Mix all ingredients together, except cheese and ¼ cup of the tomato sauce. Spread half into a greased 9x9 inch baking dish. Place a layer of cheese on top of meat. Add remaining meat and seal edges so cheese does not run out. Spread remaining tomato sauce over top. Bake at 350°F. for 65 to 70 minutes. Serves 6 to 8.

Use whatever type of cheese you want; we like either Mozzarella or Cheddar.

CHICKEN CASSEROLE

Ruthye DeWald
Bazine, KS

1 chicken, cooked, boned, and chopped
1 can cream of chicken soup
1 small onion, chopped
¾ c. Minute brand rice
1 (8 oz.) ctn. sour cream
1½ c. chicken broth
1 pkg. round buttered crackers, crushed
1 stick margarine

Combine chicken, soup, onion, rice, sour cream, and chicken broth and put in greased casserole. To prepare crumb topping combine crackers and margarine, then top chicken mixture. Bake at 350°F. for 30 minutes.

CHICKEN CASSEROLE WITH HERB DRESSING AND SAUCE

Lucile Fuller
Wichita, KS

1 (8 oz.) pkg. herb dressing, not cubed style
1 whole chicken
4 c. water
1 stick margarine
½ c. flour
4 eggs
1 can cream of mushroom soup
1 (2 oz.) jar pimento, chopped
Salt
Pepper

Stew chicken in 4 cups water until tender. When cool enough to handle, cut into bite-size pieces. Pour broth into large container and let cool until the fat can be removed from the top. Spread the herb dressing (not the cubed) in bottom of 9x13 inch pan. Add the cut up chicken. In the large pan, melt the margarine and blend in the flour, stirring until smooth. Add the broth and heat. Beat the eggs. Add small amount of hot broth; blend together and then add to the broth in the pan. Salt and pepper to taste. Pour onto top of chicken. Bake in 375°F. oven until top is set and golden brown, 30 to 45 minutes. To prepare sauce, in small saucepan, heat 1 cup of soup from the can, 1 cup of sour cream, and drained pimentos until bubbling. Cut chicken in 12 pieces and serve, topping with a spoonful or two of the sauce.

In recent years, this has been my most requested recipe. I serve it with a fruit salad, green vegetable, and rolls. The casserole may be made in two 8x8 inch aluminum pans. Place each inside a gallon freezer bag and freeze to bake later.

68

CHICKEN CORDON BLEU

Neva Jones
O'Neill, NE

3 tubes snack crackers
½ c. margarine
3 lb. skinless chicken
 breasts, sliced in thin
 strips

2 (8 oz.) pkg. Mozzarella
 cheese
1 lb. ham, thinly sliced
6 oz. lemon-lime
 carbonated beverage

Crush the crackers, put in a large bowl, and add melted margarine until all crackers are moistened. In a 9x13 inch pan, layer ½ of crackers to form a crust. Layer ½ of the chicken and cover with one 8 ounce package cheese, then add a layer of ham, the rest of the chicken, and the last package of cheese, the rest of the ham. Spread remainder of crackers over the top, pour the half can of lemon-lime carbonated beverage over all the ingredients, and bake at 350°F. for 1½ hours or until chicken is done. Let set 15 minutes. Serves 6.

CHICKEN CORN CASSEROLE

Amber Uhlenhake
Ossian, IA

4 chicken breast halves
¼ tsp. garlic powder
⅛ tsp. salt and pepper
1 (8 oz.) pkg. stuffing mix
1 can kernel corn, drained
1 c. boiling water

¼ c. margarine, melted
1 can cream of mushroom
 soup
⅓ c. milk
2 Tbsp. parsley

Cut chicken breasts up to fill a greased 9x13 inch dish. Sprinkle with the garlic, salt, and pepper. In a bowl, mix the stuffing, corn, water, and melted margarine; mix well. Pour over the chicken. In the same bowl, mix the soup, milk, and parsley; pour over top. Bake, covered, for 35 minutes at 350°F. Uncover and bake another 8 to 10 minutes.

CHICKEN CRESCENT SURPRISE

Neva Jones
O'Neill, NE

3 c. turkey or chicken,
cooked and diced
1 (8 oz.) can water
chestnuts, drained and
sliced
1 (10¾ oz.) can cream of
chicken soup
1 (4 oz.) can mushrooms,
drained

⅔ c. Cheddar cheese,
grated
4 Tbsp. margarine, melted
⅔ c. mayonnaise
¼ c. onion, chopped
½ c. sour cream
1 (8 oz.) can crescent rolls
½ c. slivered almonds

In a large saucepan, combine turkey or chicken, water chestnuts, soup, mushrooms, mayonnaise, chopped onion, and sour cream; cook until bubbly. Pour into ungreased 9x13 inch pan. Separate crescent dough into 2 rectangles and cover hot chicken mixture. Brush with melted margarine. Sprinkle with cheese and almonds. Bake at 350°F. for 20 to 25 minutes or until golden brown.

CHICKEN ENCHILADA CASSEROLE

Teresa Zimmerman
Plevna, KS

1 c. onion, chopped
2 Tbsp. margarine
½ bell pepper, chopped
¼ c. flour
2½ c. chicken broth
1 c. sour cream
1 (4 oz.) can green chili
peppers, rinsed, seeded,
and chopped

2 c. cooked chicken
4 (10 inch) flour tortillas
1 c. Cheddar cheese,
shredded

In a large saucepan, cook onion and bell pepper in the margarine until tender. Add flour. Mix until smooth. Stir in chicken broth, sour cream, and chili peppers. Cook until thickened and bubbly. Pour ½ of mixture into bowl with the chicken. Dip each tortilla into remaining sauce to soften. Fill each tortilla with ¼ cup of the chicken mixture. Roll up. Arrange rolls in a 13x9 inch baking dish that has been sprayed. Pour remaining sauce over the top and sprinkle with Cheddar cheese. Bake, covered, in a 350°F. oven for about 25 minutes or until cheese is melted.

This is a good way to use leftover turkey, too.

CHICKEN ENCHILADAS

Julie Schmidt
Smith Center, KS

1 can cream of chicken or cream of celery soup
½ c. sour cream
2 Tbsp. margarine
½ c. onion, chopped
1 tsp. chili powder
2 c. chicken, cooked and diced

1 can green chilies, chopped
8 (7 inch) flour tortillas
1 c. shredded Monterey Jack or Cheddar cheese
Fresh parsley for garnish

Preheat oven to 375°F. In small bowl, stir together soup and sour cream until smooth; set aside. In a 2 quart saucepan over medium heat in hot margarine, cook onion and chili powder until onion is tender, stirring often. Stir in chicken, chilies, and 2 tablespoons of soup mixture. Remove from heat. To make enchiladas, along center of each tortilla, spread about ¼ cup of chicken mixture; fold sides over filling and place seam side down in greased 12x8 inch baking dish. Spread remaining soup mixture over enchiladas. Cover with foil; bake 15 minutes. Sprinkle with cheese. Bake, uncovered, 5 minutes more or until cheese melts. Garnish with parsley if desired. Makes 4 servings.

CHICKEN PIZZA PACKETS

Julie Schmidt
Smith Center, KS

1 lb. boneless, skinless chicken breasts, cut into 1 inch
2 Tbsp. olive or vegetable oil
1 (small) zucchini, thinly sliced
16 pepperoni slices
1 (small) green pepper, julienned

1 (small) onion, sliced
½ tsp. dried oregano
½ tsp. dried basil
¼ tsp. salt
¼ tsp. garlic powder
¼ tsp. pepper
½ c. shredded Mozzarella cheese
½ c. shredded Parmesan cheese

In a large bowl, combine everything but the cheeses. Coat four pieces of heavy-duty foil (about 12 inch square) with nonstick cooking spray. Place a quarter of the chicken mixture in the center of each piece. Fold foil around mixture and seal tightly. Grill, covered, over medium-hot heat for 15 to 18 minutes or until chicken juices run clear. Carefully open each packet. Sprinkle with cheeses. Seal loosely; grill 2 minutes longer or until cheese is melted. Yield: 4 servings.

This is a great combination of vegetables and seasonings with the chicken that our family truly loves!

CHICKEN SALAD CRESCENT BAKE

Deb Smith
Fowler, CO

1 can refrigerated
  crescent rolls
1 (4 oz.) pkg. cream
  cheese
¼ c. mayonnaise

¼ c. celery, chopped
1 c. chicken breast,
  ground and cooked
Salt and pepper to taste

Unroll the crescent rolls and place on the bottom of an ungreased cookie sheet to form an 11x7 inch sheet. Press the perforations together to seal. In a medium-sized bowl, make a chicken salad by combining the cream cheese, mayonnaise, celery, chicken, and salt and pepper. Spread the chicken salad lengthwise down the middle ⅓ of the crescent roll dough. With a pair of scissors, cut the remaining dough into 1 inch wide strips, being careful not to cut into the chicken salad. Fold the strips criss-cross style over the chicken salad. Bake in a 400°F. oven until golden brown, between 15 to 20 minutes. Brush with melted margarine, cut into slices, and serve hot.

This is also very good with your favorite Sloppy Joe recipe or with ham salad and covered with slices of American cheese.

CHICKEN SOPA

Amy Edwards
Tulsa, OK

4 lb. chicken
1 (medium) onion,
  chopped
1 c. cream or half & half
1 c. chicken broth
2 c. tomato juice

½ lb. processed American
  cheese, cut up
1 (small) can chopped
  green chiles
1 bag tortilla chips

Boil chicken and cut into bite-size pieces. Saute the chopped onion in butter until soft and then add the cream or half & half, broth, tomato juice, cheese, and chiles. Stir over low heat until smooth. Add the chicken and mix well. Line a 13x9 inch casserole dish with tortilla chips and top with a layer of the chicken mixture.. Repeat the layering until all the chicken mixture is used. Cover and bake 35 minutes at 350°F.. Uncover and bake 10 minutes more.

My family loves this casserole and we have made it for many years. It tastes great left over, too.

CHICKEN SPAGHETTI

*Julie Klein
St. Peters, MO*

4 chicken breasts, cooked and diced
1 can diced tomatoes and green chiles
1 can cream of chicken soup

1 soup can of water
1 lb. processed American cheese
½ c. mushrooms
Spaghetti, cooked

Combine all ingredients, except spaghetti, and cook for 15 to 20 minutes; mix with spaghetti and serve.

CHICKEN TETRAZZINI

*Roxie Berning
Marienthal, KS*

1 (large) hen, cooked and deboned (or 6 boneless chicken breasts)
1 (12 oz.) pkg. spaghetti
¼ lb. butter
⅔ c. flour
1 qt. milk

1 lb. processed American cheese
1 onion, chopped
1 green pepper, chopped
6 c. chicken broth
2 cans cream of mushroom soup

Cook spaghetti in chicken broth. Prepare white sauce with butter, flour, and milk. Melt cheese into white sauce. Saute onion and green pepper. Mix together chicken, spaghetti, onion, and green pepper into the white sauce and add 6 cups of chicken broth and 2 cans cream of mushroom soup. Makes a big batch. Pour into pans and bake 45 minutes at 350°F.

This freezes really well.

73

CHILI

Elsie MacArthur
Richmond, KS

2 onions
3 garlic cloves
Butter
1 lb. ground beef

2 pkg. chili seasoning mix
2 (15 oz.) cans red beans
2 (15 oz.) cans tomato
  sauce

Saute onions and garlic cloves in butter. Add ground beef and chili seasoning; mix well. Add beans and tomato sauce. Simmer and stir often for 1 hour to get the seasonings blended well.

CHILI

Glenda Adcock
Miami, TX

2 lb. ground beef
1 (medium) onion
1 env. chili seasoning
1 (26 oz.) can Ranch Style
  beans

1 (46 oz.) can tomato juice
Salt and pepper to taste

Brown the ground beef and onion in a 6 quart pan until pink is no longer visible; drain if necessary. Add the chili seasoning and stir to mix; add tomato juice and beans. Rinse cans out with small amount of water to get all the good flavors; add salt and pepper. Bring to a boil, reduce heat, and simmer for an hour or longer.

For extra spice, add Ro-Tel to chili.

CHINESE ROAST GOOSE

Iola Egle
Bella Vista, AR

8 to 10 lb. goose, oven
  ready
2/3 c. soy sauce
1/4 c. instant minced onion
1/4 c. celery, finely chopped
1 Tbsp. sugar
1 tsp. ground cinnamon
1/2 tsp. garlic powder

1/2 tsp. aniseed, crushed
4 c. water
1/4 c. honey
1/4 c. cider vinegar
1 Tbsp. soy sauce
7 tsp. salt
2 tsp. cornstarch
2 Tbsp. water

Wash goose and wipe dry, both inside and outside. Combine soy sauce, onion, celery, sugar, cinnamon, garlic powder, aniseed with 2 cups of the water. Bring to a boiling point. Tie goose's neck tightly with a string so sauce will not seep out while cooking. Pour hot sauce into body cavity, saving 2 tablespoons for later use. Sew vent tightly with strong thread to prevent sauce from bubbling out. Rub outside skin of goose with reserved 2 tablespoons sauce. Place goose on a rack, breast side up, in a roasting pan. Cook in preheated slow oven at 325°F. for 30 minutes. Heat remaining water with honey, vinegar, the 1 tablespoon soy sauce, and salt. Brush over skin of the bird. Continue cooking for 3 to 3½ hours, basting goose with sauce at 30 minute intervals. Remove from oven, cut thread to open body cavity, and drain sauce into a saucepan. Blend cornstarch with water and add to sauce. Stir and cook for 1 to 2 minutes or until sauce is slightly thick. Serve sauce separately with goose.

This recipe is also a great way to cook a duck.

CLAM CHOWDER

Janet Keller
San Antonio, TX

2 oz. salt pork, finely
    chopped
2 cloves minced garlic
1 carrot, peeled and finely
    chopped
2 stalks celery, diced
2 (medium) onions, diced
2 leeks, finely chopped
2 Tbsp. all-purpose flour

2 (6.5 oz.) cans minced
    clams
1 Tbsp. dried parsley
    flakes
4 c. potatoes, peeled and
    diced raw
1 pt. half & half
1 tsp. salt
¼ tsp. pepper

In a large soup pot, saute salt pork. Add minced garlic to salt pork and lightly saute. Add finely chopped carrots, diced celery, diced onions, and chopped leeks. Cook until onions turn yellow. Stir flour into mixture. Drain clams. Add drained clam liquid into soup pot. Bring to boil, reduce heat, cover, and simmer for 30 minutes. Add parsley flakes, diced potatoes, and salt and pepper. Cook until potatoes are tender. Add clams the last 5 minutes. Before serving, add half & half. Heat until hot, but do not boil. Makes 4 generous servings.

A pat of butter can be placed on top of each bowl as it is served.

CLAUS NATURAL BEEF KRAUTBURGERS

Francie N. Claus
Douglas, WY

1 c. scalded milk, cooled
1 c. warm water
2 Tbsp. yeast (or 2 pkg.)
½ c. sugar (plus 1 Tbsp.)
2 tsp. salt
1 egg
½ c. oil

5 c. (plus) flour
4 lb. ground beef
½ head cabbage, chopped
2 onions, chopped head
Salt and garlic pepper to taste

Thoroughly dissolve yeast in warm water; add scalded milk (after cooling); add salt and sugar. Beat egg well and add with oil to yeast liquid. Add flour, one cupful at a time, until blended. Add more flour to make the dough into a large ball, adding a little more flour until the dough has a waxy texture. Let rise twice. On the second rise, roll out thin (¼ inch); cut into squares (about 4 to 5 inches across). Roll out each square on board to accommodate more filling. Prepare filling while the dough is rising. Brown and season beef; drain if any fat, and set meat aside. Brown onions in butter until glossy; add cabbage seasonings and more butter so cabbage won't burn. Combine and cool cooked meat, cabbage, and onions in large bowl. Add several tablespoons to the center of each square of dough and tuck the 4 corners together, pressing the seams with fingertips. Place the seam side down in a heavy baking pan so the bundles do not touch (1 to 2 inches apart), as they will come together as they bake and you do not want the dough to tear as you remove them after baking. Baste just the tops with a little melted butter before and after baking at 350°F. for 20 minutes. Cover for first ½ of the time, then remove foil, watching not to overbrown. Serve hot.

May be frozen in foil wrap, thawed, and reheated in oven or frozen in plastic bags and microwaved individually. This sweet dough is so much better than regular bread dough.

COLE'S FAVORITE PIZZA

Bobbi Higgs
Ulysses, KS

1 loaf frozen bread dough
1 c. whole wheat flour
1 can tomato sauce
1 pkg. pepperoni

3 c. Mozzarella cheese
1 Tbsp. Italian seasoning
1 Tbsp. Romano cheese

Heat oven to a hot 500°F. Spray a large round pizza pan with nonstick spray. Let 1 loaf frozen bread dough raise, then roll out to desired thickness using whole wheat flour on surface and rolling pin. Place rolled-out dough on pizza pan and flatten, then trim edges. Spread tomato sauce evenly on dough. Sprinkle Italian seasoning on pizza sauce. Sprinkle cheese evenly over sauce, then add pepperoni or meat of your choosing. Sprinkle Romano cheese on top. Place in hot oven on bottom rack for 15 minutes.

Your kids will like this better than take out pizza.

COMPANY CASSEROLE

Rita Schiefelbein
Clear Lake, SD

2 lb. ground beef
Celery and onion to taste, chopped
2 (7 oz.) boxes spiral macaroni
2 cans cream of chicken soup

2 cans cream of mushroom soup
1 can tomato soup
Salt and pepper to taste
1/3 c. green olive juice
1/2 c. green olives with pimento, sliced

Brown ground beef, celery, and onion, draining excess grease. Cook and drain macaroni. Place meat and macaroni in large roaster pan or casserole. Mix in cream of chicken soup, cream of mushroom soup, and salt and pepper to taste. Bake at 350°F. for 35 to 40 minutes. Remove from oven and pour olive juice over all, stirring lightly. Arrange sliced olives on top and return to oven for another 10 minutes.

The olive juice is the secret ingredient in this recipe.

CORN AND TUNA CASSEROLE

Jennifer Tupps
Galion, OH

2 cans whole kernel corn, drained
1 can tuna, drained

1 can evaporated milk or whole fresh milk
1 tube saltine crackers

Generously grease casserole. Spread in layers one can of corn, tuna, and second can of corn. Pour milk level with top of corn. Crush crackers and spread over top. Lightly pepper top and dot with a little pat of butter. Cover and bake at 350°F. for 45 minutes.

This recipe is easily doubled. Great for unexpected people at mealtime.

CREAM CAN PARTY DINNER

Margaret Trojan
Beaver Crossing, NE

3 doz. ears sweet corn,
husks pulled back, silks
removed, and then
layers of husks wrapped
around ears
10 lb. potatoes, peeled
and left whole
3 lb. carrots, peeled and
left whole

5 (small to medium) lb.
onions
2 heads cabbage, cut in
quarters
10 lb. Polish sausage
1 lb. butter
6 pack beer (any kind)

Butter the inside of a 10 gallon cream can. Stack corn up in the bottom of the can. Layer all other ingredients in order given. Put remaining butter on top, followed by the 6 pack of beer poured over all. Secure lid. Cook over fire for about 1 hour, until you see steam coming out, and continue cooking 45 minutes more. Take off fire and let set 5 to 8 minutes. Carefully tap on lid and get it off. Dump into a roaster and enjoy. Serves 25 people.

No taste of beer, it only keeps things moist for cooking.

CREAMIEST POTATO SOUP

Maudie Burden
Centerview, MO

3 c. potatoes, diced and
pared
½ c. celery, diced
½ c. onion, diced
1½ c. water
2 tsp. reduced sodium
instant bouillon
seasoning or 1 can
chicken broth

½ tsp. salt (or to taste)
2 c. milk
1 c. sour cream
2 Tbsp. flour
2 or 3 slices American
cheese
1 pkg. Ranch dressing mix

Combine potatoes, celery, onion, water, bouillon, and salt; cook until tender. Don't overcook potatoes. Add 1 cup milk and keep at low heat. Mix sour cream, flour, Ranch packet, and remaining milk; gradually stir into potatoes. Tear cheese into pieces and add to mix; cook over low heat until thickened, stirring constantly.

CREAMY CHICKEN ENCHILADAS

Julie Haverland
Deepwater, MO

1 (small) onion, chopped
1 (10¾ oz.) can condensed cream of chicken soup (undiluted)
1 (10 oz.) can tomatoes with green chile, diced and undrained
1 c. sour cream

1 c. Cheddar cheese, shredded
1 c. Mozzarella cheese, shredded
6 (8½ inch) flour tortillas
2 c. cooked chicken, cubed

In a skillet coated with a nonstick cooking spray, saute onion until tender. Remove from heat to cool. Add soup, tomatoes, sour cream, ¾ cup Cheddar cheese, and ¾ cup Mozzarella cheese; mix well. Place 3 tablespoons on each tortilla and top with ⅓ cup of chicken. Roll up tightly. Place seam side down in a 13x9 inch baking dish coated with nonstick cooking spray. Top with remaining soup mixture and sprinkle with remaining cheeses. Bake, uncovered, at 350°F. for 20 to 25 minutes or until heated through. Yields 6 servings.

CREAMY CHICKEN-POTATO BAKE

Kathy Heinrich
Grainfield, KS

3 to 4 (medium) potatoes, cubed, peeled or unpeeled (whichever you prefer)
4 to 6 chicken breasts
1 jar creamy Parmesan-Mozzarella sauce

Onion powder
Garlic powder
Pepper
Poultry seasoning
Parsley flakes

Heat oven to 350°F. Spray bottom and sides of 8x12 inch baking dish with cooking spray. Season chicken breasts with onion and garlic powder, pepper, and poultry seasoning. Lightly brown on both sides in a nonstick pan. Place potatoes in bottom of pan and place chicken on top of potatoes. Pour creamy sauce over all. Sprinkle with parsley flakes. Cover with foil and bake for 1 hour.

For an all-in-one dish, layer frozen asparagus spears over the top of the chicken and spray with butter.

79

CRESCENT CRISTO SANDWICH LOAF

Iola Egle
Bella Vista, AR

2 (8 oz.) cans crescent
   dinner rolls
2 Tbsp. butter, melted
2 Tbsp. honey
6 oz. turkey breast,
   smoked, cooked, and
   thinly sliced

6 oz. (medium) cooked
   ham, thinly sliced
½ c. red raspberry
   preserves
2 Tbsp. honey
1 Tbsp. sesame seed

Separate dough into 4 long rectangles. Place rectangles crosswise on large ungreased cookie sheet (rectangles must not touch). Firmly press perforations to seal. In small bowl, combine butter and 2 tablespoons honey; mix well. Brush over dough. Bake at 375°F. for 8 to 12 minutes or until light golden brown. Cool 15 minutes. Grease 15x10x1 inch baking pan. Carefully place 1 crust on pan. Top evenly with turkey. Place second crust over turkey; top with cheese and ham. Place third crust over ham; spread evenly with preserves. Top with fourth crust; brush top with 2 tablespoons honey. Sprinkle the honey with sesame seeds. Bake at 375°F. for 10 to 15 minutes or until crust is deep golden brown and loaf is hot clear through. Let stand 5 minutes. Cut into 8 slices and serve.

CROCKPOT ITALIAN BEEF

Julie Klein
St. Peters, MO

3 to 5 lb. roast
2 pkg. brown gravy mix
   (dry)

2 pkg. Italian dressing
   (dry)
2 c. water

Put roast in crockpot. Mix all other ingredients and pour over roast. Cook on high 4 to 6 hours or low 6 to 8 hours. Remove roast, shred up, and put back into juice.

CROCKPOT STEAK AND POTATOES

Cynthia Lambert
Palco, KS

1 lb. round steak	⅛ tsp. pepper
5 c. potatoes, diced	1 can mushroom soup
⅛ tsp. salt	1 c. milk

Cut steak into serving size pieces and place in crockpot. Place potatoes on top. Mix milk and soup; pour over steak and potatoes. Add salt and pepper to taste. Cook for 4 hours on low.

CROCKPOT STEAK SOUP

Kathy Hogue
Topeka, KS

1½ lb. ground beef, browned and drained	1 (16 oz.) can tomatoes, diced
3 c. water	1 tsp. pepper
2 (small) onions, chopped	1 Tbsp. monosodium glutamate (optional)
3 stalks celery, chopped	2 Tbsp. beef bouillon granules
2 carrots, sliced	
1 (10 oz.) pkg. frozen mixed vegetables	

Put all ingredients in crockpot and stir. Cover and cook on low 8 to 10 hours. This soup can also be thickened. One hour before serving, turn to high. Make a paste of ½ cup melted margarine plus ½ cup flour. Stir into crockpot; cook until thickened.

CROCKPOT STUFFED PEPPERS

Felicia Leary
Topeka, KS

6 to 8 (small) peppers (green, red, or yellow)	½ tsp. garlic salt
1 lb. ground beef	¼ tsp. pepper
¼ c. onion, chopped	½ c. Parmesan cheese
1 c. white rice (uncooked)	2 (8 oz.) cans tomato sauce
1 can whole kernel corn, drained	2 cans tomatoes, diced

Wash peppers; remove tops and seeds. Drain well. Brown beef and onion in a skillet. Drain fat. Combine remaining ingredients with beef and onion mixture in large skillet, except 1 can diced tomatoes. Heat through. Stuff peppers ⅔ full. Pour 3 tablespoons water in crockpot. Arrange peppers in crockpot. Pour can of diced tomatoes over top of peppers. Cover and cook on low 7 to 9 hours or high 3 to 4 hours. Garnish with Mozzarella cheese if desired.

CROCKPOT SWEET AND SOUR PHEASANT

Merrill Powers
Spearville, KS

1 to 2 lb. pheasant
¾ c. brown sugar
⅔ c. white vinegar
¼ c. lemon-lime soda pop
3 tsp. minced garlic
2 Tbsp. soy sauce
1 tsp. black pepper

3 stalks celery, diced
1 green pepper, thinly sliced
1 onion, thinly sliced
2 c. chicken broth
3 to 4 Tbsp. cornstarch
6 c. cooked white rice

Cut raw pheasant into bite-size pieces. Combine pheasant, brown sugar, vinegar, soda pop, garlic, soy sauce, and black pepper in crockpot; cook on low for 8 hours. Transfer crockpot mixture to large saucepan and bring to a simmer on stove top; add celery, green pepper, and onion. Simmer till vegetables are tender-crisp, 3 to 5 minutes. Mix cornstarch with small amount of cold water and add to pheasant mixture to thicken. Cook only till thickened. Pour pheasant/vegetable mixture over bed of fluffy hot rice; serve immediately. Serves 6 to 8.

You may substitute chicken for pheasant. You may also substitute any of the following vegetables: Oriental pea pods, mushrooms, yellow squash. We like to top this with chow mein noodles and soy sauce to taste.

CROCKPOT CUBE STEAK

Kolleen R. Dome
Munjor, KS

1 to 2 lb. cube steak
1 pkg. dry onion soup mix
1 (10½ oz.) can cream of mushroom soup

1 c. water

Cut cube steaks into one inch size pieces and place in crockpot. Mix in dry onion soup mix, cream of mushroom soup, and water. Mix well. Bake on low for 6 to 8 hours. When complete, remove steak from crockpot with slotted spoon. Pour juices from crockpot into a saucepan.

If the gravy is thick enough for your preference, serve. If not, bring the gravy to a boil and add 1 tablespoon of flour at a time to thicken it up. Serve with mashed potatoes.

I have tried it with noodles, but my family likes it better with mashed potatoes. Also, the steak will be very tender and break apart easily.

CURLEY CHICKEN

Margaret Goss
Carmen, OK

1 lb. skinless, boneless chicken breast, cut into cubes
1 can mushroom soup
3 to 4 c. water
½ c. onion, chopped
½ c. celery, chopped
½ c. carrots, chopped
½ c. broccoli, chopped
4 c. corkscrew pasta
1 to 2 c. processed cheese, cubed
Salt, pepper, garlic to taste

In a large saucepan, boil the chicken until done. Add onion, celery, carrots, and broccoli; cook until almost tender. Add the pasta and cook until tender. Drain the excess water. Add the soup and seasonings to taste. Pour mixture into a large casserole that has been sprayed with cooking spray. Add cheese. Bake in 350°F. oven until cheese is melted.

My family likes this dish for one-dish harvest meal. Turkey may be substituted.

DELICIOUS RUMP ROAST BEEF

Cynthia Ann Mitchell
Fall River, KS

1 to 5 lb. rump roast
4 to 6 carrots, each cut in fourths
1 (medium) onion
1 (4 oz.) can mushrooms, sliced
2 stalks celery
½ tsp. seasoned salt
1 tsp. beef bouillon grains
1 tsp. pepper
1 clove garlic

Place roast with fat side up in a roaster. Place garlic clove, celery stalks, and sliced onion on top of meat. Sprinkle meat with salt, pepper, bouillon on roast. Cover and cook at 300° to 325°F. until tender, 3 to 4 hours, depending on size. Use juices from pan for gravy.

Makes a wonderful Sunday meal. Serve with mashed potatoes, green salad, and hot rolls.

DELUXE HAM OMELET

Gary Kasel
Adams, MN

3 eggs
2 Tbsp. milk
Salt and pepper to taste
1 Tbsp. olive oil or
  vegetable oil
1 to 2 Tbsp. butter
½ c. ham, cooked and
  finely chopped
2 Tbsp. onion, chopped

2 Tbsp. green pepper,
  chopped
2 mushrooms, sliced
2 Tbsp. tomato, chopped
  (optional)
2 Tbsp. Cheddar cheese,
  shredded
2 Tbsp. Mozzarella
  cheese, shredded

In a skillet, saute ham, onion, green pepper, and mushrooms in butter for 6 to 8 minutes or until tender. Add tomatoes about 2 to 3 minutes after vegetables. In a small bowl, beat eggs and milk, salt and pepper. Heat oil in 10½ inch nonstick skillet; add the egg mixture and cook over medium heat. As the eggs set, lift edges, letting uncooked portion flow underneath. Sprinkle with ham and vegetable mixture. When eggs are set, remove from heat and fold omelet in half. Sprinkle with cheeses; cover for 1 to 2 minutes or until cheese melts. Yields 1 to 2 servings.

When my brothers are home, we make this omelet recipe for the rest of the family. Turns out so good it's like eating out.

DONNA'S QUICK RISE BREAD SANDWICH

Donna L. Thorp
Kismet, KS

2½ c. flour
2 Tbsp. sugar
½ tsp. salt
1 pkg. quick rise yeast
½ c. milk
¼ c. water

½ c. butter
1 egg (room temperature)
½ lb. ham
1 lb. turkey
½ lb. favorite cheeses
Italian salad dressing

Mix flour, sugar, salt, and yeast together. Cook milk, butter, and water till very hot. Add to dry ingredients; add egg. Mix with dough hooks. Cover with towel and let rise 10 minutes. Turn dough out on bed of flour. Roll around enough so it will spread without being too sticky. Do not overknead. Spread dough out on greased cookie sheet. Add meat, cheese, and dressing in a heap down the center. Cut slits on both sides of dough to crisscross over stuffing. Let rise 10 minutes. Bake at 375°F. for about 20 minutes until golden brown.

Before baking, glaze bread with one egg white for a nice shine; sprinkle top with poppy or sesame seeds. Layer meat on bread first; cheese makes the bottom doughy.

EASY CASSEROLE

Kimberly Chambers
Norcatur, KS

1 lb. ground beef (raw)
½ pkg. dry onion soup mix
Shredded cheddar cheese

1 can cream of mushroom soup
Tater tots

In 8x8 inch pan, put the following in layers, beginning with ground beef with tater tots on top. Bake 1 hour at 350°F.

ENCHILADA CASSEROLE

Kim Due
Friend, NE

1½ lb. ground beef
1 c. onion, chopped
2 tsp. cumin
½ tsp. garlic salt
½ tsp. pepper
4 tsp. chili powder
1 c. water

1 c. picante sauce
2 to 3 (7 inch) flour tortillas
½ c. sour cream
1 c. Cheddar cheese, shredded

Brown and drain ground beef; add onion, cumin, garlic salt, pepper, chili powder, and water. Simmer for 5 minutes. Layer in a greased 9x13 inch baking dish: Picante sauce, tortillas, picante sauce, beef mixture, sour cream, and cheese.

FINGER LICKIN' SPARERIBS

Iola Egle
Bella Vista, AR

6 to 6½ lb. country-style
  spareribs
½ c. apple cider
½ c. water
1 tsp. chili powder
1 tsp. celery seed
3 c. water
¾ c. onion, finely chopped

1 tsp. sea salt
1 c. ketchup
¼ c. vinegar
¼ c. Worcestershire sauce
½ lemon, sliced thin
⅛ tsp. black pepper
½ c. light brown sugar

Brown spareribs in a large frying pan (do not flour). Add apple cider and water. Simmer, covered, for 1 hour. In another pan, combine all sauce ingredients and simmer for 2 to 3 hours. Let ribs cool in liquid long enough to skim off excess fat. Remove ribs and drain. Lay drained ribs in large casserole dish; cover with sauce and bake at 300°F. for 1 hour.

Get your lickin' fingers ready with the traditional wet cloth next to you.

FIRE HOUSE CASSEROLE

Keith Mueller
Halstead, KS

1 lb. ground beef
1 (8 oz.) container sour
  cream
1 pkg. Doritos tortilla
  chips
1 pkg. taco seasoning

1 small onion, chopped
1 can crescent rolls
1 can chiles, chopped
1 pkg. cheese, grated
½ c. water

Brown ground beef and onion. Drain. Spread unbaked crescent rolls over the bottom and ½ way up the sides of a 9x9 inch ungreased pan, pressing with fingers. Crush a layer of Doritos over the unbaked rolls. Mix taco seasoning, ½ cup water, sour cream, and chopped chiles with the browned ground beef and onion mixture. Spread the meat mixture over the crushed Doritos. Top with more crushed Doritos. Bake 15 minutes at 350°F. Top with grated cheese and bake until cheese melts. Can serve with chopped lettuce and salsa if desired.

Double the above recipe for a 9x13 inch pan. My son is a fireman and he gave this recipe to me.

GERMAN MEATBALLS

Carol Price
Cordell, OK

3 lb. ground beef
1 (12 oz.) can evaporated
  milk
2 c. quick oats
2 eggs
1 c. onions, chopped
1 tsp. chili powder
2 tsp. salt

1 tsp. garlic powder
3 c. ketchup
½ tsp. garlic powder
½ c. onions, chopped
1½ c. brown sugar
1 tsp. monosodium
  glutamate
½ tsp. liquid smoke

Mix ground beef, evaporated milk, quick oats, eggs, onions, chili powder, salt, and garlic powder together. Shape into golf size balls (about 50). Place in large layer cake pan, 1 layer only. To prepare sauce, mix together ketchup, garlic powder, onions, brown sugar, monosodium glutamate, and liquid smoke. Pour on meatballs. Bake at 350°F. for 45 minutes, covered with foil. Remove foil and bake an additional 15 minutes.

This family favorite can be divided, frozen, and used as needed.

GERTIE'S BREAKFAST CASSEROLE

Coleen Koch
Summerfield, KS

1 (32 oz.) pkg. frozen hash
  browns
2 c. shredded American
  cheese
1 stick margarine

1½ c. cooked bacon or
  ham, chopped
1 doz. eggs
1 c. milk

Melt margarine in bottom of 9x13 inch baking dish. Add hash browns, cheese, and meat. Beat eggs with milk and pour over all ingredients. Bake at 350°F. for about 1 hour. Stir after 10 minutes. Bake until eggs are set.

My family likes a mixture of ham and bacon, both.

GOOD POTATO SOUP

Diane Meisinger
Hillsboro, KS

6 to 8 large potatoes
1 (large) onion
3 to 4 stalks celery
½ c. carrots, shredded
½ lb. processed American
   cheese spread

3 Tbsp. butter
Salt and pepper
Milk

Dice potatoes, onion, and celery and place in large pot, along with shredded carrots. Add water just until vegetables are covered. Cook until tender, about 20 minutes. Turn to low heat and add cheese, butter, and seasoning to taste. Add milk to desired thickness.

This soup makes a nice addition to Sloppy Joes or hamburgers.

GORGONZOLA, TOMATO, AND BASIL TUNA STEAK

Aubrey
Canonsburg, PA

2 (1 lb.) tuna steaks
½ c. Gorgonzola,
   crumbled
1 large tomato, seeded
   and diced
2 to 3 leaves fresh basil,
   chopped
1 c. packed fresh baby
   spinach

Olive oil to taste
Sea salt, ground to taste
Peppercorns, ground to
   taste
½ clove garlic, minced
   walnuts, chopped for
   garnish

Find thinnest section of tuna. Slice a pocket with sharp, non-serrated knife, leaving about ¼ inch of fish as is. Lightly season pocket with salt and pepper. Set aside. Combine tomato dices, crumbled cheese, and basil. Season. Stuff into tuna steak; either prop up with crumpled foil or seal with metal skewer or toothpicks soaked in water. Broil until fish is done to your liking. Pack spinach leaves in serving dish; add olive oil, sea salt, peppercorns, and minced garlic. This will be a bed to serve the tuna on. Garnish with chopped walnuts.

GRANNY'S UPSIDE-DOWN BBQ
Jennifer Tupps
Galion, OH

Your favorite sloppy joe recipe

1 pkg. cornbread mix

In an 8 or 10 inch cast iron skillet, make sloppy joe mixture, letting liquid cook down. Mix cornbread as package directs. Remove skillet from heat and top hot barbecue with the cornbread batter. Place, uncovered, in preheated oven and bake as cornbread directs. Remove from oven and let set a few minutes. Place serving plate upside down over skillet. Invert all, lifting skillet away; cut in wedges to serve.

If you prefer you can assemble this in an 8x8 inch baking pan. Can also serve from pan/skillet and flip over onto individual plate as being served.

GREEN CHILI CASSEROLE
Anna Mae Lancaster
Wray, CO

2 lb. ground beef
1 onion, minced
10 oz. Cheddar cheese, grated
1 large can canned milk
2 to 4 cans chopped green chiles

2 cans cream of mushroom soup
12 flour tortillas
Salt and pepper to taste

Brown ground beef and onion together; drain grease. Add milk, green chiles, and soup; simmer for 5 minutes. Layer tortillas and meat mixture in a 1½ quart baking dish and top with cheese. Bake until cheese melts.

This has been a family favorite for a long time.

GRILLED FLANK STEAK
Margaret Trojan
Beaver Crossing, NE

1 c. soy sauce
2 c. barbecue sauce
1 Tbsp. Worcestershire sauce

1 (1½ to 2 lb. size) flank steak

Combine soy sauce, barbecue sauce, and Worcestershire sauce in shallow glass pan or heavy zipper-style plastic bag. Add meat. Marinate 1 hour or overnight in refrigerator. Remove meat from marinade and discard leftover marinade. Grill over direct heat, using medium-hot coals in covered barbecue or on gas grill 5 to 6 minutes each side. Allow meat to set for a few minutes, then cut in diagonal slices. Makes 4 servings.

This cut of meat is less expensive and tastes as good as any steak.

GROUND BEEF AND CHEESE CASSEROLE

Christy Kleffner
Brinktown, MO

1½ lb. ground beef
½ c. onion, chopped
½ tsp. salt
⅛ tsp. pepper
5 slices bacon, cooked
   and drained
¾ c. water

1 can condensed cream of
   mushroom soup
1 (8 oz.) box corn muffin
   mix
1 egg
⅓ c. milk
½ c. grated cheese

Brown ground beef. Saute onion. Mix beef, onion, salt, pepper, bacon, water, and soup. Put in a 1½ quart casserole. Combine corn muffin mix, egg, milk, and cheese and put over top of casserole. Bake for 40 minutes or until corn bread is done in a 350°F. to 375°F. oven.

GROUND BEEF BEAN CASSEROLE

Barbara Koelling
Paradise, KS

1 lb. ground beef
1 tsp. salt
1 (16 oz.) can pork and
   beans
¾ c. barbecue sauce

2 Tbsp. brown sugar
1 Tbsp. minced onion
1 can refrigerated biscuits
1 c. Cheddar cheese,
   shredded

Brown ground beef; drain. Stir in salt, beans, barbecue sauce, brown sugar, and onion; heat until bubbly. Pour in a 2 quart casserole. Cut biscuits in halves to form 20 half-circles. Place cut side down around edges of casserole. Bake at 375°F. for 25 to 30 minutes until biscuits are brown. Melt cheese on top.

GROUND BEEF CASSEROLE

Eleanor Odle
Prairie View, KS

1 lb. ground beef
Salt and pepper to taste
¼ c. onion, chopped
1 tube biscuits
1 (16 oz.) can pork and
  beans

¾ c. barbecue sauce
1 Tbsp. brown sugar
¾ c. Cheddar cheese,
  grated

Brown ground beef with salt, pepper, and onion. Drain off liquid, if any. Add pork and beans, barbecue sauce, and brown sugar. Simmer 5 minutes. Pour into 8x11 inch baking dish. Cut biscuits in halves, placing the cut sides down on top of mixture. Sprinkle grated cheese on top of biscuits. Bake in preheated 350°F. oven for 20 to 30 minutes or until biscuits are done.

GROUND BEEF TURNOVERS

Alice P. Boehme
Mullinville, KS

4 c. flour
1 Tbsp. sugar
1 tsp. salt
1¾ c. shortening
½ c. cold water
1 egg, lightly beaten
1 Tbsp. vinegar
2 lb. ground beef
  (uncooked)

1 c. carrots, diced
2 (medium) potatoes, cut
  into ¼ inch cubes
1 medium onion, chopped
1 tsp. salt
¼ tsp. pepper

In a bowl, combine flour, sugar, and salt; cut in shortening until mixture resembles coarse crumbs. Combine the water, egg, and vinegar; mix well. Add to shortening mixture, 1 tablespoon at a time, tossing lightly with a fork until mixture forms a ball. Cover and chill for 30 minutes. Meanwhile, combine the filling ingredients, ground beef, carrots, potatoes, onion, and salt and pepper. Divide pastry into 15 portions. On a lightly floured surface, roll out one portion into a 6½ inch circle. Mound a heaping ⅓ cup filling on ½ of circle. Moisten edges with water; fold dough over filling and press edges with a fork to seal. Transfer to a greased baking sheet. Repeat with remaining pastry and filling. Cut 3 slits in the top of each turnover; brush with butter flavored shortening. Bake at 375°F. for 40 to 45 minutes or until vegetables are tender and crust is golden brown.

I usually use my ground deer meat instead of ground beef.

HAM, CHEESE, AND NOODLE CASSEROLE

Ruthye DeWald
Bazine, KS

1 (14 oz.) bag noodles, cooked and drained
2 c. ham, cubed
8 oz. Cheddar cheese, cubed
1 can water chestnuts, sliced and drained
1 (medium or large) onion, diced

1 can cream of chicken soup
1 c. sour cream
Salt and pepper to taste
1 pkg. round buttery crackers, crushed
1 stick margarine

Combine noodles, ham, cheese, chestnuts, onion, soup, sour cream, and salt and pepper in a 3 quart greased casserole. Top with crumb mixture of crackers and margarine. Bake at 350°F. for 30 minutes.

HAM AND CHEESE MEAL

Connie M. Terry
Ellsworth, KS

10 to 15 (medium) potatoes, peeled and sliced
1½ ham steaks, cut into bite-sized pieces
1 onion, chopped

1 lb. processed American cheese
1 can cream of mushroom soup
Salt and pepper to taste

In a 6 quart crockpot, fill half full of potatoes, ham, and onion. Add grated processed cheese. Continue filling crockpot with potatoes, ham, and onion, leaving enough room for can of soup. Add soup to the top at the last. Cook on low until potatoes are done. Stir occasionally so the mixture does not stick to the sides of crockpot.

This is great to take to a potluck dinner.

HASH BROWN CASSEROLE

Maudie Burden
Centerview, MO

2 lb. frozen hash brown
  potatoes, thawed
12 oz. sharp Cheddar
  cheese, shredded
1 (16 oz.) tub sour cream

1 can cream of mushroom
  soup
1 stick margarine, melted
½ (small) onion, diced
  (optional)

Mix all together in a large bowl, then pour into a 13x9 inch greased pan. Bake at 375°F. for 1 to 1¼ hours or until golden brown.

HAWAIIAN CHICKEN

Shelley Fangman
Hereford, TX

1 tsp. cornstarch
1 Tbsp. cold water
½ c. sugar
½ c. soy sauce
¼ c. vinegar

1 clove garlic, minced
½ tsp. ginger
½ tsp. pepper
6 chicken breasts
1 (10 oz.) can pineapple

Spray a 9x13 inch pan with cooking spray. Place chicken in pan and put into a preheated 425°F. oven. Bake for 30 minutes. While chicken starts to cook, prepare sauce. In a small saucepan, mix cornstarch and water, then add sugar, soy sauce, vinegar, garlic, ginger, and pepper. Cook over medium heat, stirring until thick. Turn chicken and brush with sauce every 10 minutes for 30 minutes. Add pineapple the last 10 minutes of baking. Serve while hot with rice and a vegetable salad. Yields 6 servings.

HEARTY BAKED POTATO SALAD

Dana K. Reese
Fyffe, AL

8 red salad potatoes
½ c. onion, chopped
2 Tbsp. parsley, chopped
1 (11 oz.) can Cheddar
  cheese soup

½ c. mayonnaise
½ c. plain yogurt
4 oz. bacon, cooked,
  drained, and crumbled
Paprika for garnish

Peel potatoes; boil until soft. Cut in 1½ inch chunks. Spread potatoes evenly over bottom of 13x9x2 inch baking pan. Combine onions, parsley, soup, mayonnaise, and yogurt; pour over potatoes. Sprinkle cooked bacon on top; garnish with paprika. Cover with aluminum foil and bake at 350°F. for 1 hour, uncovering the last 30 minutes. Yields 10 to 12 servings.

HOMEMADE TURKEY SAUSAGE
Judy Hall
McCook, NE

1 Tbsp. cumin, ground
2 tsp. oregano, ground
2 tsp. thyme, ground
2 tsp. sage, ground
2 tsp. rosemary, ground
2 tsp. basil, leaf or ground
1 tsp. black pepper
2 tsp. paprika
2 tsp. salt

1 Tbsp. garlic powder or
   to taste
1 Tbsp. onion powder or
   to taste
4 (1.2 lb.) pkg. ground
   turkey
1 to 4 tsp. water or as
   needed

Combine spices; knead into ground turkey, adding a little water at a time if needed to help incorporate the spices. Divide into freezer bags. Size will depend on number of servings that you want per meal. Use a portion fresh and freeze remainder for future use. Makes 4.8 pounds.

This is not a real spicy sausage and you may tweak it to your liking.

HONEY MUSTARD CHICKEN
Diane Meisinger
Hillsboro, KS

⅓ c. Dijon style mustard
¼ c. honey
½ tsp. dried dill

1 tsp. orange peel, freshly
   grated
1 chicken, cut up

Combine mustard, honey, orange peel, and dill in small bowl. Line baking sheet with foil. Place chicken skin side down on prepared pan. Brush sauce on both sides of chicken. Gently pull back skin and brush sauce over the meat. Bake at 400°F. for 30 minutes until juices run clear when thickest portion of meat is pierced with a knife.

May also use chicken breast for a quicker meal.

HORSERADISH DRESSING FOR PRIME RIB

Janet Rauch
Deep River, IA

Prime rib
1 c. half & half
1 pt. sour cream
1 Tbsp. salt
¾ c. sugar

⅛ c. vinegar
3½ oz. frozen lemon juice
2 Tbsp. dried parsley
⅛ tsp. garlic powder
3 oz. horseradish

Mix well all ingredients and refrigerate until used. Keeps well. Cook prime rib to taste and serve with sauce.

HOT PARTY DISH

Thelma Maxwell
Dodge City, KS

1 (7 oz.) pkg. ring or
  alphabet macaroni
  (uncooked)
1½ c. American or
  Cheddar cheese, grated
½ c. green pepper
½ c. black olives, chopped
2 Tbsp. onion, chopped
1 (small) jar pimentos,
  diced

2½ c. milk
2 cans cream of
  mushroom or celery
  soup
2 c. chicken, turkey, ham,
  or roast beef, cooked
  and diced
½ c. water chestnuts,
  sliced

Combine all ingredients and bake in 350°F. oven for 1 hour. Can be made the day before serving and refrigerated until 1 hour before baking.

This is a one dish meal that serves 12 or more.

HOT SPICED CHICKEN SALAD WITH JALAPENO CREAMED ACCOMPANIMENT

Iola Egle
Bella Vista, AR

4 boneless chicken breast halves
1 pkg. dry onion soup mix
2 Tbsp. virgin olive oil
1 (15 oz.) can pinto beans, drained and rinsed
1 c. whole kernel corn, drained
½ c. picante sauce (thick 'n chunky style)
1 (4.5 oz.) can green chiles, chopped
¼ c. green onions, chopped (including tops)

2 c. lettuce leaves, torn
2 c. romaine lettuce leaves, torn
1 red pepper, cut in thin slices
¼ c. fresh cilantro, chopped
½ c. jalapeno pepper jelly
½ c. sour cream
1 Tbsp. lemon juice
2 jalapeno peppers, sliced

Sprinkle onion soup on both sides of all four chicken breasts and press firmly. In frypan, bring virgin olive oil to bubbly hot stage. Add chicken and cook about 12 minutes over medium heat until chicken is no longer pink. Remove chicken to platter. Add pinto beans, corn, and picante sauce to frypan. Heat through and remove from frypan to bowl. Add chiles and onions. Arrange chopped lettuce leaves on large platter. Cut strips on each chicken breast to within ½ inch of one side and fan out. Place chicken on lettuce with fans toward outside. Top each chicken breast with mixture of jalapeno pepper jelly, sour cream, lemon juice, and 3 slices of jalapeno pepper. Spoon warm vegetable mixture around outside of chicken breasts. Pour remaining jalapeno accompaniment in small relish dish and place on side of platter so guests can add additional hot spice if desired. Serve immediately to 4 guests.

This is so yummy.

IMPERIAL GLAZED CHICKEN

Barb Kasel
Adams, MN

4 chicken breasts
¾ c. flour
1 tsp. curry powder
½ tsp. salt
¼ tsp. pepper
6 Tbsp. butter
2 Tbsp. sherry
⅓ c. orange marmalade

Bone chicken. Mix flour, curry powder, salt, and pepper. Melt butter in a frying pan. Dip chicken in seasoned flour and brown in butter. Reduce heat and cook until tender. Just before chicken is done, add marmalade and sherry.

This is easy to make. I serve it with pasta or potatoes.

JOHN WAYNE EGGS

Keith Mueller
Halstead, KS

1 lb. bulk pork sausage
1 doz. eggs
¼ c. milk
1 can cream of chicken
  soup
¼ c. milk
3 c. chunky style frozen
  hash browns
1 pkg. Cheddar cheese,
  grated

Brown sausage and drain. Crumble the sausage in the bottom of an ungreased 9x12inch pan. Beat eggs with ¼ cup milk and softly scramble in same skillet that sausage was browned in. Spread eggs over sausage. Brown hash browns in same skillet and spread over eggs. Mix cream of chicken soup with ¼ cup milk. Pour soup mixture over hash browns and top with grated Cheddar cheese. Bake at 350°F. for approximately 25 minutes or until cheese melts and the casserole is heated.

KALUA PORK

Clara Ough
Hebron, NE

4 lb. pork roast
¼ c. soy sauce
1½ Tbsp. salt
1 clove garlic, minced
1 Tbsp. ginger, grated
¼ tsp. liquid smoke

Combine all ingredients, except pork, in a small bowl. Put pork in foil-lined 9x9x2 inch pan and rub sauce over entire surface. Cover pan. Bake at 325°F. for 4 hours. Shred. You may use a crockpot.

KARMEN'S BARBECUE

Karmen Krug
Waldo, KS

1 (3 to 4 lb.) boneless
rump roast
1 (1 lb.) pork loin
2 c. water
1 pkg. onion soup mix
1 garlic clove, minced

¼ c. celery, chopped
½ c. barbecue sauce
½ c. ketchup
1 Tbsp. brown sugar
10 to 14 sandwich buns

Place beef and pork in a Dutch oven. Combine the water, soup mix, and garlic; pour over meat. Cover and bake at 325°F. for 2½ to 3 hours or until the meat is very tender. Remove meat; cool. Cut into small cubes. Skim fat from drippings. Saute celery in the drippings until tender. Add the barbecue sauce, ketchup, and brown sugar. Bring to boil; stir in cubed meat. Heat through. Serve on buns. Yields 10 to 14 servings.

LASAGNA STYLE MACARONI AND CHEESE

Mrs. D. Lynd
Ellis, KS

1 (4 serving size) box
macaroni and cheese
1 lb. ground beef
1 onion
1 (37 oz.) jar mushroom
spaghetti sauce
1 (15 oz.) can chili with
beans
6 to 8 stuffed sliced olives

½ tsp. jalapeno peppers,
snipped
1 (12 oz.) container
cottage cheese
1 tsp. dried parsley,
oregano, and basil
1 (16 oz.) pkg. Mozzarella
cheese, shredded

Cook macaroni and cheese according to box; brown ground beef and onion. Add meat mixture to spaghetti sauce, chili, olives, and jalapeno peppers. Combine cottage cheese, parsley, oregano, and basil, and ½ of Mozzarella cheese. In a 2 quart casserole, first layer ½ of spaghetti sauce mixture; second, layer ½ of macaroni mixture. Third, layer all of the cottage cheese mixture; fourth, layer remaining macaroni mixture. Fifth layer: Remaining spaghetti sauce mixture. Top with remaining Mozzarella cheese. Bake till bubbly, about 20 to 30 minutes. Yields 8 servings.

Use plastic gloves when snipping the jalapeno peppers and keep hands away from face.

LASAGNE

Arlene Bontrager
Hutchinson, KS

1½ to 2 lb. sausage
½ tsp. instant garlic, minced
1 Tbsp. whole basil
1 Tbsp. Italian seasoning
1 tsp. sugar
1 tsp. salt
1 qt. tomatoes, cut up
2 (6 oz.) cans tomato paste
10 lasagne noodles

2 eggs
3 c. Ricotta or cottage cheese
½ c. Parmesan cheese, grated
2 Tbsp. parsley flakes
½ tsp. salt
½ tsp. pepper
1 lb. Mozzarella cheese, sliced thin or grated (about 3 to 4 c.)

Brown meat slowly; spoon off excess fat. Add garlic, basil, Italian seasoning, sugar, salt, tomatoes, and tomato paste. Simmer, uncovered 30 minutes, stirring occasionally. Cook noodles in large amount of boiling salted water until tender; drain and rinse. Beat eggs; add Ricotta or cottage cheese, Parmesan cheese, parsley flakes, salt, and pepper. Layer half of the noodles in 13x9x2 inch baking dish; spread with half the Ricotta filling. Add half the Mozzarella cheese and half the meat sauce. Repeat. Bake at 375°F. about 30 minutes. Let stand 10 minutes before serving. Serves 8 to 10.

MARCY'S ROAST

Velma Twyman
Boise City, OK

1 can cream of mushroom soup
1 pkg. beefy onion soup mix

1 (medium size) roast, frozen

Place frozen roast on heavy aluminum foil (enough to completely wrap the roast). Mix the mushroom and beefy onion soup mix and pour over the roast. Wrap the roast and seal tightly. Place in oven directly on the rack. You might want to place a cookie sheet on the rack below. Bake at 250°F. for 10 to 12 hours.

Our family likes this because it is easy to fix and is ready when we get home from church.

MARINATED RIB-EYE STEAKS

Marilyn Barner
Belle Plaine, KS

⅓ c. hot water
3 Tbsp. onion, chopped
2 Tbsp. cider or red wine
  vinegar
2 Tbsp. cooking oil
2 Tbsp. soy sauce
½ tsp. liquid smoke

1 tsp. beef bouillon
  granules
½ tsp. garlic powder
½ tsp. paprika
½ tsp. black pepper,
  coarsely ground
3 or 4 rib-eye steaks

Combine all ingredients, except steaks, in a small bowl. Put steaks in a Ziploc bag. Pour marinade over steaks and marinate several hours or overnight. Discard marinade and grill steaks to your desired doneness.

MEAL IN A DISH

Rita Schiefelbein
Clear Lake, SD

1 lb. ground beef
½ c. ketchup
Celery and onion to taste,
  chopped
Salt and pepper to taste
1 can cream of chicken
  soup

1 can cream of celery
  soup
1 (small) bag frozen peas
1 (small) bag frozen
  carrots
Tater tot potatoes

Brown ground beef, celery, and onion, draining off excess grease. Season to taste with salt and pepper and add the ketchup. Put in large casserole or baking dish and stir in chicken soup, celery soup, and peas and carrots. Top with tater tots. Bake, covered, in 350°F oven for 45 minutes.

MEATBALLS

Rita Schiefelbein
Clear Lake, SD

1½ to 2 lb. cooked
  meatballs (using your
  favorite meatball recipe
  or deli-prepared ones)
1 bottle chili sauce

1 bottle water
1 c. brown sugar
1 can whole cranberries
1 (15 oz.) can sauerkraut

Stir together the chili sauce, water, sugar, cranberries, and sauerkraut. Pour over meatballs and bake in slow oven at 250°F. for 1½ hours.

Your guests will definitely ask for the recipe and they will be surprised when you tell them there is sauerkraut in the sauce.

MEXICAN LASAGNA

Iola Egle
Bella Vista, AR

Flour tortillas
1 (16 oz.) jar tomato salsa
¾ lb. ground beef
1 medium Vidalia onion, chopped fine

1 c. lettuce, shredded fine
1 tomato, peeled, seeded, and chopped
2 c. Cheddar cheese, grated

Preheat oven to 425°F. Brown beef with onion; drain well. Put 2 tablespoons salsa on the bottom of a sprayed 9x13 inch baking dish. Cover with a layer of flour tortillas. Layer meat, tomato, lettuce, 1½ cups cheese, and all but ½ cup salsa. Cover with another layer of tortillas and top with remaining salsa and cheese. Cover with foil and bake for 20 to 30 minutes or until cheese melts.

This recipe is made in just a few minutes and is so different.

MEXICAN MEATLOAF

Janet Rauch
Deep River, IA

1½ lb. ground beef
2 eggs
¼ c. onion, chopped
½ c. cheese, diced

¾ c. oatmeal
1 c. picante sauce
1 tsp. salt
⅛ tsp. pepper

Mix all ingredients together and bake at 350°F. for 1 hour.

MEXICAN PIZZA

Deb Smith
Fowler, CO

1 lb. ground beef
1 (16 oz.) can tomatoes
(undrained)
½ c. onions, chopped
1 (6 oz.) can tomato paste
¼ c. water
2 Tbsp. chili powder
¼ tsp. salt

¼ tsp. pepper
12 corn tortillas
2 c. sharp Cheddar
cheese, shredded and
divided
1 c. lettuce, shredded
1 avocado, sliced
Sour cream (optional)

In a large skillet, brown the ground beef. Drain. Stir in the canned tomatoes and their juice, onions, tomato paste, water, and seasonings. Simmer for 10 minutes. Cover the bottom and sides of a 14 inch pizza pan with the tortillas. Spread the meat sauce evenly over the tortillas. Bake at 350°F. for 20 minutes. Remove from the oven. Sprinkle with 1 cup cheese and return to the oven. Continue baking until the cheese is melted. To serve, top with lettuce and the remaining cheese. Garnish with the avocado. Sour cream may also be used as a garnish.

MOM'S MEATLOAF

Maudie Burden
Centerview, MO

½ c. onion, diced
½ c. green pepper, diced
½ tsp. hot sauce
2 tsp. dry oregano

1 tsp. garlic powder
2 tsp. black pepper
1 lb. ground round beef
4 egg whites

In a nonstick skillet over medium heat, simmer onion, green pepper, oregano, garlic powder, pepper, and hot sauce in ½ cup water until vegetables are tender; drain and mix by hand with beef and egg whites. Transfer to small loaf pan or casserole dish and bake in a preheated 400°F. oven until no longer pink in the middle, 20 to 30 minutes.

MOUTHWATERING SPARERIBS

Belinda Nichols
Edmond, OK

1 slab pork ribs
1 green pepper
1 red pepper
1 clove garlic

1 (medium) onion
1 Tbsp. seasoning salt
1 Tbsp. barbecue spice

Place ribs in foil and sprinkle with seasoning salt and barbecue spice. Top with peppers, garlic, and onions. Let marinate overnight. Bake at 350°F. for 8 hours.

MUSHROOM SALISBURY STEAK
Maudie Burden
Centerview MO

¼ c. cornstarch
2 (10½ oz.) cans beef consomme (undiluted)
1 (6 oz.) jar mushrooms, sliced and drained
4 tsp. Worcestershire sauce
1 tsp. dried basil
1 egg, beaten

½ c. soft bread crumbs
1 (medium) onion, finely chopped
½ to 1 tsp. salt
¼ tsp. pepper (optional)
1½ lb. ground beef
Hot mashed potatoes or cooked noodles

In a bowl, combine cornstarch and consomme until smooth. Stir in mushrooms, Worcestershire sauce, and basil; set aside. In another bowl, combine egg, bread crumbs, onion, seasoned salt, and pepper if desired. Add beef and mix well. Shape into six oval patties. Place in a shallow 1½ quart microwave-safe dish. Cover and microwave on high for 6 minutes; drain. Turn patties, moving the ones in the center to the outside of the dish. Pour consomme mixture over patties. Cover and microwave on high for 8 to 10 minutes or until meat is no longer pink. Let stand for 5 minutes. Serve with potatoes or noodles. Yields 6 servings.

ONE-POT SPAGHETTI
Flo M. Burtnett
Gage, OK

1 lb. ground beef
1 (small) onion, chopped
2 (14 oz.) cans chicken broth
1 (6 oz.) can tomato paste
½ tsp. salt

½ tsp. dried oregano
⅛ tsp. garlic powder
¼ tsp. pepper
7 oz. uncooked spaghetti, broken
Grated Parmesan cheese

Cook ground beef and onion in very large skillet over medium heat, stirring until beef crumbles and is no longer pink. Drain off any fat. Return beef to skillet. Stir in broth, tomato paste, salt, oregano, garlic powder, and pepper. Bring to a boil. Add uncooked spaghetti. Reduce heat and simmer, stirring often, 15 minutes or until spaghetti is tender. Sprinkle with cheese. Makes 4 servings.

ONION BEEF AU JUS

Stacy Menges
Watsontown, PA

1 (4 lb.) boneless beef
  rump roast
2 Tbsp. vegetable oil
2 (large) sweet onions,
  cut into ¼ inch slices
6 Tbsp. butter or
  margarine, softened,
  divided
5 c. water

½ c. soy sauce
1 pkg. onion soup mix
1 garlic clove, minced
1 tsp. browning sauce
  (optional)
1 (1 lb.) loaf French bread
1 c. (4 oz.) shredded
  Swiss cheese

In a Dutch oven over medium-high heat, brown roast on all sides in oil; drain. In a large skillet, saute onions in 2 tablespoons butter until tender. Add the water, soy sauce, soup mix, garlic, and browning sauce if desired. Pour over roast. Cover and bake at 325°F. for 2½ hours or until meat is tender. Let stand 10 minutes before slicing. Return meat to pan juices. Slice bread in ½ lengthwise; cut into 3 inch sections. Spread remaining butter over bread. Place on baking sheet. Broil 4 to 6 inches from the heat for 2 to 3 minutes or until golden brown. Top with beef and onions; sprinkle with cheese. Broil 4 to 6 inches from the heat for 1 to 2 minutes or until cheese is melted. Serve with pan juices. Yield: 12 servings.

The flavor of the meat gets with the garlic, soy sauce, and onion soup mix is out of this world. The tasty rich broth used for dipping makes it even better. The leftover beef makes delicious sandwiches, too.

ORIENTAL HOT CHICKEN

Marilyn Barner
Belle Plaine, KS

1 c. soy sauce
1 tsp. garlic salt
1 tsp. sesame seed oil
1 tsp. monosodium
  glutamate
3 green onions, chopped

2 jalapeno peppers,
  chopped
2 Tbsp. oriental hot
  peppers, chopped
½ c. sugar
1 whole chicken

Cut chicken into small pieces, bone and all, or cut as you would for frying chicken. Mix ingredients together and pour over chicken. Let set at least 2 hours or overnight. Stir now and then. Cook in saucepan about 40 minutes or until chicken is done. Serve over cooked rice.

This is very good, but very hot.

ORIENTAL PEPPER STEAK

Thelma Maxwell
Dodge City, KS

1½ lb. beef (sirloin or rib), cut in thin strips
1½ tsp. monosodium glutamate
1 c. beef bouillon
½ tsp. sugar
½ tsp. ginger
1 tsp. soy sauce
2 green peppers, cut in strips
1 (medium) onion, sliced
2 tomatoes, peeled, cut in wedges
2 tsp. cornstarch
2 Tbsp. water

Sprinkle beef with 1 teaspoon monosodium glutamate. Brown beef in hot oil in skillet. Add bouillon, sugar, ginger, and soy sauce. Bring to a boil, then reduce heat. Simmer for 15 minutes. Add peppers, onion, tomatoes, and remaining ½ teaspoon monosodium glutamate. Cook 5 minutes longer. Combine cornstarch and water. Stir until smooth. Add slowly to beef mixture. Cook, stirring, until mixture comes to a boil.

Serve with rice and grape tapioca pudding.

ORTEGA TACO CASSEROLE

Joan Stegman
Offerle, KS

1 lb. ground beef
½ c. onion, chopped
1 (8 oz.) bottle taco sauce (any flavor)
¾ c. water
1 (4 oz.) can green chiles, diced
1 (1.25 oz.) pkg. taco seasoning mix
1 (12 count) pkg. taco shells, broken and divided

Grease 11x17 inch baking dish. Cook beef and onion in large skillet until beef is browned; drain. Stir in taco sauce, water, chiles, and seasoning mix; bring to a boil. Reduce heat to low; cook, stirring occasionally, for 3 to 4 minutes. Layer ½ of broken shells on bottom of prepared baking dish. Cover with ½ of meat mixture; sprinkle with 1 cup cheese.

Repeat with remaining ingredients. Bake at 350°F. for 20 to 25 minutes or until bubbly and cheese is melted. Top with tomato, green pepper, and other desired garnishes. Makes 8 servings.

PARTY POTATOES

Phylis Carlson
Clarinda, IA

1 (8 oz.) pkg. cream
  cheese
1 (8 oz.) pkg. French onion
  dip

⅛ tsp. garlic salt
12 servings instant
  mashed potatoes

Mix instant potatoes according to directions to serve 12 people. Use a mixer to blend cream cheese and French onion dip. When blended, add to mashed potatoes. Add garlic salt to taste. Pour into a buttered casserole dish, dot with butter, and sprinkle with paprika on top. Bake 30 minutes at 350°F. until heated through.

I put these in my crockpot on medium heat to heat through. I get lots of compliments on these.

PASTA TUNA MELT

Wendy Uhlenhake
Ft. Atkinson, IA

3 c. uncooked pasta
1 can chicken broth
½ soup can water
1 can cream of mushroom
  soup

1 c. milk
1 can tuna, drained
1 c. cheese, shredded

Cook the pasta in the chicken broth and water in a skillet until it's tender. Don't drain. Add the soup, milk, and tuna. Top with the cheese and heat through.

PEPPER STEAK

Pauline Riley
Dodge City, KS

1 lb. beef (London Broil or sirloin), trimmed of all fat and sliced thin
2 Tbsp. olive oil
2 bell peppers, red or green

1 onion, sliced
1 clove garlic, chopped
½ c. mushrooms, sliced (optional)

Pat meat dry with paper towel. Heat oil in wok or frying pan. Add onion and saute over medium heat until golden brown, about 10 minutes. Add garlic and peppers and saute additional 3 minutes. Add the beef; stir until meat is cooked. Stir in mushrooms and cook about 2 more minutes. Season with soy sauce and salt to taste.

PEPPERONI PIZZA SOUP

Joan Stegman
Offerle, KS

4 (large) Italian or sourdough rolls
1 Tbsp. olive oil
2 Tbsp. fancy Parmesan cheese, shredded
1 (14½ oz.) can chunky pasta-style stewed tomatoes
1 (14½ oz.) can chicken broth
2 c. zucchini, sliced ½ inch thick

1 (large) red bell pepper, cut into ¾ inch pieces
1 (2¼ oz.) can sliced black olives, drained
2 oz. pepperoni, thinly sliced
1½ c. (6 oz.) pizza double cheese, shredded
Fresh basil sprigs (optional)

Hollow out rolls, leaving ½ inch shell. Brush with oil; sprinkle with Parmesan cheese. Place on baking sheet. Bake in preheated oven at 400°F. for 6 minutes or until golden brown. Combine tomatoes, chicken broth, zucchini, and bell pepper in large saucepan. Heat to a boil; reduce heat. Simmer uncovered 5 minutes or until vegetables are crisp-tender. Stir in olives and pepperoni. Simmer 1 minute. Ladle soup into four bread bowls; sprinkle evenly with double pizza cheese. Garnish with basil sprigs if desired. Preparation time: 15 minutes. Cooking time: 8 minutes. Serves 4.

PICANTE MEATLOAF

Jean Lorenz
Sanford, CO

1½ lb. ground beef
1 egg, beaten
½ c. bread crumbs
¼ c. onions, chopped
¾ c. picante salsa

½ tsp. sugar
1 tsp. salt
1 tsp. chili powder
½ tsp. garlic powder
¼ c. salsa

Stir together egg, bread crumbs, onions, salsa, sugar, salt, chili, and garlic powder. Add ground beef and mix well. Pat meat mixture into an 8x4x2 inch oval and place in a loaf pan. Bake in 350°F. oven for 1 hour. Remove from oven and spoon ¼ cup salsa over loaf; cook for 5 minutes more.

PIZZA ROLL

Brenda Smith
Allen, TX

½ lb. ground beef
½ lb. sausage
½ tsp. basil
½ tsp. oregano
½ tsp. salt
¾ c. onion, chopped
1 (6 oz.) can tomato paste

⅛ tsp. garlic powder
1 egg
1 c. cottage cheese
¼ c. Parmesan cheese
1 pkg. Mozzarella cheese
2 pkg. crescent rolls

Brown beef, sausage, basil, oregano, salt, onion, tomato paste, and garlic powder together. Mix egg, cottage cheese, and Parmesan cheese together. Place crescent rolls in a large square on pan. In the middle of crescent rolls, add the ground beef/sausage mix, then the egg/cottage cheese mix. You will layer this several times. Put Mozzarella cheese on the top layer and then close the crescent rolls. Seal it with milk and then sprinkle sesame seeds on top. Bake at 375°F. for 25 minutes.

POOR MAN'S BEEF STROGANOFF

LaDonna Miller
Wichita, KS

½ c. onion
1 lb. ground beef
1 Tbsp. butter
2 Tbsp. flour
1 tsp. salt
¼ tsp. monosodium glutamate

¼ tsp. pepper
½ tsp. paprika
1 can mushrooms
1 can mushroom soup
1 c. sour cream
Rice or Chinese noodles

In skillet, saute minced onion in butter. Add ground beef; saute 5 minutes. Drain. Add flour, salt, monosodium glutamate, pepper, paprika, mushrooms, and soup. Simmer, uncovered, 10 minutes, then stir in sour cream. Serve over cooked rice or Chinese noodles.

POOR MAN'S LOBSTER

Sandi Loiseau
Frankfort, KS

2 lb. codfish
1 tsp. salt
3 slices lemon
Water

½ c. white wine
3 slices onion
1 bay leaf
¼ to ½ c. melted butter

Put fish in skillet; add salt, lemon, wine, onion, bay leaf, and enough water to cover the fish. Bring to a boil and reduce heat. Simmer for 12 minutes. Melt butter; pour some in bottom of broiler pan. Put in the fish and baste with remaining butter. Broil until golden. Serve with butter.

PORCUPINE MEATBALLS

Betty Mead
Paradise, KS

4 c. tomato juice
2 Tbsp. chili powder
¼ tsp. allspice
½ tsp. celery seed
1 tsp. Worcestershire
  sauce
1 tsp. brown sugar
1 lb. ground beef

½ c. rice (uncooked)
1 c. green pepper,
  chopped
½ c. celery, finely chopped
1 egg
2 tsp. prepared mustard
1½ tsp. salt
¼ tsp. pepper

Combine all sauce ingredients, tomato juice, chili powder, allspice, celery seed, Worcestershire sauce, and brown sugar. Cover and simmer 10 minutes. Combine all ingredients for meatballs, ground beef, rice, green pepper, celery, egg, mustard, and salt and pepper. Mix well and form into 1½ inch meatballs. Place in baking dish. Pour sauce over meatballs. Cover and bake at 350°F. for 1 hour. Yields 6 servings.

PORK CASSOULET

Thelma Maxwell
Dodge City, KS

1 lb. dried pinto beans
6 c. water
1½ tsp. salt
2 cloves garlic, minced
2 carrots, diced
2 onions, sliced
1 bay leaf
½ tsp. pepper
½ tsp. thyme

3 slices salt pork or
  bacon, diced
1 pork steak
1 Polish ring sausage
1 c. celery, sliced
1 can tomato sauce
1 (8 oz.) ½ c. dry white
  wine (optional)
6 whole cloves (optional)

Sort and wash beans, place in heavy kettle, and add water. Bring to boil; remove from heat. Let stand 1 hour, covered. Add seasonings, salt pork, carrots, and onions to beans. Cover; bring to boil. Lower heat and simmer 1 hour. Add meats, celery, tomato sauce, and wine. Simmer 1 hour or until meats are tender. Cut pork into cubes; skin and slice sausage. Remove bay leaf and cloves. Return meats to beans and simmer, uncovered, to thicken slightly. Serves 12 or more.

Ham may be used instead of the sausage.

POTATOES, KRAUT AND SAUSAGE MEAL

Tammy Bell
Osawatomie, KC

10 baking potatoes
¾ to 1 lb. Polish sausage
1 (large) can sauerkraut
1 onion, chopped

2 Tbsp. vegetable oil
½ tsp. salt
¼ tsp. pepper
½ tsp. garlic powder

In a skillet, fry potatoes and onion in oil until almost done. Slice sausage and add to potatoes and onion; continue cooking until all are done. Add sauerkraut, salt, pepper, and garlic powder. Cover and simmer until sauerkraut is heated through.

QUICHE

Barb Kasel
Adams, MN

3 eggs
½ c. prepared biscuit mix
¼ c. butter, melted
1½ c. milk
¼ tsp. salt

⅛ tsp. pepper
1 c. Swiss cheese
1 c. broccoli
½ c. bacon, ham and/or
   mushrooms

Mix the eggs, prepared biscuit mix, butter, milk, and salt and pepper together. Pour mixture into a greased quiche dish or pie pan, then add the cheese, broccoli, ham, mushrooms, etc. Bake at 350°F. for 45 minutes or until brown on top.

This goes well for family brunch.

QUICK CREAMED HAMBURGER

Amy Edwards
Tulsa, OK

1 lb. ground beef
1 (small) onion, chopped
Flour

Milk
Salt
Pepper

Brown the beef with the onion. When cooked, add flour until all the liquid is absorbed and cook until flour turns light brown. Salt and pepper to taste. Add milk to cover the beef and cook until gravy thickens. Serve over roast.

This is a very quick meal - great for a busy night. Just heat up a can of green beans and you have a great meal that kids love!

111

QUICK TACO TATERS

Juanna Beth Lewis
Darlington, ID

6 to 8 (medium) potatoes,
  peeled, sliced, and
  boiled until tender
2 lb. ground beef,
  browned in skillet
1 (small) onion, chopped
1 pkg. taco seasoning mix
  (optional homemade
  seasoning in directions)

¼ c. water
¼ c. margarine, melted
¼ c. flour
2 c. milk
1 tsp. salt
⅛ tsp. pepper
1 c. cheese, grated

Simmer together potatoes, ground beef, onion, taco seasoning mix, and water for 10 minutes. Stir into sauce; fold in cooked potatoes. Spread half in buttered 7x11 inch casserole dish. Spread meat mixture over potatoes, then layer remaining potatoes over meat. Sprinkle cheese over casserole. Bake 15 minutes at 400°F until cheese melts. To prepare homemade taco seasoning: 1 teaspoon salt, 1 teaspoon chili powder, ½ teaspoon cumin, ½ teaspoon crushed dried red pepper, ½ teaspoon minced garlic, ½ teaspoon oregano, 2 tablespoons minced onion, 1 tablespoon cornstarch. Mix all together and use in place of 1 package purchased taco seasoning mix.

I often make 4 times the homemade taco seasoning recipe and store in a covered jar. It's so handy for recipes.

R.J.'S VEGETABLE MEDLEY

Ruthye DeWard
Bazine, KS

½ stick margarine, melted
½ c. water
½ c. Worcestershire sauce
1 (small) head cabbage,
  chopped
1 yellow squash, chopped
1 zucchini, chopped

1 (large) onion, chopped
1 (29 oz.) can tomatoes,
  diced
1 green pepper, chopped
1½ lb. ground beef,
  browned

Combine all ingredients in a large stock pot. Cook 1 hour on low heat. Stir often. Add any vegetables you like to the above ingredients.

I made this recipe up one day, and my family loves it.

ROUND STEAK AND POTATO CASSEROLE

Gwenda Batterman
Amarillo, TX

2 lb. tenderized round
   steak
4 to 5 (medium) potatoes,
   peeled and sliced thin
2 cans cream of
   mushroom soup
2 cans hot water
1 lb. Mozzarella cheese,
   shredded
Salt and pepper to taste

Cut steak into bite-size pieces. Flour and fry in small amount of oil until done. Spread meat into 9x13 inch casserole dish. Boil potatoes in water until done. Place potatoes on steak. Mix 2 cans of mushroom soup with 2 cans hot water and salt and pepper to taste. Pour over steak and potatoes. Top with shredded Mozzarella cheese. Bake at 400°F. for 30 to 45 minutes or until brown on top. Let stand 10 minutes before serving.

RUNZA CASSEROLE

Jenny Pachta
Belleville, KS

2 lb. ground beef
1 can cream of mushroom
   soup
2 cans ready to bake
   crescent rolls
1 pkg. (about 8 slices)
   Swiss cheese
1 head cabbage, finely
   shredded
1 medium onion

Grease 9x13 inch pan. Cover the bottom of the pan with 1 package of crescent rolls. Brown ground beef with cabbage and onions. Drain grease off ground beef; combine ground beef, cabbage, and onion with cream of mushroom soup. Pour over crescent rolls. Layer top of ground beef mixture with Swiss cheese. Open second package of crescent rolls and layer over top of Swiss cheese. Try to cover all the cheese so the cheese does not get a brown crust on it. Bake at 350°F. for 20 to 25 minutes.

SALMON CROQUETTES

Thelma Baldock
Delphos, KS

1 (16 oz.) can salmon, drain about half the liquid
¼ c. onion, chopped
2 eggs, beaten
3 Tbsp. whole wheat bread crumbs
¼ tsp. thyme
¼ tsp. oregano
⅛ tsp. garlic powder
1 c. flour
½ c. olive oil
4 Tbsp. butter
4 Tbsp. flour
1 c. milk
1 c. chicken broth
Salt and pepper to taste

Place salmon in large mixing bowl. Add onion and seasoning. Mix well. Add eggs, then bread crumbs. Form into small patties. Heat oil in heavy skillet. Dip patties into flour; shake off excess flour. Fry 2 to 3 minutes per side until golden brown. Serve with Bechamel sauce made of butter, flour, milk, and chicken broth. Melt butter in a heavy saucepan over medium heat. Add flour to hot butter to make a paste; remove from heat and cool. Heat milk and broth together; gradually add to cooled flour mixture. Return to low heat and cook 15 minutes. Stir often. Season with salt and pepper.

SALMON LOAF

Eileen Locke
Paola, KS

½ c. celery, chopped
1 Tbsp. onion, chopped
3 Tbsp. butter, melted
2 Tbsp. flour
1½ c. milk
1 tall can salmon
1 c. bread crumbs
1 egg, beaten
½ tsp. salt
1 Tbsp. fresh lemon juice

In a small saucepan, stir and cook celery, onion, and butter. Continue cooking and stirring; add flour and milk. Cook until sauce thickens, stirring constantly. Do not boil. Add to sauce salmon, bread crumbs, egg, salt, and lemon juice. Mix together and place in lightly sprayed loaf pan. Bake about 1 hour at 350°F. or until lightly browned. Garnish with the remainder of the lemon.

SALMON SCRAMBLE

Elsie Mac Arthur
Richmond, KS

1 onion, chopped
1 Tbsp. butter
2 cloves garlic, chopped
⅔ c. fresh mushrooms,
 sliced

1 c. fresh frozen peas
2 c. smoked salmon,
 chopped
1 egg (for each person
 serving)

Saute onion and garlic in butter until done. Add mushrooms, peas, salmon, and beaten eggs. Cook and stir until eggs are done. Serve garnished with parsley. Add a salad and you have a complete meal.

SALMON/OYSTER CASSEROLE

Lucile Fuller
Wichita, KS

1 (14.75 oz.) can red
 salmon
1 (8 oz.) can oysters,
 whole or pieces

40 saltine crackers
Half & half
2 or 3 pats margarine

Grease 2½ quart or larger casserole. Begin with a layer of crumbled crackers, then a layer of salmon, then one of oysters. Make about 3 layers, ending with cracker crumbs and pats of margarine. Add liquid from salmon and oysters, then pour on half & half until you can see the liquid. Bake in 350°F. oven about 45 minutes until the top is golden brown and liquid is absorbed.

This was my mother's recipe, and she usually served it with mashed potatoes, creamed peas, pickled beets, and relishes.

SAUSAGE CASSEROLE

Arlene Bontrager
Hutchinson, KS

1 c. elbow macaroni
1 lb. bulk pork sausage
1 (medium) onion,
 chopped
1 (14.5 oz.) can tomatoes,
 diced
3 Tbsp. margarine

4 Tbsp. flour
¼ tsp. pepper
1 c. milk
1 c. cheese, shredded
 (Cheddar, Jack, or
 Mozzarella)

Cook macaroni according to package directions. Drain and set aside. In large skillet, cook sausage and onion till browned. Drain off fat. Stir in tomatoes; set aside. In large saucepan, melt margarine; stir in flour and pepper. Add milk all at once and cook and stir until thick and bubbly. Stir meat mixture and macaroni into white sauce. Transfer mixture into an ungreased 9x13 inch baking pan. Sprinkle top with cheese. Bake, uncovered, in 350°F. oven about 30 minutes until bubbly.

SAUSAGE CASSEROLE

Carol F. Mandrell
Olton, TX

1 lb. smoked sausage, sliced
1 (large) onion, cut into short, thin strips
2 (large) green peppers, cut into short, thin strips
3 Tbsp. vegetable oil
1 (16 oz.) can tomatoes and green chilies
2 (16 oz.) cans black-eyed peas, drained
1 pkg. corn muffin mix
¼ tsp. ground cayenne pepper
⅔ c. milk
1 egg, beaten

In a large skillet over medium heat, cook sausage, onion, and green pepper in 1 tablespoon oil until vegetables are tender and sausage is done. Stir in tomatoes and peas; reduce heat and simmer for 5 to 10 minutes. Pour into lightly sprayed 13x9 inch baking dish. In a small bowl, combine corn muffin mix, cayenne pepper, milk, egg, and remaining 2 tablespoons of oil. Stir until smooth. Pour over sausage mixture. Bake at 400°F. for 25 to 30 minutes or until golden brown.

SAVORY SLOW-COOK BEEF-VEGETABLE SOUP

Betty Mead
Paradise, KS

1 c. potatoes, chopped
1 c. onion, chopped
1 c. carrots, chopped
1 c. celery, chopped
2 lb. beef
1 Tbsp. salt
⅛ tsp. pepper
3 c. water
2 tsp. beef-flavored base
1 (16 oz.) can cut green beans
1 (16 oz.) can whole kernel corn

In slow cooker, combine potatoes, onions, carrots, celery, beef, salt, pepper, and water. Cover and cook on low heat for 10 to 12 hours. Turn on high heat and add undrained corn and green beans; cook for 30 minutes longer. Yields 10 to12 servings.

SAVORY SWISS EGGS

Barb Kasel
Adams, MN

8 eggs, slightly beaten
1 (4 oz.) pkg. Cheddar
 cheese, shredded
2 Tbsp. butter, melted
⅔ c. milk
¼ tsp. prepared mustard

½ tsp. salt
⅛ tsp. pepper
1 (4 oz.) can mushroom
 pieces (optional)
Green peppers, chopped
 (optional)

Combine all ingredients. Pour into a greased 8x8 inch pan. Bake at 350°F. for 25 to 30 minutes.

I have made this egg bake for over 25 years; they will reach for seconds. For 9x13 inch pan double recipe.

SEAFOOD ENCHILADAS

Donna Evans
Turpin, OK

1 (10 oz.) can cream of
 chicken soup
½ c. onion, chopped
1 (8 oz.) bag imitation
 crabmeat
1 (8 oz.) bag small shrimp
2 c. Monterey Jack
 cheese, shredded

8 flour tortillas
1 c. milk
⅛ tsp. nutmeg
⅛ tsp. ground black
 pepper

In a mixing bowl, stir together soup, onion, nutmeg, and black pepper. In another bowl, place ½ of the soup mixture, crab, shrimp, and 1 cup of the Monterey Jack cheese; stir until combined and set aside. Wrap the tortillas in paper towels; microwave on 100% power for 30 to 60 seconds. Place ⅓ cup mixture on each tortilla; roll up. Place seam side down in a greased 12 x 7½ inch dish. Stir milk into the reserved soup mixture; pour over enchiladas. Microwave, covered, on high for 12 to 14 minutes. Sprinkle with the remaining cheese. Let stand for 10 minutes.

I have also substituted canned chicken for the crabmeat and shrimp. Serve with a tossed salad, tortilla chips, and salsa.

SIMPLE LASAGNA

Johnna Lambert
Palco, KS

1 (8 oz.) pkg. mini lasagna
noodles
1½ lb. ground beef
1 clove garlic, minced
Butter
3 (8 oz.) cans tomato
sauce
1 Tbsp. sugar
1 c. cottage cheese

1 (8 oz.) pkg. cream
cheese
¼ c. sour cream
⅓ c. onion, finely chopped
¼ c. green pepper,
chopped
2 c. Cheddar cheese,
grated

Brown ground beef and drain well; stir in garlic and butter. Add tomato sauce, salt, pepper, and sugar; set aside. Blend cottage cheese with cream cheese; add sour cream, onion, and green pepper to cheeses. Grease a 13x9 inch baking dish. Layer in the following order: ½ of noodles in bottom, cheese mixture, one cup of Cheddar cheese, rest of noodles, and then ground beef mixture. Top with remaining Cheddar cheese and bake 30 minutes at 350°F. Remove from oven and let set for 5 minutes before serving.

SKI BREAKFAST

Nanette Conger
Fairfield, IA

1 stick butter
1 (24 oz.) pkg. O'Brien
potatoes
1½ c. bacon, ham, or
sausage

12 eggs, beaten
1 c. milk
4 c. Cheddar cheese,
shredded

Melt butter or margarine in 10x15 inch pan. Mix potatoes, bacon, ham or sausage, eggs, milk, and cheese together and stir into melted butter. Bake at 350°F. for 45 to 60 minutes or until tests done. Cool slightly before serving.

This recipe is great to freeze and serve later.

SLOPPY JOE DINNER

Mary Jeans
Blackwell, OK

1½ lb. ground beef
1 (15½ oz.) can Sloppy
　Joe sauce
2 c. Cheddar cheese,
　shredded

2 c. Bisquick
2 beaten eggs
1 c. milk
1 Tbsp. sesame seeds

Brown meat and drain. Stir in Sloppy Joe sauce. Pour into lightly greased 9x13 inch baking dish. Sprinkle with cheese. In separate bowl, combine Bisquick, eggs, and milk just until blended. Pour over cheese. Sprinkle with sesame seeds. Bake, uncovered, at 400°F. for 25 minutes or until golden brown. Serves 8.

SLOW COOKER NOODLE CASSEROLE

Beth Zucker
Bucyrus, OH

2½ c. dry noodles
1 tsp. salt
½ c. onion, finely chopped
1 (8 oz.) can peas with
　liquid
1 can tuna or other meat
　(ham, beef, chicken)

1 (10¾ oz.) can cream of
　mushroom soup
½ can water
¼ c. almonds
½ c. cheese, shredded
　(any kind)

Put ingredients in slow cooker in order listed. Cover and cook on low for 6 to 8 hours or on high 2 to 3 hours. Stir occasionally.

SMOKED BRISKET

Anna Mae Lancaster
Wray, CO

1 brisket
⅓ c. Worcestershire sauce
⅓ c. liquid smoke

Savory salt
Celery salt
Garlic powder or flakes

Marinate overnight and cook in oven at 275°F. for 10 to 12 hours. Cover the baking pan tight with foil for about 8 hours; remove from oven and slice. Return to oven to complete cooking to desired degree of doneness. At this point, barbecue sauce can be added if desired.

SOUR CREAM ENCHILADAS

Ruthye DeWald
Bazine, KS

12 corn tortillas
⅓ c. oil
1 (medium) onion, finely chopped
1 (10 oz.) pkg. Monterey Jack cheese, shredded
¼ c. margarine

¼ c. flour
1 c. chicken broth
1 (8 oz.) container sour cream
7 oz. chiles, chopped (mild)

Fry tortillas in oil in skillet 3 to 5 seconds each side (not crisp). Combine onion and cheese. Place 3 tablespoons of cheese and onion mixture on each tortilla; roll tortillas up and place seam side down in greased 13x9x2 inch dish. Melt margarine in saucepan on low heat; add flour, stirring until smooth. Cool one minute, stirring constantly; gradually add broth. Cook over medium heat, stirring, until thick (like gravy). Stir in sour cream and chiles. Pour over tortillas. Bake at 375°F. for 15 to 20 minutes.

SOUTH-OF-THE BORDER CASSEROLE

Kathy Hogue
Topeka, KS

1 (7 oz.) pkg. macaroni
1 lb. ground beef
1 (medium) onion, chopped
1 c. celery, sliced
1 clove garlic, minced
1 (7 oz.) can green chiles, diced
1 (16 oz.) can diced tomatoes (undrained)

2 tsp. instant beef bouillon
½ tsp. seasoned salt
2 tsp. ground cumin
1 (16 oz.) can tomatoes, crushed
⅓ c. picante sauce
2 oz. Cheddar cheese
2 oz. Muenster cheese, cubed

Prepare macaroni according to package directions; drain. In large skillet, combine ground meat, onion, celery, and garlic. Cook until meat is browned. Stir in all ingredients except cheeses. Simmer 10 minutes. Combine macaroni, meat mixture, and cheeses. Pour into glass casserole dish. Cover. Bake in 350°F. oven until cheese melts, about 20 minutes.

I like to divide this into two 8 inch square casserole dishes and freeze one.

SOUTHERN STYLE SCALLOPED CHICKEN

Clara Ough
Hebron, NE

1 chicken, salted and
  boiled
6 c. broth from chicken
  (add water if not
  enough broth)
½ c. butter
¾ c. flour
3 eggs, beaten

6 to 8 c. corn bread
  crumbs
2 Tbsp. celery flakes
2 Tbsp. minced onion
1 Tbsp. parsley flakes
1 tsp. salt
1 tsp. sage
½ tsp. pepper

Debone chicken and cut into cubes. Grease a 9x13 inch pan. Layer bread crumbs and chicken. To make custard, melt butter; add flour and blend. Slowly add broth and stir so it does not lump. Cook until thick. Add to beaten eggs; pour over bread crumbs and chicken. Bake for 45 minutes in a 350°F. oven. Shredded cheese can be sprinkled over casserole about 6 minutes before it is done.

SPAGHETTI AND MEATBALLS

Donna Fisk
Montezuma, IA

1½ lb. ground beef
¾ c. oatmeal
1 Tbsp. onion, chopped or
  dried
½ c. milk
1 egg, beaten

1 Tbsp. parsley flakes
½ tsp. Italian seasoning
¼ tsp. pepper
1 tsp. salt
½ tsp. garlic salt

Mix all ingredients and form into balls. Brown in skillet and add one large jar of spaghetti sauce. Serve over cooked spaghetti.

SPAGHETTI AND MEATBALLS WITH GARDEN SQUASH

Lisa Petzold
Elmer, OK

1½ lb. ground beef
1 (small) onion, chopped
1 (small) green pepper, chopped (optional)
5 to 7 saltine crackers, crushed

1 egg
2 (15 oz.) cans tomato sauce
1½ (15 oz.) cans water
1 tsp. garlic
2 to 3 (medium) squash

For meatballs, mix ground beef, onion, green pepper, crackers, and egg. Form into balls and drop onto heated skillet. Cook on medium heat until no longer pink. While meat is cooking, prepare sauce. Stir tomato sauce, water, and garlic together in a medium size mixing bowl. Pour sauce over meatballs when meat is cooked through. Slice squash over meatballs and sauce. Cover with skillet lid. Simmer until squash is done. Serve over spaghetti noodles.

This is a great one dish meal.

STEVE'S CALF FRIES

Bobbi Higgs
Ulysses, KS

1 disgusting day of cutting fresh calf fries
1 box Zatarain's fry mix seasoning

6 (large) eggs
8 c. oil

After you have convinced your husband to clean the fries (you get to clean up the mess). Slice half frozen fries into ¼ inch slices. Heat oil till hot. Mix eggs and dip fry slices in egg, seasoning mix, and fry till golden brown.

The worst part of this recipe is really for the bull calves.

STEW FOR YOUR CROCKPOT

Alene Fosler
Sublette, KS

1½ to 2 lb. roast
Potatoes, sliced
Carrots, sliced
Celery, sliced

1 pkg. dried onion soup
1 can mushroom soup
1 can tomato soup

Cut up roast or use stew meat and put into your crockpot. Put potatoes, carrots, and celery on top of meat. Sprinkle dried onion soup over the meat and vegetables. Mix cream of mushroom soup and tomato soup together. Pour over the meat mixture, but do not mix. Cover and cook for 8 to 10 hours. Cook on high the first hour, then turn to low for the remaining time.

Very easy, but it is very good.

STUFFED GREEN PEPPER SOUP
Julie Schmidt
Smith Center, KS

2 lb. ground beef
1 (28 oz.) can tomato
    sauce
1 (28 oz.) can diced
    tomatoes (undrained)
2 c. cooked converted or
    long grain white rice

2 c. green pepper,
    coarsely chopped
2 beef bouillon cubes
¼ c. packed brown sugar
2 tsp. salt
1 tsp. pepper

In a large saucepan or Dutch oven, brown beef; drain. Add remaining ingredients; bring to a boil. Reduce heat; cover and simmer for 30 to 40 minutes or until peppers are tender. Yield: 10 servings.

If you like traditional stuffed green peppers, you will love this soup. I couldn't believe how similar it tasted. Also, people that have tried the soup who normally don't like stuffed peppers because of the large amount of green pepper thought this was a great way to get smaller portions of green pepper per bite.

STUFFED GREEN PEPPERS
Glennys Bruning
Ellsworth, KS

6 (large) green peppers
2 Tbsp. onions, chopped
⅛ tsp. garlic salt
1 (15 oz.) can tomato
    sauce

¾ c. Mozzarella cheese,
    shredded
1 lb. ground beef
1 tsp. salt
1 c. cooked rice

To microwave, cut thin slices from stem end of each pepper. Remove seeds and membranes. Rinse. Place peppers cut sides up in ungreased 9 or 10 inch glass pie plate. Cover with plastic wrap; microwave until hot, 3 to 3½ minutes. Mix cooked rice, uncooked ground beef, onion, salt, and garlic salt. Fill peppers with one cup ground beef mixture. Pour sauce over peppers. Cover with plastic wrap. Microwave 6 minutes. Turn plate ¼ turn; microwave until mixture is done, 6 to 7 minutes longer. Sprinkle with cheese.

SUGAR FREE SPAGHETTI SAUCE

Norma Weber
Grainfield, KS

1 lb. lean ground beef
2 (28 oz.) cans tomatoes, diced
2 (6 oz.) cans tomato paste
1 (large) onion, chopped
2 stalks celery, chopped
2 green peppers, chopped
1 (8 oz.) pkg. fresh mushrooms, sliced

4 Tbsp. Italian seasoning
½ tsp. dried red pepper flakes
3 cloves garlic, minced
1 Tbsp. dried basil
4 Tbsp. sugar substitute
2 c. water

In a large skillet, brown beef over medium heat. In a large (Dutch oven size) kettle, combine remaining ingredients; add browned beef. Cover; bring to a boil. Reduce heat and simmer over low heat. Simmer 4 to 6 hours or all day. Stir occasionally. Serve with spaghetti or as sauce for pizza.

SUPER SHRIMP CREOLE

Pat Habiger
Spearville, KS

½ c. onion, chopped
½ c. celery, sliced
1 clove garlic, minced
2 Tbsp. vegetable oil
1 (16 oz.) can whole tomatoes (undrained)
½ c. tomato sauce
½ c. picante sauce
1 Tbsp. Worcestershire sauce

½ tsp. chili powder
¼ tsp. salt
¼ tsp. sugar
1 Tbsp. cornstarch
2 Tbsp. cold water
1 lb. large shrimp, peeled and deveined
½ c. green pepper, chopped

Cook onion, celery, and garlic in oil in large skillet until tender, but not brown. Add tomatoes, tomato sauce, picante sauce, and seasonings. Simmer, uncovered, 15 minutes. Combine cornstarch and water; add to sauce and stir until smooth and thickened. Add shrimp and green pepper. Cover and simmer 10 minutes. Serve over rice if desired.

Simple to make and elegant to serve. Oh, the smiles when they taste!

SWEET AND SOUR CHICKEN

Donna Sawyer
McCook, NE

4 chicken breast halves
  (boneless and skinless)
½ c. flour
½ tsp. salt
¼ tsp. pepper
½ c. canola oil
1 c. orange juice
½ c. chili sauce

½ c. red pepper, chopped
1 tsp. prepared mustard
1 tsp. garlic salt
3 Tbsp. soy sauce
1 Tbsp. honey
1 can mandarin orange
  sections

Place flour, salt, and pepper in a plastic bag. Add chicken and shake to coat well. Place canola oil in fry pan over medium-high heat. Add chicken and brown on both sides, about 5 minutes. Remove chicken to 3 quart casserole. Drain oil from fry pan and add orange juice, chili sauce, bell pepper, mustard, garlic salt, soy sauce, and honey. Simmer, stirring about 5 minutes, and pour over chicken; cover casserole with foil. Bake chicken at 350°F., covered, for 55 minutes. Remove foil and top chicken with mandarin orange sections and additional orange juice if thinner sauce is desired. Return to oven and bake 10 minutes. Serve over rice. Makes 4 delicious servings.

I like to serve this with a green salad and garlic bread followed with frozen yogurt dessert.

SWISS CHICKEN CASSEROLE

Kimberly Chambers
Norcatur, KS

8 to 9 boneless chicken
  breasts
1 can cream of chicken
  soup

8 oz. Swiss cheese
Seasoned bread crumbs

In 9½ x 11 inch pan, spray with cooking spray. Place chicken breast flat; cover with soup, then cheese. Generously sprinkle with bread crumbs. Bake at 350°F. for 45 minutes.

Instead of the bread crumbs, I use Stove Top stuffing mix. It's great!

TACO CASSEROLE

Joyce Sievers
Slater, IA

1 bag Doritos tortilla
  chips
1 lb. ground beef,
  browned
¾ c. sour cream

¾ c. salsa
1 pkg. taco seasoning
1 to 2 c. Cheddar cheese,
  shredded

Grease a 9x13 inch pan. Layer ½ of crushed Doritos chips to cover bottom of pan. Add ground beef, sour cream, and salsa. Sprinkle taco seasoning over the layers and top with Cheddar cheese, using as much as you desire. Bake at 350°F. for 30 minutes. Remove from oven and place more crushed Doritos chips on top. Return to oven for 5 minutes.

TACO SOUP

Roxie Berning
Marienthal, KS

2 lb. ground beef
1 (large) onion
1 pkg. taco seasoning
1 (1.6 oz.) pkg. Ranch
  salad dressing (dry)
1 can red beans
1 can hominy

1 can chili beans
3 cans stewed tomatoes,
  chopped
3 cans water
Salt, pepper, garlic
  powder to taste

Brown ground beef and onion together; drain. Add taco seasoning, salad dressing, red beans, hominy, chili beans, tomatoes, and water. Cook and simmer until hot and blended. Add salt, pepper, and garlic powder to taste. Serve with shredded Cheddar cheese, sour cream, and tortilla chips.

TAMALES

Aron Fangman
Hereford, TX

1¼ lb. pork shoulder roast
1½ lb. Masa Harina
¼ lb. lard or shortening
⅛ tsp. salt

⅛ tsp. garlic
½ lb. corn husks
2 lb. ground red chili

Cook meat in a roaster on the stove between medium-low and medium-high heat or in the oven. Cook meat until tender with enough water to cover meat. Cool and shred. Mix chili powder with meat; add salt and enough broth from meat to soften. Add garlic salt. Simmer 15 minutes. Preparation of dough: Add to Masa Harina, meat broth, melted lard, and salt. Cream well to spreading consistency. Preparation of corn husks: Open up the husks, clean by shaking, soak in hot water (not boiling) for 15 minutes, until soft and pliable, and drain well. How to prepare tamales: Spread dough (about 1 tablespoon) on one end of the husks. Spread chili meat mixture on top of that; fold edges in and fold husks over the filling. Stand the tamales up (don't lay them down) in a pan with just enough water to cover the bottom and steam until the dough is done. The dough is done when firm and will come away from the husk when you open it up. Makes about 24.

You may use ready mixed Masa Harina instead of making it yourself.

THAI PASTA

Iola Egle
Bella Vista, AR

1 c. salsa
½ c. chunky peanut butter
2 Tbsp. honey
2 Tbsp. orange juice
1 tsp. soy sauce
1 tsp. red pepper, crushed

½ tsp. ground ginger
3 c. (about 6 dry oz.) fettuccine, cooked
2 c. chicken, cooked and cubed
16 oz. salad greens

In a large skillet, combine the salsa, peanut butter, honey, orange juice, soy sauce, crushed red pepper, and ginger over low heat and cook until heated through, stirring occasionally. Stir in the fettuccine and chicken until evenly coated. Place on a serving platter and top with the fettuccine mixture. Toss just before serving.

I like to garnish this salad with red bell pepper and chopped fresh cilantro. Linguine, bow tie pasta, or almost any flat noodle can be used instead of fettuccine.

THRIFTY MEAT BALLS

Gary Kasel
Adams, MN

1 lb. ground beef
1 egg, beaten
¼ c. onion, chopped
½ c. soda cracker crumbs
⅓ c. milk
½ tsp. salt

⅛ tsp. pepper
¼ tsp. poultry seasoning
1 (10¾ oz.) can cream of mushroom, chicken, or celery soup
½ can milk

Combine ground beef, egg, onion, cracker crumbs, milk, salt, pepper, and poultry seasoning; mix well. Shape into small balls and put into baking dish. Mix soup with milk and pour over top of meat balls. Bake in a 325°F. oven for 1 hour. Yields 4 servings.

These are my favorite meat balls.

TORTILLA SOUP

Julie Schmidt
Smith Center, KS

1 green bell pepper, chopped
1 onion, chopped
2 cloves garlic, minced
1 (4 oz.) can green chiles, chopped, drained
2 Tbsp. vegetable oil
6 c. chicken broth
3 c. chicken, chopped and cooked
1 (10 oz.) can tomato soup
1 (10 oz.) can Ro-Tel tomatoes

1 (14 oz.) can stewed tomatoes
1 (10 oz.) pkg. frozen whole kernel corn
2 tsp. Worcestershire sauce
1 tsp. ground cumin
1 tsp. chili powder
Salt and pepper to taste
1 (8 oz.) bag tortilla chips
Monterey Jack cheese, shredded
Avocado slices

Saute green pepper, onion, garlic, and chiles in oil in large saucepan until tender. Add chicken broth, chicken, soup, tomatoes, corn, Worcestershire sauce, cumin, chili powder, salt, and pepper. Simmer for 3 hours, stirring occasionally. Place tortilla chips in soup bowls. Ladle in soup. Garnish with cheese and avocado. Yield 10 to 12 servings.

TUNA CAKES

Juanita Gross
Clearwater, KS

1 (medium) zucchini
1 (7 oz.) can tuna
1½ c. bread crumbs
1 egg
2 tsp. onion, grated

1 tsp. lemon juice
¼ tsp. salt and pepper
2 Tbsp. salad oil
Lettuce and small tomato, sliced

Shred zucchini; pat with paper towel in bowl. Mix zucchini, tuna, bread crumbs, egg, onion, lemon juice, salt, pepper, and salad oil. Shape into patties. Over medium heat in nonstick skillet, cook patties until brown on each side, 8 to 10 minutes. Serve on lettuce with tomato slice on top.

TUNA CHEESE TWIST

Jennifer Mitchell
Columbia, MO

2 (6 oz.) cans chunk tuna
1 (2½ oz.) can sliced black olives
½ c. celery, chopped
¼ c. onion, chopped
1 egg
½ c. cold water
1 can mushroom soup

2 c. Bisquick
1½ c. shredded Cheddar cheese
¼ c. milk
½ c. green pepper, chopped
1 Tbsp. water

Heat oven to 425°F. Mix tuna, olives, celery, green pepper, onion, and ¼ cup soup. In another bowl, Mix Bisquick with ½ cup water to make soft dough. Knead 5 minutes and roll into a 14x11 inch rectangle. Place dough in center of a cookie sheet. Spoon tuna mixture lengthwise in center of dough and sprinkle with cheese. Clip dough at 1 inch intervals and lap over from side to side. Brush with egg and 1 tablespoon water. Bake 15 to 20 minutes or until golden brown. Mix remaining soup, cheese, and milk over low heat for sauce.

TUNA PIE

Marilyn Scott
Van Buren, AR

1 (9 inch) pie crust
1 can tuna
1 c. Swiss cheese
½ c. onion, sliced

3 eggs
1 c. mayonnaise
½ c. milk

In a bowl, toss tuna, cheese, and onion; spoon into pie crust. In another bowl, beat eggs gently and mix mayonnaise and milk. Pour over tuna mix. Bake at 350°F. for 60 minutes.

TUNA PUFF

Maudie Burden
Centerview, MO

1¾ c. biscuit mix
¾ c. mayonnaise
1 egg
¼ c. onion

3 Tbsp. lemon juice
1 (6½ oz.) can tuna
2 c. cheese, shredded
¼ c. celery

Mix biscuit mix, mayonnaise, and egg; fold in onion, lemon juice, tuna, cheese, and celery. Place in 8x11 inch pan. Bake at 350°F. until fluffy or a golden brown. Cut into 9 servings.

TURKEY AND TORTILLA CASSEROLE

Ann Kane
Wichita, KS

2½ c. leftover turkey, cut up
½ to 1 large onion
1 stick margarine
1 can evaporated milk

1 can cream of chicken soup
½ lb. mild Cheddar cheese
6 tortillas

Preheat oven to 350°. In large skillet, cook onion slowly in 4 tablespoons of margarine. Add milk, soup, and cheese; cook slowly until cheese melts. Cut 6 tortillas in quarters. Melt the other 4 tablespoons of margarine; dip the tortillas in melted margarine and line the bottom of a 9x13 inch pan with them. Add the turkey and pour sauce over it. Bake 45 minutes at 350°F.

TUSCAN STUFFED CHICKEN

Jennifer Bender
Sarasota, FL

1 c. fresh sage, chopped
4 oz. roasted red peppers, chopped
1½ c. Feta cheese
Black pepper
Kosher salt
4 chicken breasts (skinless and boneless)

2 c. all-purpose flour
2 eggs
5 c. water
2 c. seasoned bread crumbs
3 Tbsp. olive oil

Combine chopped sage, red peppers, Feta cheese, salt, and pepper until incorporated. Cut a lengthwise pocket into each chicken breast. Be careful not to cut all the way through. Fill each pocket in the chicken with the Feta mixture. Use a spoon or pastry bag to fill; it may require a toothpick to hold the opening closed after filling. In three separate bowls, arrange as follows: Flour, eggs and water (whisked together), seasoned bread crumbs. Dip each piece of chicken in each bowl. First with the flour and shaking off any excess, then through the egg mixture and dripping off excess and finally, through the bread crumbs. Make sure all sides of the breast are coated in bread crumbs, even the pocket opening. Heat olive oil in large skillet over medium heat. Once the oil is hot, sear the first side of each breast one or two at a time. Don't overcrowd the pan. Cook on first side for 1 to 2 minutes. Do not touch or flip until after 2 minutes. After 2 minutes, flip onto other side. Let cook untouched for another 2 to 3 minutes. Once both sides of all chicken breast have golden brown crusts, arrange them on baking sheet without sides touching. Bake in 350°F. oven for 10 to 15 minutes or until juices run clear.

Serve the stuffed chicken breasts with Tuscan style vegetables and you will have a wonderful meal.

VEGETABLE STEW

Flo M. Burtnett
Gate, OK

Roast beef, cut up
2 c. water
2 to 3 carrots, chopped
2 (large) potatoes,
   chopped

1 onion, cut into rings
Salt and pepper to taste
1 (16 oz.) can tomatoes

Cook roast in water, along with carrots, potatoes, and onion until vegetables are done. Add the tomatoes; cook to boiling point.

The amount of vegetables you use depends on the amount of roast you have.

VERENIKA CASSEROLE

Arlene Bontrager
Hutchinson, KS

4 c. cooked noodles
1 (24 oz.) container
  cottage cheese
2 eggs
½ tsp. salt
¼ tsp. pepper
3 to 4 c. cooked ham,
  diced

¼ c. margarine
¼ c. flour
½ tsp. salt
2 c. milk
1½ c. sour cream

Mix cottage cheese, eggs, salt, and pepper together in bowl; set aside. In skillet melt margarine; add flour and salt, stirring, then add milk; stir until thick and bubbly. Remove from heat; add sour cream. In 9x13 inch baking pan, layer ½ of noodles, then ½ cottage cheese mixture, then ½ of ham, then ½ of gravy. Repeat layers, ending with gravy. Bake at 350°F., covered with foil, for 45 minutes or until done.

WESTERN PIZZA RICE CASSEROLE

Ruthe Zimmerman
Tunas, MO

2 lb. ground beef
1 onion, chopped
1 (26½ oz.) jar spaghetti
  sauce
1 tsp. salt
1½ tsp. smoke flavor
1½ c. cottage cheese

5 c. cooked brown rice
1 (3½ oz.) pkg. pepperoni,
  divided
½ c. Parmesan cheese,
  divided
4 c. cheese, shredded and
  divided

Brown meat and onion. Drain off any remaining liquid. Mix in the spaghetti sauce (pizza sauce may be used); add the salt and smoke flavor. Simmer for 15 minutes. In a big bowl, mix the cottage cheese into the rice. Add the meat and sauce mixture; stir well. Into 2 buttered 1½ to 2 quart casserole dishes, divide half of the meat and rice mixture. Divide half of the pepperoni between the 2 bowls. Sprinkle with ¼ cup Parmesan cheese, divided between the 2 casserole dishes. Take a cup of shredded cheese and sprinkle over each dish. Add the remaining rice mixture carefully, dividing between the 2 dishes. Top this second layer of rice mixture by repeating. Pop the 1 dish into the oven; bake at 325°F. for 30 minutes. Store the other dish in the refrigerator or freezer until a later date.

We like this casserole fresh from the oven. But we like it even better once the leftovers are warmed up.

WINTER WONDERLAND SALAD
Joan Stegman
Offerle, KS

1 (12 oz.) bottle
  vinaigrette dressing
1 red pear, cored and
  diced
1 (7 oz.) bag European-
  style salad mix
1 lb. oven roasted turkey
  breast, cut into strips

1 (6 oz.) bag honey
  roasted sliced almonds
1 c. dried cranberries
⅓ c. Gorgonzola or Blue
  cheese, crumbled
  (optional)
1 small julienne-cut
  orange squash

In small bowl, combine vinaigrette dressing and pears; set aside. Divide salad mix among 4 plates. Top each plate with turkey, almonds, cranberries, and cheese. Evenly divide pears among the salads. Drizzle each salad with the pear vinaigrette dressing. Garnish with julienne squash. Makes 4 salads.

WONDERFUL CHICKEN POT PIE
Donna L. Thorp
Kismet, KS

1 (10 oz.) pkg. frozen peas
  and carrots
1 can mixed vegetables
¼ c. butter
⅓ c. flour
½ tsp. salt
⅛ tsp. pepper

2 c. water
¾ c. milk
1 Tbsp. chicken bouillon
3 c. cooked chicken
¼ c. parsley, snipped
Pastry for double crust

Cook peas and carrots; drain. Melt butter; stir in flour, salt, and pepper. Add water, milk, and chicken bouillon. Cook and stir until thickened and bubbly. Cook and stir 1 to 2 minutes more. Stir in vegetables, chicken, and parsley. Heat until bubbly. Pour into pie crust. Cut slits in top crust. Bake at 450°F. for 15 minutes or until crust is golden brown.

Make a fancy top crust by using festive cookie cutters. This pot pie is also great with that leftover holiday turkey. Double the recipe and have 1 to freeze.

133

WORKPERSON'S ROAST

Betty Mead
Paradise, KS

1 roast (can be beef or
  pork)
1 pkg. onion soup mix
2 Tbsp. Worcestershire
  sauce

1 can cream of mushroom
  soup
1 section fresh garlic

Place the roast in center of large sheet of aluminum foil wrap; cut slits
in roast and push in cut sections of garlic. Pour mushroom soup over
roast; pour the Worcestershire sauce over soup. Sprinkle dry soup over
that. Add seasoning salt and pepper to taste. Pull foil up and seal,
leaving space above and around roast. Place in pan and bake at 300°F.
for 8 to 10 hours (depending on size of roast). Put on in the morning
and it will be ready for supper when you get home from work.

Roast will be tender and juicy and your gravy is made, too.

YUMMY TURKEY CASSEROLE

Sheri Holthus
McPherson, KS

1 lb. ground turkey
1 (15 oz.) can tomato
  sauce
1 tsp. granulated sugar
1 (8 oz.) container sour
  cream

1 (8 oz.) pkg. cream
  cheese
1 (12 oz.) pkg. uncooked
  egg noodles
2 c. Cheddar cheese,
  shredded

Preheat oven to 350°F. Over medium-high heat, saute the ground turkey
in a large skillet for about 10 minutes or until browned. Drain turkey
juices; add tomato sauce and sugar to browned turkey. Combine sour
cream and cream cheese, mixing well. Set aside. Cook noodles according to package directions. Place cooked noodles in a salad oil-
sprayed 9x13 inch baking dish. Layer turkey mixture alternately with
sour cream mixture over noodles. Top with cheese. Bake at 350°F. for
30 to 35 minutes until cheese is melted and bubbly.

*This recipe can be frozen ahead of time and brought out 4 hours before
baking. Serve with corn bread and a green salad.*

Side Dishes

Side Dishes
Recipe Contest Winners

First
Strawberry Chicken Salad
Treva Gangwish, Wood River, Nebraska
Page 168

Second
Ritz Cracker Salad
Eleanor Odle, Prairie View, Kansas
Page 164

Third
Greek Tomato Olive Salad
Norma Weber, Grainfield, Kansas
Page 156

SIDE DISHES

ANTIPASTA SALAD

Amy Edwards
Tulsa, OK

1 lb. seashell or rotini
  pasta
8 oz. Cheddar cheese
1 pkg. pepperoni slices
1 bell pepper
2 stalks celery
1 can black olives
1 (small) jar green olives
3 Roma tomatoes

1 (small) onion
1 tsp. dry oregano
1 Tbsp. salt
1 tsp. fresh ground black
  pepper
⅛ tsp. crushed red pepper
¾ c. oil
½ c. vinegar

Combine oregano, salt, pepper, red pepper, oil, and vinegar in a shaker and mix well to make the dressing. Cook pasta and drain. Chop all other ingredients and mix together with the dressing and pasta. Keep the salad in the refrigerator overnight for best flavor.

This recipe makes enough for at least 10 people and has become a family favorite at our picnics and cookouts.

APRICOT SALAD

Kimberly Chambers
Norcatur, KS

1 (3 oz.) box apricot jello
1 (small) can crushed
  pineapple with juice
½ c. sugar

8 oz. cream cheese
1 (large) jar apricot baby
  food
8 oz. whipped topping

Mix and boil 2 minutes. While cooling some, combine one 8 ounce package cream cheese (softened), 1 large jar apricot baby food, and 8 ounce container whipped toping. Fold mixture into cooled mixture and refrigerate till set.

APRICOT SALAD

Jenny Pachta
Belleville, KS

1 pkg. apricot gelatin
1 c. hot apricot nectar
1 c. small marshmallows
1 c. canned apricots, diced
1 c. apricot juice/nectar (off apricots)
1 egg, slightly beaten

2 tsp. flour
¼ c. sugar
½ c. apricot nectar
2 Tbsp. butter or margarine
½ c. sour cream
1 c. Cheddar cheese
⅛ tsp. salt (optional)

Dissolve gelatin in 1 cup hot apricot nectar. Add 1 cup apricot juice/ nectar. Chill until partially set, then add diced apricots and marshmallows. Chill in refrigerator while making topping. For topping, cook egg, slightly beaten; add flour, sugar, and apricot nectar until thickened. Remove from heat and add butter. Let cool. Fold sour cream into this mixture. Fold cooled mixture into gelatin mixture. Top with grated cheese and chill 1 to 2 hours or until set firmly.

Enjoy. This recipe has been passed down from my grandmother to my mother and now to me. I remember at family gatherings, this was always my Dad's favorite salad.

ASPARAGUS CASSEROLE

Maudie Burden
Centerview, MO

2 Tbsp. butter
2 tsp. flour
1 c. milk
2 c. asparagus, cooked partially and drained
¼ tsp. salt
Pepper to taste

2 hard cooked eggs, diced
1 pimento, cut fine
1½ Tbsp. onion, grated
½ c. cheese, grated
Cereal crumbs or cracker crumbs, crushed and buttered

Make a white sauce with melted butter and stir in flour and cook over moderated heat, stirring while the mixture bubbles and cooks. Gradually stir in milk and continue cooking until mixture thickens. Combine with remaining ingredients, with exception of crumbs. Spoon into casserole and top with buttered crumbs. Bake at 350°F. for about 30 minutes.

AUNT BERTIE'S CAULIFLOWER SALAD

Amy Edwards
Tulsa, OK

1 head cauliflower
1 bunch green onions
1 (small) can black olives, sliced

1 c. mayonnaise

Wash cauliflower and cut into bite-size pieces. Chop green onions very thin. Combine all ingredients and refrigerate overnight.

My great aunt shared this treasured recipe with me at our family reunion recently. It is quite simple and always a favorite with the family. She did say that you must use Hellmann's mayonnaise or it just won't turn out.

AVOCADO GELATIN SALAD

Gwenda Batterman
Amarillo, TX

4 or 5 avocados, depending on size
1 (3 oz.) box lime gelatin
1 (20 oz.) can pineapple (crushed or tidbits), drained

1 (8 oz.) pkg. cream cheese (room temperature)
1 (8 oz.) container whipped topping

Peel, core, and coarsely mash avocados. Set aside. Mix gelatin in drained pineapple until dissolved. Stir in cream cheese, avocado, and whipped topping. Cover and refrigerate.

AVOCADO SALAD

Clara Hinman
Flagler, CO

1 (3 oz.) pkg. lime gelatin
2 c. hot water
1 (medium) avocado
1 (3 oz.) pkg. cream cheese (may use low fat)

½ c. low fat mayonnaise
¼ c. celery, cut fine
½ c. green pepper, chopped fine
A few drops onion juice
⅛ tsp. salt

Mix gelatin with boiling water; let stand until it is partially set. Smash together the avocado and cream cheese. Add mayonnaise, celery, green pepper, onion juice, and salt to the partially set gelatin and pour into a shallow pan. When completely set (several hours), cut into squares and serve on salad plates. Makes 8 servings.

I serve this salad for a special dinner.

BAKED BEANS

Angela L. Brown
Monett, MO

2 (15 oz.) cans pork and
  beans
¼ c. ketchup
¼ c. mustard
¼ c. barbecue sauce
½ c. brown sugar

1 (medium) green bell
  pepper
1 (medium) onion
3 slices bacon
1 dash Worcestershire
  sauce

Chop veggies and bacon. Combine all ingredients. Bake in 375°F. oven for 40 to 45 minutes.

BAKED BEANS

Diane Meisinger
Hillsboro, KS

6 strips bacon, fried crisp,
  diced
3 cans pork and beans
¼ c. celery, chopped
½ c. onion, diced

½ c. bell pepper, diced
⅓ c. ketchup
3 Tbsp. molasses
2 Tbsp. brown sugar
1 tsp. hot sauce

Drain liquid off the beans. Add all ingredients to a crock pot and cook on medium heat for 4 to 5 hours. Can also be baked at 375°F. for 45 minutes.

BAKED KRAUT

Beverly Long
Lowry City, MO

1 can kraut
1 (small) can tomatoes
1 (medium) onion,
  chopped

1 c. brown sugar
3 slices bacon (raw), diced

Place kraut, tomatoes, onion, and brown sugar in baking dish. Put bacon on top. Bake at 350°F. for 1½ hours.

BAKED POTATO CASSEROLE

Lori Zimmerman
Ulysses, KS

5 (medium) potatoes,
cleaned with skins on
2 Tbsp. butter or
margarine
½ c. onion, chopped

1 (8 oz.) pkg. Cheddar
cheese, shredded
⅓ c. real bacon pieces
Sour cream (optional)

Prick potatoes and wrap in foil. Bake at 375°F. for 1 hour. Lightly coat a casserole dish with cooking spray. When potatoes are done, unwrap and cut into cubes. Drizzle potatoes with butter or margarine. Evenly top with cheese, onion, and bacon. Return to oven until cheese is melted, 15 to 20 minutes. Serve with sour cream if desired.

I have made this for get-togethers and it disappears quickly.

BANANA SPLIT SALAD

Julie Haverland
Deepwater, MO

1 can sweetened
condensed milk
1 (12 oz.) container
whipped topping
1 (20 oz.) can crushed
pineapple, drained

6 bananas, sliced to ¼
inch slices
½ c. nuts, chopped
2 c. mini marshmallows

Remove label from unopened can of condensed milk and boil 3 hours. Keep covered with water. Cool to room temperature before opening the can of milk. This will create a caramel sauce; sauce may be thick. Mix milk and whipped topping together; add pineapple, bananas, nuts, and marshmallows. Chill at least 1 hour. Make smaller or larger by using different size of whipped topping.

This will make a very large salad.

BASIL TOMATO SALAD

Margaret Trojan
Beaver Crossing, NE

2 Tbsp. olive oil
2 Tbsp. cider vinegar
2 Tbsp. fresh basil leaves,
   chopped*
½ tsp. salt
¼ tsp. black pepper
3 c. cooked rice

2 (medium) tomatoes,
   chopped
1 (medium) cucumber,
   peeled, seeded, and
   chopped
1 (small) red onion,
   chopped

Whisk together oil, vinegar, basil, salt, and pepper in large bowl. Add rice, tomatoes, cucumber, and onion. Toss and serve chilled.

* Dried basil leaves can be used.

BEAN/BANANA SALAD

Kathy Hogue
Topeka, KS

1 (15 oz.) can pork and
   beans
2 heaping teaspoons
   sweet pickle relish

1 heaping Tbsp.
   mayonnaise
1 (large) banana (firm),
   sliced

Mix relish and mayonnaise together. Drain beans and add to mixture. Just before serving, add banana.

This recipe will surprise you.

BEST SAUERKRAUT EVER

Teresa Uhlenhake
Ossian, IA

1 can sauerkraut
½ lb. bacon

½ to 1 c. sugar

Drain and wash the sauerkraut. Chop up the bacon and mix it into the sauerkraut. Add the sugar to your preference, and pour in a loaf pan. Bake 1 hour at 350°F.

BLUEBERRY SALAD WITH TOPPING

Lucile Fuller
Wichita, KS

1 (3 oz.) pkg. raspberry
  gelatin
1 (3 oz.) pkg. cherry
  gelatin
1 c. boiling water
1 (16½ oz.) can
  blueberries in light
  syrup

1 (20 oz.) can crushed
  pineapple in natural
  syrup
1 (8 oz.) pkg. cream
  cheese
½ c. sugar
1 tsp. vanilla

In large mixer bowl, dissolve gelatin in boiling water. Add blueberries and pineapple with juice. Pour into 11x17 inch glass pan (or two smaller dishes) and chill until firm. Top with the cream cheese beaten together with sugar and vanilla. Keeps several days.

BO'S OYSTER DRESSING

Tracy Vonderschmidt
Leona, KS

6 c. bread crumbs
6 Tbsp. butter
½ c. celery, chopped
½ c. onion, chopped
½ tsp. salt

1¼ tsp. poultry seasoning
⅛ tsp. black pepper
1 (8 oz.) can oysters,
  drained

Melt butter in a large skillet; when hot, stir in the bread crumbs. Cook until all the crumbs are coated in butter and slightly browned. Add celery, onion, salt, poultry seasoning, pepper, and oysters. Stir until mixed. Put in an 8 inch square baking dish and bake for 20 to 30 minutes at 350°F.

BQ GREEN BEAN CASSEROLE

Phyllis Carlson
Clarinda, IA

4 (15 oz.) cans green
  beans, drained
1 lb. bacon

½ c. onion, chopped
¾ c. brown sugar
1 c. ketchup

Fry bacon in pan. Remove bacon; drain and cut up in small pieces. In bacon grease, brown onion; drain and remove. Mix together brown sugar, ketchup, onion, and bacon. In 9x13 inch pan, place green beans. Add the ketchup mixture over the top. Bake at 250° to 300°F. Can make the night before or bake ahead and rewarm in microwave.

I have given this recipe to almost everyone who has eaten at my house. My husband doesn't care for green beans but this is his favorite.

BROCCOLI AND CAULIFLOWER PASTA SALAD

Tracy Vonderschmidt
Leona, KS

1 lb. bacon
1¼ c. salad dressing
2 Tbsp. sugar
½ tsp. garlic salt
1 (16 oz.) pkg. tri-color vegetable pasta
½ head fresh cauliflower, broken into bite-size pieces

½ head fresh broccoli, broken into bite-size pieces
1 red pepper, chopped
2 to 3 carrots, shredded
1 onion, chopped

Cook pasta until done and drain under cold water. Cook bacon until crisp. Reserve 2 tablespoons of the drippings and crumble the bacon for later. Mix the dressing, sugar, garlic salt, and 2 tablespoons of drippings in a large bowl. Add the remaining vegetables. Stir well until everything is well coated. Add the bacon crumbles last on top of the salad.

Use your judgment to determine how much of the broccoli and cauliflower you need in this salad. This is a very large salad that makes good use of what is fresh in the garden. It can be a meal in itself.

BROCCOLI AND RED GRAPE SALAD

Amber Uhlenhake
Ossian, IA

1 c. mayonnaise
½ c. sugar
1 tsp. vinegar
3½ c. broccoli, chopped
2 c. seedless red grapes
1 c. celery, diced

½ c. bacon, cooked and chopped
½ c. raisins
½ c. onion
½ c. slivered almonds

Mix and chill the mayonnaise, sugar, and vinegar. Combine all the other ingredients in a large serving bowl. Toss with the dressing and serve.

I use golden raisins and adjust the amount according to preference.

BROCCOLI AND CAULIFLOWER SALAD

Shana Lambert
Palco, KS

2 stalks broccoli
1 head cauliflower
1 (small to medium)
  onion, diced
1 c. salad dressing

¼ c. sugar
¼ c. milk
Salt to taste
Pepper to taste

Cut up broccoli and cauliflower into small pieces. Add diced onion. Mix up sugar, salad dressing, and milk. Pour over vegetables. Salt and pepper to taste. Best made the day before serving.

Good salad for potlucks or beside a sandwich on a hot summer day.

BROCCOLI AND CHEESE CASSEROLE

Shelley Fangman
Hereford, TX

2 (10 oz.) boxes broccoli
  (frozen), chopped
1 onion, chopped
1 c. celery, chopped
1 stick margarine
2 (10¾ oz.) cans cream of
  mushroom soup

1 c. milk
1 (15 oz.) jar processed
  cheese spread
2 c. rice

Melt butter. Add onion and celery; brown. Add broccoli and cook a few minutes. Add cream of mushroom soup, milk, processed cheese, and rice. Mix. Put in bowl and bake in oven at 350°F. for 30 to 45 minutes or until bubbly.

BROCCOLI IN CHEESE

Stacy Menges
Watsontown, PA

2 (10 oz.) boxes chopped
   broccoli
1 (1 lb.) box processed
   American cheese
2 Tbsp. butter

⅓ c. milk
¼ tsp. salt
1 pkg. butter crackers,
   crushed

Cook broccoli as directed on package. Drain. Melt cheese, butter, milk, and salt in top of double boiler till smooth (can also melt in microwave). Layer broccoli, cheese, and crackers in buttered 2 quart casserole, using two layers of each. Cover and bake at 350°F. for ½ hour.

This dish is often requested at family gatherings. It is usually the first dish empty.

BROCCOLI SALAD

Julie Haverland
Deepwater, MO

4 c. fresh broccoli, cut
   into bite-size pieces
½ c. raisins
2 Tbsp. red onion,
   chopped
⅓ c. sunflower seeds

5 slices bacon, cooked
   and crumbled
3 Tbsp. white sugar
2 Tbsp. white vinegar
1 c. mayonnaise

Place bacon in a large deep skillet. Cook over medium high heat until evenly brown. Crumble and set aside. In a salad bowl, toss together broccoli, raisins, sunflower seeds, crumbled bacon, and red onions. In a separate bowl, whisk together white sugar, vinegar, and mayonnaise. Pour over broccoli mixture and toss to coat.

CALIFORNIA RICE CASSEROLE

Marilyn Barner
Belle Plaine, KS

¼ c. margarine
1 c. onions, chopped
4 c. freshly cooked rice
2 c. sour cream
1 c. small curd cottage
   cheese

2 (4 oz.) cans green
   chilies, chopped
2 c. Cheddar cheese,
   grated
Salt and pepper to taste

Saute onions in margarine until golden. Remove from heat and stir in hot cooked rice. Add sour cream, cottage cheese, salt, and pepper and toss lightly. In a greased 2 quart baking dish, layer with rice mixture, green chilies, cheese, then repeat. Bake at 375°F., uncovered, until hot and bubbly.

This recipe can be frozen and baked later. It is one of our family favorites that I use for almost every family gathering.

CELERY CASSEROLE

*Thelma Maxwell
Dodge City, KS*

6 c. celery, diced
1 can water chestnuts, diced
1 (small) jar pimento
2 (10 oz.) cans cream of chicken soup
1 pkg. Chicken in a Biskit crackers, crushed
½ c. butter
½ c. slivered almonds

Cook celery; bring to a boil and cook approximately six minutes. Place in casserole alternately with water chestnuts and pimentos. Pour soup over top. Melt butter, crush crackers, and mix with butter and almonds. Place on top and bake 25 minutes at 350°F. Serves 12 or more.

CHEESE AND MARSHMALLOW SALAD

*Kim Oborny
Durham, KS*

1 or 2 (approx. 15 oz.) cans pineapple tidbits, well drained, reserving juice
2 Tbsp. flour
4 Tbsp. sugar
⅛ tsp. salt
1 egg, beaten
Juice from pineapple
1 Tbsp. butter
2 c. marshmallows (miniature)
¼ lb. processed American cheese

Drain pineapple juice and place in a medium saucepan. In a small bowl, combine flour, sugar, and salt. Add to beaten egg. When well blended, stir into heated pineapple juice. Add butter; stir until thickened. Cut cheese into ¼ inch cubes. Put cheese, pineapple, and marshmallows in serving bowl and while pineapple juice mixture is hot, pour over, mix, and chill at least 3 hours before serving. Overnight is better.

CHEESE CAKE SALAD

Rita Schiefelbein
Clear Lake, SD

1 (small) box instant vanilla pudding
½ c. milk
1 (8 oz.) pkg. cream cheese, softened
1 (8 oz.) pkg. sour cream
1 (8 oz.) container whipped topping
1 can cherry or blueberry pie mix

Mix together pudding and milk. In separate bowl mix together cream cheese, sour cream, and whipped topping. Add this to the pudding and beat together until smooth. Put in a pretty clear glass bowl or serving dish and top with pie mix. Refrigerate several hours before serving.

CHICKEN PASTA SALAD

Kathy Hogue
Topeka, KS

1 (8 oz.) pkg. rotini, uncooked
1 (11 oz.) can white shoe peg corn
1 (medium) red bell pepper, chopped
1 c. celery, peeled and chopped
½ c. (plus ¼ c.) Italian salad dressing
1 c. mayonnaise
¼ tsp. pepper
½ c. mild Cheddar (small chunks)
½ c. Monterey Jack (small chunks)
2 cans breast of chicken

Prepare rotini following package directions and drain in colander. Place in large bowl and toss with ½ cup dressing. Combine corn, pepper, and celery. Mix ¼ cup dressing with mayonnaise and pepper. Add to veggies and toss. Add this mixture to rotini and toss. Gently stir in cheese and chicken. Chill before serving.

CHICKEN SALAD

Roxie Berning
Marienthal, KS

1½ lb. boneless chicken breasts, cooked and chopped
1 (small) onion, chopped
1½ tsp. tarragon
½ to ¾ c. mayonnaise
20 green grapes, cut in halves
⅓ c. almonds, slivered
Salt and pepper to taste

Mix all together and serve on croissants.

CINNAMON APPLE SALAD

Lois Mills
Lake City, KS

1 c. water
⅔ c. Red Hots
1 box strawberry gelatin
1 can (1½ c.) applesauce

1 (3 oz.) pkg. cream
  cheese
2 Tbsp. milk
1 Tbsp. salad dressing

In a pan, put water and Red Hots. Boil this until Red Hots are dissolved. Add gelatin. Let cool, then put into a bowl and add applesauce. In another bowl, blend softened cream cheese, milk, and salad dressing. Stir cheese mixture into partially set gelatin and applesauce so that it will create a marble effect. Let set in refrigerator overnight. Serve completely hardened.

CINNAMON RED HOTS SALAD

Rita Schiefelbein
Clear Lake, SD

2 (3 oz.) pkg. raspberry
  gelatin
2 c. hot water

½ c. Red Hots candy
1 qt. applesauce

Dissolve gelatin in hot water in a large saucepan. Add the Red Hots and stir over low heat until melted. Remove from burner and cool slightly, then add the applesauce. Put into glass bowl and refrigerate overnight.

This is a pretty red salad to serve during the holidays and one most kids also like.

COPPER CARROT PENNIES

Thelma Baldock
Delphos, KS

2 lb. carrots, sliced
1 (small) green pepper,
  sliced in rings
1 (medium) onion, sliced
1 can tomato soup
½ c. olive oil

Salt and pepper to taste
1 c. sugar
¾ c. vinegar
1 tsp. prepared mustard
1 tsp. Worcestershire
  sauce

Boil carrots in salted water until fork-tender; cool. Alternate vegetables in salad bowl. Combine other ingredients; stir well. Pour over vegetables. Refrigerate.

Canned carrots may also be used.

CORN CASSEROLE

Janet Maltbie
Burlington, OK

1 (large) bag frozen corn
½ (8 oz.) pkg. cream cheese

¼ to ½ stick margarine
Salt to taste

Cook corn in microwave as directed on bag. Add cream cheese, margarine, and salt to taste. Microwave all ingredients until melted. Stir well.

This recipe is fast, easy, and delicious.

COUNTRY CREAM CORN

Carla Nemecek
Copeland, KS

½ pkg. bacon
1 (large) onion
1 (large) green bell pepper
2 pkg. frozen sweet corn
6 Tbsp. water

½ stick butter
1 (8 oz.) pkg. cream cheese
½ tsp. salt

Saute bacon with onion and green pepper until bacon is done and onion is soft. Mix saute, including bacon drippings, with all other ingredients in crockpot and cook on low for 4 to 5 hours, stirring often.

Because we love fresh sweet corn and we raise pigs, this recipe is a great combination of our 2 favorite things. It is especially good in the summer with fresh vegetables.

CRANBERRY SALAD WITH CREAM CHEESE

Lucile Fuller
Wichita, KS

1½ c. boiling water
2 (small) pkg. cherry
  gelatin
1 pkg. cranberries, ground
2 c. sugar
3 bananas
1 (large) can pineapple
  (crushed)

4 apples, ground
1 (8 oz.) pkg. cream
  cheese
Milk
½ c. pecan or walnut
  pieces

In large mixer bowl, dissolve cherry gelatin in boiling water. In food processor, grind cranberries, bananas, and apples with the sugar. Add crushed pineapple with juice, then add all to the gelatin. Pour into 9x13 inch pan or 2 smaller bowls. Refrigerate until firm. To prepare topping, in a small bowl, mix cream cheese with a little milk to thin. Spread on firm salad and sprinkle with nuts.

CREAMED CORN

Connie M. Terry
Ellsworth, KS

9 (No. 2) cans whole
  kernel corn
3 (8 oz.) pkg. cream
  cheese

2 tsp. sugar
Salt and pepper to taste

Drain corn and put in crockpot. Add sugar, salt, pepper, and cream cheese. Heat on low for 4 hours. May add chopped red or green pepper for color.

When our family has a get together, all of the nieces and nephews request this dish. It is one of their favorites.

CREAMY GARLIC DRESSING

Margaret Trojan
Beaver Crossing, NE

¼ c. lemon juice
¾ c. salad oil
⅔ c. light cream
2 cloves garlic

1 tsp. salt
½ tsp. sugar
½ tsp. paprika
¼ tsp. white pepper

Put all ingredients into blender. Cover and process and whip until blended. Makes 2 cups.

Excellent on crispy tossed lettuce salad.

CREAMY SLICED CUCUMBERS
Arlene Bontrager
Hutchinson, KS

4 to 5 (medium)
cucumbers, peeled and
sliced
1 onion, sliced

1 tsp. dill weed
Salt to taste
Pepper to taste
1 c. sour cream

Prepare cucumbers and put in bowl. Add onions and dill. Add salt and pepper according to taste. Stir and let sit for about 15 to 20 minutes. They should get watery. Add sour cream and stir well. Refrigerate until ready to serve. These should be prepared within 2 to 3 hours of serving.

CROCKPOT CORN
Cynthia Lambert
Palco, KS

1 (20 oz.) pkg. frozen corn
1 (8 oz.) pkg. cream
cheese

2 Tbsp. sugar
6 Tbsp. water
½ stick margarine

Mix all ingredients together and cook in crockpot on low for four hours, stirring occasionally.

CROCKPOT CORN
Rita Schiefelbein
Clear Lake, SD

2 (16 oz.) bags frozen corn
1 (8 oz.) pkg. cream
cheese

1 stick butter
2 Tbsp. sugar
2 Tbsp. water

Place frozen corn in crockpot. Cut cream cheese and butter into small cubes and add to corn, along with sugar and water. Cook on high for 45 minutes. Turn down to low and cook for 3¼ hours more, stirring occasionally.

This is a family favorite because it is different than "just plain corn."

CROCKPOT SWEET POTATOES

Kathy Hogue
Topeka, KS

5 sweet potatoes, boiled
½ c. brown sugar
½ c. sugar
2 eggs
¾ c. butter, softened
¼ tsp. allspice
1 tsp. cinnamon

½ c. evaporated milk
1 c. miniature marshmallows
1 (8 oz.) can crushed pineapple, drained and pureed in blender
½ tsp. salt

Cut potatoes in 2 inch pieces; boil, cool, and peel. With electric mixer, cream potatoes with sugar, eggs, and butter. Add spices and evaporated milk. Mix in ½ cup marshmallows, pineapple, and salt. Stir until well blended. Pour into crockpot and cook on low one hour; put ½ cup marshmallows on top just before serving, or prepare night before and heat on high 2 hours. Stir and keep on low; add marshmallows on top.

CROCKPOT POTATO SOUP

Brittany Habiger
Spearville, KS

8 c. potatoes, chopped, peeled
1 (small) onion
½ lb. bacon, crisp cooked
1 (8 oz.) pkg. cream cheese, softened

3 (14 oz.) cans chicken broth
1 (10 oz.) can cream of chicken soup
¼ tsp. pepper

In a 4 quart electric crockery cooker, stir together the potatoes and onion. Stir in bacon. In large mixing bowl, combine the cream cheese, the chicken broth, the cream of chicken soup, and pepper. Add the mixture to the crockpot. Cover and cook the soup on low heat for 8 to 10 hours. If you like, mash the potatoes slightly for a thicker consistency before serving. Yield: 8 servings.

This is a hearty, thick soup and is great for a side dish for any meat.

DELICIOUS MIXED LETTUCE SALAD

Kim Robinson
Dexter, NM

1 (large) bag assorted lettuce greens
2 (small) cans mandarin oranges
½ c. walnut halves or pieces
½ (small) purple onion, sliced thinly
4 slices cooked bacon, crumbled

6 Tbsp. seasoned rice vinegar
½ c. oil
1 tsp. soy sauce
1½ tsp. dark sesame oil
⅓ c. sugar
1 tsp. salt
1 tsp. pepper
1 tsp. parsley flakes

Mix together in a dressing container the seasoned rice vinegar, oil, soy sauce, dark sesame seed oil, sugar, salt, pepper, and parsley flakes. Heat in microwave 60 seconds on high. Stir until sugar is dissolved and refrigerate. In a large bowl, add assorted lettuce greens, mandarin oranges, walnuts, and cooked bacon. Ten minutes before serving, marinate sliced onions in a little bit of the prepared dressing. Pour dressing and marinated onions on salad; toss and serve.

Optional: Sliced mushrooms or diced avocado.

EASY BAKED BEANS

Madeline Fangman
Hereford, TX

4 slices bacon
½ c. onion, chopped
2 (16 oz.) cans pork and beans in tomato sauce
2 Tbsp. brown sugar

2 Tbsp. ketchup
1 Tbsp. Worcestershire sauce
1 Tbsp. prepared mustard

Cook bacon till crisp. Remove bacon, reserving about 3 tablespoons drippings in skillet. Drain and crumble bacon; set aside. Cook onion in reserved drippings till tender. Stir in pork and beans, brown sugar, ketchup, Worcestershire sauce, and mustard. Turn into a 1½ quart casserole dish. Bake, uncovered, in a 350°F. oven for 1½ to 1¾ hours. Stir; top with bacon. Let stand a few minutes before serving. Makes 6 servings.

EASY CREAM CHEESE CORN

Tammy Bell
Osawatomie, KS

1 lb. bag frozen corn
½ stick margarine
1 (4 oz.) pkg. cream
  cheese, softened

Salt and pepper to taste

Melt margarine in pan. Add frozen corn. Stir. Add cream cheese and stir over heat until hot and cream cheese is melted.

This recipe is ideal for a family of four. I double the recipe to take to gatherings.

EGGPLANT DISH

Eileen Locke
Paola, KS

¼ c. olive oil
1 (large) onion, sliced
1 or 2 eggplants, no need
  to peel
1 or 2 bell peppers, cut
  into strips
1 or 2 zucchini, sliced
Fresh or dried basil (be
  generous)

1 or 2 cloves garlic
1 or 2 bay leaves
Celery (optional)
1 or 2 c. okra
Fresh tomatoes, sliced
Parmesan or Romano
  cheese

In bottom of large pot place olive oil; add onion, eggplant, pepper, zucchini (basil between layers), garlic, bay leaves, celery, and okra; top with tomatoes. No need to stir. Cover; simmer slowly for 1 or 2 hours or until vegetables are tender.

Measurements aren't exact as this recipe uses garden produce as available.

EXTRA CHEESY POTATO CASSEROLE

Donna L. Thorp
Kismet, KS

2 lb. frozen hash browns
½ c. butter
1 can cheese soup
1 soup can milk
1 pt. sour cream

2 Tbsp. instant onions
2 c. Cheddar cheese, grated
½ tsp. pepper
2 c. dried onion rings

Mix together ingredients, except the dried onion rings, and bake in a 9x13 inch pan. Bake at 350°F. for 45 minutes. The last 15 minutes, add the dried onion rings.

This recipe is similar to other potato casseroles, with the exception of the soup.

FLUFFY FRUIT SALAD

Maudie Burden
Centerview, MO

1 (3 oz.) box instant vanilla pudding
1 (8 oz.) container whipped topping

1 can pineapple, crushed and drained
1 c. miniature marshmallows

Mix whipped topping and dry pudding together. Add pineapple and marshmallows. Chill.

Can also add mandarin oranges, coconut, cherries, and nuts.

FRESH SPINACH STRAWBERRY SALAD

Roxie Berning
Marienthal, KS

2 bunches spinach
1 pt. fresh strawberries, sliced
½ c. honey roasted pecans
½ c. purple onion, chopped
½ c. oil

¼ c. red wine vinegar
½ c. sugar
1 Tbsp. poppy seed
½ tsp. dry mustard
1 tsp. sesame seed
1 tsp. Worcestershire sauce

Combine spinach, strawberries, pecans, and onion. To prepare dressing, mix together oil, vinegar, sugar, poppy seed, mustard, sesame seed, and Worcestershire sauce. Pour over salad.

FROZEN APRICOT SALAD

Lucile Fuller
Wichita, KS

1 (6 oz.) can frozen
  orange juice, thawed
1 juice can water
1 c. sugar
1 Tbsp. lemon juice
1 (small) can pineapple,
  crushed

1 (17 oz.) can apricots,
  drained and chopped
3 bananas, sliced
1 jar maraschino cherries

Mix all ingredients in large bowl, including pineapple juice. Fill foil muffin cups in large muffin pans. Top each with ½ maraschino cherry. Place pans in freezer and freeze. May be taken out of the pans and placed in a large plastic bag. Use as needed. Will make at least 18, maybe more, depending on size of muffin pans.

GELATIN JEWEL

Juanita Gross
Clearwater, KS

1 (3 oz.) pkg. orange
  gelatin

1 c. boiling water
1 c. plain yogurt

Dissolve gelatin with water; add yogurt. Mix together. Chill until set.

Any flavor of gelatin can be used. Quick, simple, and delicious.

GRANDMA SINGER'S CRANBERRY SALAD

Donna J. Walker
Kismet, KS

1 pkg. fresh cranberries
1 container whipped
  topping
1 pkg. small
  marshmallows

1 c. sugar
1 c. nuts

Grind cranberries; add 1 cup sugar. Let set 30 minutes. Mix whipped topping and add to cranberries, then nuts and marshmallows. Best if chilled overnight.

GRAPE SALAD

Margaret Trojan
Beaver Crossing, NE

2 to 4 lb. seedless grapes (either red, green, or both)
1 c. sour cream

½ c. brown sugar
½ c. whipped topping
Slivered almonds

Mix sour cream and brown sugar; fold in whipped topping and almonds. Fold in grapes.

Red and green grapes mixed together look nice for Christmas.

GREEK TOMATO OLIVE SALAD

Norma Weber
Grainfield, KS

1 (6 oz.) pkg. cherry or grape tomatoes
1 (6 to 7 oz.) jar green olives
1 can black olives
1 (small) red onion

½ c. olive oil
2 Tbsp. red wine vinegar
1 Tbsp. white sugar
1 tsp. oregano
Salt and pepper to taste

Cut tomatoes and olives in halves. Finely chop onion. Place all in large bowl. In a small bowl or glass jar, mix together olive oil, vinegar, sugar, and oregano. Pour over tomato-olive mixture. Salt and pepper to taste. Gently stir to coat. Chill to combine flavors.

GREEN BEAN DISH

Eileen Locke
Paola, KS

2 (16 oz.) cans green beans
1 (small) onion, chopped
¼ c. parsley, chopped
¼ c. butter
¼ c. flour

2 Tbsp. sugar (or sweetener)
1 c. sour cream
2 Tbsp. vinegar
3 to 4 strips bacon, fried, drained, and chopped

Drain beans and save the liquid. Saute onion and parsley in the butter. Add flour and blend. Add bean liquid, sugar, and vinegar. Stir together. Add sour cream and beans and cook, stirring, until hot. Place in hot serving dish and top with the bacon.

HOLIDAY WILD RICE SCALLOP

Lora Lackaff
Bassett, NE

1 c. wild rice
¼ c. diced onion
¼ c. diced green onion

½ c. diced celery
2 c. cream
Salt and pepper

Cook wild rice in 3 to 4 cups salted water (½ teaspoon salt) for 40 minutes, until tender and fully open. Drain rice. Add onion, green onion, celery, and cream. Add salt and pepper to taste. Lightly spray small casserole with oil (or butter lightly) and add rice mixture. Bake at 325°F. for 1 hour until golden.

Wild rice is difficult to find here and is expensive. The wild rice mixes are not a good substitute.

HOT PEPPER DISH

Sherri Straub
Hobart, OK

1 c. milk
1 can cream of mushroom
  soup
1 c. cheese, grated
3 hot peppers, cayenne or
  jalapeno (can adjust the
  number of peppers
  used)

1 bag corn chips (regular
  size)

Warm milk and soup, then mix in cheese, hot peppers, and corn chips. Bake in oven for 10 to 15 minutes at 350°F.

This recipe has been in my family for over 20 years. It's a good side dish for hamburgers and hot dogs.

JUANITA'S OLD SETTLERS BAKED BEANS

Patricia Gale
Flagler, CO

½ lb. ground beef
½ lb. bacon, chopped
1 whole onion, chopped
¼ c. brown sugar
¼ c. granulated sugar
¼ c. ketchup
¼ c. barbecue sauce
2 Tbsp. mustard
2 Tbsp. molasses

½ tsp. chili powder
1 tsp. salt
¼ tsp. pepper
1 (16 oz.) can red kidney beans
1 (32 oz.) can pork and beans
1 (16 oz.) can butter beans

Cook ground beef; drain and set aside. Cook bacon; drain and set aside. Brown onions. In large kettle, combine brown sugar, granulated sugar, ketchup, barbecue sauce, mustard, molasses, chili powder, salt, pepper, red beans (drained), pork and beans, and butter beans (drained). Bake at 350°F. for one hour or in slow cooker or crockpot on low 4 to 5 hours.

This recipe doubles nicely and is perfect for pot lucks and family dinners.

JUNE'S NOODLES

June Wescott
Brewster, NE

2 c. flour
1 tsp. salt
2 eggs

¼ c. cream
¼ tsp. yeast, dissolved in
¼ c. water

Combine flour and salt. Beat eggs with fork; add cream and dissolve yeast. Stir into flour, adding more flour until very stiff. Roll out on floured board, cut into ¼ inch strips, and drop into boiling broth.

MACARONI, CHEESE 'N PEA SALAD

Barbara Koelling
Paradise, KS

½ c. (6 oz.) c. macaroni
1 (10 oz.) pkg. frozen peas
2 c. Cheddar cheese,
  shredded
4 (½ c.) green onions,
  sliced

1 (½ c.) medium stalk
  celery, sliced
¾ c. mayonnaise or salad
  dressing
⅓ c. sweet pickle relish
½ tsp. salt

Cook macaroni. Rinse frozen peas under cold water to separate. Mix macaroni, peas, cheese, onions, celery, mayonnaise, relish, and salt. Cover and refrigerate.

MACARONI SALAD

Alene Fosler
Sublette, KS

2 c. macaroni
1 c. radish, sliced
½ c. green pepper,
  chopped
½ c. sweet pickles, diced
1 c. carrots, coarsely
  grated

1 c. celery, chopped
4 to 6 hard-boiled eggs,
  diced
⅓ c. sweet pickle juice
1 c. salad dressing
1 tsp. seasoning salt
½ c. dry mustard

Cook macaroni; wash and rinse in cold water and drain. Mix all other ingredients together.

MACARONI SALAD

Barbara Koelling
Paradise, KS

1 lb. macaroni, cooked,
  drained, and cooled
2 c. cucumber, chopped
1 c. onion, chopped
1½ c. vinegar
1½ c. sugar

1 tsp. salt
1 tsp. monosodium
  glutamate
1 tsp. garlic salt
Pimento and parsley

Mix together cucumber, onion, vinegar, sugar, salt, monosodium glutamate, and garlic salt. Stir in macaroni. Sprinkle with pimento and parsley flakes. Let stand several hours before serving.

MARINATED MUSHROOMS AND VEGETABLES

Pat Habiger
Spearville, KS

⅔ c. vinegar
⅔ c. olive or salad oil
¼ c. onion, chopped
2 cloves garlic, minced
1 tsp. sugar
1 tsp. dried basil, crushed
1 tsp. dried oregano, crushed
8 oz. fresh mushrooms, halved

1 (16 oz.) can whole carrots, drained
1 (14 oz.) can artichoke hearts, drained and halved
1 c. ripe olives, halved
1 c. celery, sliced
1 (2 oz.) jar pimiento, sliced, drained

In saucepan, combine the vinegar, oil, onion, garlic, sugar, basil, oregano, and salt and pepper to taste. Bring to boiling. Simmer, uncovered, 10 minutes. In bowl, combine remaining ingredients. Pour hot marinade over vegetables; stir to coat. Cover; chill several hours, stirring occasionally. Drain vegetables; serve in a lettuce-lined bowl.

Mix and match veggies if you like, but I really like this combination. It is easy because of the canned ingredients which you can keep on hand.

MEXICAN CAESAR SALAD

Donna Sawyer
McCook, NE

2 Anaheim chiles, roasted, peeled, and seeded
⅓ c. roasted pumpkin seeds
2 cloves garlic, peeled
¼ tsp. ground black pepper
1 tsp. salt
12 oz. canola oil
¼ c. red wine vinegar
5 Tbsp. Parmesan cheese, grated
2 Tbsp. stemmed cilantro, cut fine

1½ c. mayonnaise
¼ c. water
2 corn tortillas
¼ c. canola oil
1 (large) head romaine lettuce, rinsed and dried
1⅓ c. Parmesan cheese, finely grated
1 roasted red bell pepper, peeled and cut into julienne strips
½ c. pumpkin seeds

Place all dressing ingredients, except mayonnaise and water, in a blender and process about 15 seconds. Add to blended mayonnaise and water in a large mixing bowl with a whisk until smooth. To assemble salad, cut corn tortillas into matchstick size strips. Heat canola oil in a saute pan; add tortilla chips and fry until crisp. Remove and drain on paper towels. Set aside. Tear romaine lettuce into bite-sized pieces. Place on 4 to 6 salad plates and ladle approximately 2 ounces of dressing on each salad. Sprinkle with Parmesan cheese and tortilla strips. Arrange red pepper strips like spokes on top of each salad.

This makes a nice salad luncheon served with Club crackers. More salad dressing may be placed in a small pitcher and served optionally to your guests.

MY MISTAKE SALAD

Maudie Burden
Centerview, MO

1 box orange gelatin
1 small) container cottage cheese
1 can mandarin oranges
1 (8 oz.) container whipped topping

Pineapple, crushed
1 c. miniature marshmallows

Mix gelatin and cottage cheese until gelatin is dissolved. Add oranges, whipped topping, pineapple, and marshmallows; chill a few hours. May also add nuts.

ORANGE TAPIOCA GELATIN

Pauline Riley
Dodge City, KS

1 pkg. orange gelatin
1 pkg. tapioca pudding
2½ c. water

1 can mandarin oranges
1 (small) container whipped topping

Cook gelatin, tapioca pudding, and water until tapioca is clear. Cool. Fold in mandarin oranges and carton of whipped topping. Use the juice from oranges as part of liquid. Chill.

PATIO POTATOES

Jacob Fangman
Hereford, TX

6 (medium) potatoes
4 Tbsp. butter
¼ c. milk
Dash of salt (to taste)
⅛ tsp. pepper (to taste)

¼ c. onion, chopped (to taste)
1 c. Cheddar cheese, grated

Can peel or leave skin on potatoes, but cut like French fries. Place cut potatoes in greased casserole dish. Add milk, butter, salt, pepper, and onion. Bake at 350°F. until done, 45 to 60 minutes. Add Cheddar cheese or cheese of your choice on top. Let cheese melt and serve. Yield: 8 to 10 servings.

Can use ⅛ teaspoon of onion powder instead of onion.

POTATO LOGS

Lori Zimmerman
Ulysses, KS

5 (medium) potatoes, washed (skins on)
2 Tbsp. vegetable oil
1 tsp. dill weed

1 tsp. garlic salt
1 tsp. onion powder
1 tsp. Nature's Seasoning
Sour cream (optional)

Cut potatoes lengthwise into fourths. Place in large resealable bag. Combine dill weed, garlic salt, onion powder, and Nature's Seasoning in small bowl. Add vegetable oil to bag, then spices. Seal bag and shake well until potatoes are well coated. Place potatoes, skin sides down, on cookie sheet. Bake at 350°F. for 45 minutes or until potatoes begin to turn golden brown. Serve with sour cream if desired.

POTATO SALAD

Rochelle Fangman
Hereford, TX

8 (medium) potatoes
5 boiled eggs, diced
1½ c. pickles, chopped
¾ c. celery
1 c. salad dressing

1 Tbsp. mustard
1 tsp. salt
¼ tsp. pepper
1 to 2 tsp. paprika (optional)

Boil potatoes until tender; cool. Dice potatoes. Boil eggs; cool and dice hard-boiled eggs. Add eggs, pickles, and celery to potatoes. Mix together salad dressing, mustard, and salt and pepper; add to potato mixture and toss well. Chill 2 to 4 hours or overnight. Sprinkle top with paprika if desired and serve. Makes 10 to 12 servings.

POTATO SALAD

Ivy Maltbie
Amorita, OK

6 (medium) potatoes
6 hard-boiled eggs
½ c. onion, chopped
1 (10 oz.) jar sweet relish
3 Tbsp. dill pickle relish

1 to 2 Tbsp. mustard
½ tsp. salt
2 Tbsp. vinegar
1 to 2 c. salad dressing

Boil eggs in cold water and cook 20 minutes until hard boiled. Peel the egg shell off. Wash potatoes off and cook until they are done. Dice eggs, potatoes, and onion in small chunks, then add one small jar of sweet relish, salt, vinegar, mustard, and salad dressing. Mix it up and stir well. Chill overnight.

POTATO SOUP

Shana Lambert
Palco, KS

4 slices ham
3 c. potatoes, peeled and cubed
1 can chicken broth
1 (small) carrot, grated
½ c. onion, chopped

½ tsp. celery salt
½ tsp. pepper
2 c. milk
½ c. cream
½ c. Cheddar cheese, grated

In a large saucepan, put potatoes, broth, carrots, onion, parsley, celery, and salt and pepper. Cover and simmer until potatoes are tender, about 15 minutes. Add milk, cream, ham, and cheese to soup. Bring to a boil and stir for 2 minutes.

POTATOES O'BRIEN

Arlyss Alexander
Clay Center, KS

1 pkg. frozen hash browns with peppers and onions
1 can cheese soup

1 can mushroom soup
1 (8 oz.) container sour cream

Mix all together and bake 1½ hours at 350°F.

RICE DRESSING

Norma Weber
Grainfield, KS

2 c. long grain white rice
5 c. chicken broth
½ stick butter
6 to 8 oz. chicken gizzards
¾ c. onion, finely chopped

1 stalk celery, chopped
2 cloves garlic, chopped
½ tsp. black pepper
¼ tsp. cayenne pepper

Chop gizzards into small pieces. Brown gizzard pieces in a large frying pan with ¼ cup of the butter. Add the remaining butter, onion, celery, garlic, and pepper. Cook for 5 minutes. Put rice, broth, and gizzard mixture into a roaster pan or 9x13 inch pan sprayed with cooking spray. Cover tightly and bake at 350°F. for 50 to 60 minutes until liquid is absorbed and rice is tender. Stir before serving.

RITZ CRACKER SALAD

Eleanor Odle
Prairie View, KS

60 Ritz crackers, rolled
¼ c. butter, melted
1 c. sugar
1 (small) can frozen orange juice, partly thawed

1 can sweetened condensed milk
1 (small) can mandarin oranges, drained
1 (9 oz.) container whipped topping

Mix together crackers, butter, and sugar to make crust; press all but 1 cup into bottom of 9x13 inch pan. Mix juice with milk; add small can mandarin oranges. Fold in whipped topping; spread on top of crust. Top with 1 cup of leftover crumbs. Refrigerate.

ROASTED VEGGIES

Elsie MacArthur
Richmond, KS

Carrots, chopped
Zucchini, chopped
Onion, chopped
Celery, chopped

Potato, chopped
Olive oil
1 pkg. dry onion soup mix

Mix carrots, zucchini, onion, celery, and potato. Drizzle with olive oil. Sprinkle on dry onion soup mix. Bake at 350°F. until veggies are tender.

SANTA FE CORN

Teresa Zimmerman
Plevna, KS

½ green pepper, chopped
¼ c. green onion, sliced
⅛ tsp. garlic powder
⅛ tsp. cayenne pepper

2 tsp. margarine
1 (17 oz.) can sweet corn, drained

In a saucepan, cook green pepper, onions, garlic powder, and cayenne pepper in the margarine for 2 minutes. Add corn; cover and cook for 5 additional minutes.

SANTA FE SCALLOPED POTATOES

NanCee Maynard
Box Elder, SD

6 c. potatoes with skins, thinly sliced
¼ c. green pepper, chopped
¼ c. red onion, chopped
1½ c. ham, cut into ¼ inch cubes
2 Tbsp. flour

½ c. milk
1 (10 oz.) can condensed nacho cheese soup
1 (15 oz.) can Mexican style corn, drained
1½ c. shredded Cheddar cheese

Heat oven to 325°F. Grease a 4 quart casserole. Wash and thinly slice potatoes; put into large saucepan and cover with water. Add green pepper and onion. Bring to a boil and simmer for 6 minutes. Combine flour and milk; stir until smooth and add the nacho cheese soup mix. Stir well until smooth. Drain potato mixture; add the ham and corn. Pour into casserole and stir in the cheese mixture and cover. Bake 40 minutes. Remove from oven; top with shredded cheese and bake 5 to 8 minutes more until cheese melts.

This is a colorful dish and a change from traditional scalloped potatoes. Great on cold winter evenings with crescent rolls and a fruited jello salad.

SCALLOPED CORN (KANSAS STYLE)

Betty Mead
Paradise, KS

1½ c. whole kernel corn
¾ c. cream
2 Tbsp. flour
⅛ tsp. pepper
½ c. bread or cracker crumbs

2 Tbsp. butter
1 tsp. salt
2 eggs, beaten

Drain liquid from corn into measuring cup. To this, add thin cream to make 1 cup. Melt butter; add flour, salt, and pepper. Stir until smooth. Add liquid gradually; cook until thickened. Add corn mixed with beaten eggs. Pour into buttered baking dish (quart size). Sprinkle top with crumbs; place dish in shallow pan of water. Bake in 350°F. oven 45 to 50 minutes. Yields 5 to 6 servings.

SCALLOPED POTATOES

Clara Hinman
Flagler, CO

1½ pkg. frozen hash browns with onions and peppers
½ c. butter, melted
1 can cream of chicken soup

½ c. sour cream
2 c. cheese, grated
¼ c. butter
2 c. Corn Flakes cereal, crushed

Mix all ingredients, except ¼ cup butter and Corn Flakes together and place in a greased 9x13 inch pan. Top with melted butter and 2 cups crushed Corn Flakes. Bake, uncovered, for 45 minutes or 1 hour at 350°F.

May be mixed ahead of time and stored in refrigerator until ready to bake. It's great for pot luck dinners and church dinners.

SEVEN LAYERED LETTUCE SALAD

Ivy Maltbie
Amroita, OK

1 (small) head lettuce
¾ c. onion, diced
¾ c. green pepper, diced
1 (10 oz.) pkg. frozen peas

1 pt. salad dressing
1 (8 oz.) pkg. processed American cheese
1 (3.25 oz.) jar bacon bits

Chop lettuce into bite-size pieces and lay on bottom of a 9x13 inch glass dish, then layer with onion, green pepper, and frozen peas. Spread salad dressing all over it to seal it, then sprinkle with a layer of cheese and bacon bits. Refrigerate.

This salad will keep 3 to 4 days. When my family comes home, this is one of their favorite dishes.

SQUASH DRESSING

Annilee Kniffen
Lorena, TX

2 lb. yellow squash, cooked and mashed
1 pkg. cornbread mix, baked according to directions on pkg.
2 c. milk
1 can cream of chicken soup

1½ sticks butter
½ c. celery
½ c. onions
½ c. green peppers
1 tsp. salt
1 tsp. sage

Crumble cornbread in 2 cups milk. Use a bit more if it seems too dry. Add to squash. Saute celery, onions, and peppers in the butter. Add to squash and bread mixture with soup (undiluted), sage, and salt. Mix well and bake in greased pan at 350°F. about 1 hour or until lightly browned.

STRAWBERRY CHICKEN SALAD

Treva Gangwish
Wood River, NE

2 lb. boneless, skinless
  chicken breast, grilled
1 bunch romaine lettuce
1 bunch green leaf or
  iceberg lettuce
½ red onion
1 (15 oz.) can mandarin
  oranges

1 (6 oz.) can chow mein
  noodles
1 lb. fresh strawberries
1 bottle sweet and sour
  dressing

Cut chicken breasts in ¼ inch strips. Cut or tear lettuce. Slice onion into rings and cut in ½. Drain mandarin oranges and slice strawberries. If not serving within 1 or 2 hours, prepare all ingredients and keep in separate covered containers or plastic bags. When serving, layer all ingredients in a large bowl and toss with the dressing. Makes 10 servings.

This salad is a "big hit" at pot luck dinners. It is colorful and pretty. Sometimes I sprinkle in a cup of fresh blueberries.

STRAWBERRY PUDDING SALAD

Martha Ritter
Marquette, KS

2 boxes instant vanilla
  pudding mix
2 (10 oz.) pkg. frozen
  strawberries with juice
2 (8 oz.) containers
  whipped topping

2 c. miniature
  marshmallows
1 c. English walnuts,
  chopped

Mix all ingredients together and chill.

Makes a good Christmas salad.

STRAWBERRY SALAD WITH TOPPING

Lucile Fuller
Wichita, KS

2 (3 oz.) pkg. strawberry
  gelatin
2 c. boiling water
1 (large) pkg. frozen sliced
  strawberries
1 (large) can crushed
  pineapple

2 (large) bananas
2 c. sugar
4 Tbsp. flour
1 c. pineapple juice
2 eggs
1 c. whipping cream

In large mixer bowl, dissolve gelatin in the boiling water. Add frozen sliced strawberries with juice, but drain juice from crushed pineapple before adding. Add the bananas, sliced. Pour into 13x9 inch glass pan and chill until firm. In small saucepan, mix sugar, flour, drained pineapple juice, and eggs, slightly beaten. Cook over medium heat until slightly thick. Cool and pour over salad; add the whipped topping.

This recipe serves 12 or more, but can be cut in half easily.

STRAWBERRY WHIP

Lois Mills
Lake City, KS

1 box strawberry gelatin
1½ c. boiling water
1 pt. vanilla ice cream

1 pt. strawberries
½ c. nuts or walnuts
½ lb. vanilla wafers

Mix gelatin and water; add vanilla ice cream. Stir until dissolved; let set until mixture begins to thicken Whip until fluffy. Add strawberries and let set, then whip again. Add nuts. Line pan with ½ of vanilla wafers that have been crushed. Pour mixture over wafers and top with rest of vanilla wafers. Chill overnight.

My mom made this every Christmas for my son, who is 53 years old now, so you know it is an old family recipe.

STRAWBERRY-BANANA SALAD
Theresa Fangman
Hereford, TX

3 (3 oz.) pkg. strawberry
  gelatin
1 c. boiling water
1 (10 oz.) pkg. frozen
  strawberries, thawed
  and drained

1 (15 oz.) can crushed
  pineapple (undrained)
3 bananas, sliced
2 c. sour cream, divided
½ c. pecans or walnuts,
  chopped (optional)

Dissolve gelatin in boiling water; stir in fruit. Pour ½ of gelatin mixture into an 8 inch pan and refrigerate until firm. Store remaining gelatin mixture at room temperature. Spread congealed gelatin with 1 cup sour cream. Spoon remaining gelatin over sour cream and refrigerate until firm. Top with remaining sour cream, spreading evenly; sprinkle with pecans if desired. Yields 8 to 10 servings.

Can double and put in 9x13 inch dish and take it to family get-togethers or to church dinners.

SUMMER SALAD
NanCee Maynard
Box Elder, SD

1 (large) cucumber
1 (large) tomato
1 (small) yellow pepper
1 (small) red pepper
1 (small) green pepper

1 (medium) red onion
¼ c. balsamic vinegar
½ c. Italian dressing
⅛ tsp. black pepper
⅛ tsp. garlic powder

Wash the cucumber and with a fork, make stripes down the peel. Slice thinly. Cut the tomato, peppers, and onion into ½ inch pieces. Pour the balsamic vinegar over vegetables and add the dressing. Sprinkle with pepper and garlic powder and stir. Refrigerate and stir vegetables to blend.

The longer it blends, the better the taste. This salad is light and colorful.

SWEET SOUR COLESLAW

Arlyss Alexander
Clay Center, KS

1½ lb. green cabbage,
  shredded
⅓ c. cider
1 c. whipping cream (do
  not whip)

1 tsp. salt
⅔ c. sugar

Place shredded cabbage in covered dish in refrigerator for several hours. Mix cider, whipping cream, salt, and sugar together 30 minutes before serving. Chill. Pour over cabbage and serve.

TACO PASTA SALAD

Nanette Conger
Fairfield, IA

6 oz. rotini
1 lb. ground beef
1 pkg. taco seasoning mix
½ (medium) tomato,
  chopped
½ (medium) green pepper,
  chopped

½ (medium) onion,
  chopped
½ c. taco sauce
½ c. salsa
1 c. 3-blend cheese,
  shredded

Cook rotini; cool completely. Brown ground beef; drain. Add taco seasoning and prepare according to directions. Cool beef completely. Mix rotini, ground beef, tomato, green pepper, onion, taco sauce, salsa, and cheese together. Refrigerate at least 2 hours before serving. Yield: 6 to 8 servings.

This recipe is great because it can be made ahead for picnics, family gatherings, potlucks, etc. Any type of taco sauce and salsa can be used to make it hotter or with a mild flavor.

TOMATO CUCUMBER SALAD

Ann V. Gallentine
Clayton, KS

4 (large) tomatoes
1 cucumber
1 red onion
2 pinches dried basil

2 pinches dried oregano
Salt to taste
½ c. olive oil

Cut tomatoes into bite-size pieces. Peel and cut cucumbers into bite-size pieces; add onion, basil, oregano, and salt. Toss all ingredients together, except the oil. Chill for ½ hour. Add olive oil and mix. Let stand for 10 minutes.

This is especially good with tomatoes from the garden.

TORTELLINI GRATIN

Kathy Hogue
Topeka, KS

¾ c. Ricotta cheese
1 c. Parmesan cheese, freshly grated
1 c. whipping cream
¼ tsp. nutmeg, grated
1 lb. cheese tortellini
½ c. white bread crumbs

1 Tbsp. Romano cheese, grated
1 Tbsp. olive oil
1 Tbsp. fresh basil and oregano leaves, chopped (or 1 tsp. dried)

Combine the Ricotta, Parmesan, cream, and nutmeg in a large heavy-based pan. Heat slowly until smooth, stirring frequently. Cook tortellini in salted boiling water until tender, stirring frequently to prevent from sticking together. Just before tortellini are cooked, remove some of the cooking water with a ladle and add as much as necessary to cheese sauce to obtain a thin sauce consistency. Drain tortellini well and add to cheese sauce. Allow to heat through, stirring constantly. Transfer the mixture to an oiled baking dish and sprinkle with the combined bread crumbs, Romano, oil, and herbs. Place under a preheated broiler and broil until the top is golden. Serve immediately.

TRIPLE MUSHROOM TART

Joanie Slaughter
Columbia, MO

1 unbaked pie crust
1 c. fresh brown mushrooms
1 c. fresh oyster mushrooms
1 c. fresh shiitake mushrooms
¼ tsp. marjoram
2 Tbsp. butter

¾ c. shredded Gruyere cheese
¾ c. shredded Swiss cheese
½ c. Canadian bacon (or ham)
2 slightly beaten eggs
½ c. milk
1 Tbsp. chives

Place pie crust in 9 inch pie pan and line with 2 layers of foil and bake in 450°F. oven for 8 minutes. Remove foil; bake 4 to 5 minutes until set and dry. Reduce heat to 375°F. Cook mushrooms, marjoram, and butter in skillet at medium-high heat till tender and liquid is evaporated. Remove from heat. Combine cheese and ham in a large bowl. Add mushroom mixture, eggs, milk, and chives. Stir. Pour into pastry shell. Bake at 375°F. for 40 minutes or until set and golden. Cool on wire rack 10 to 15 minutes. Cut into wedges.

Use any combination of mushrooms-whatever is available. They all work. If you can't find Gruyere cheese, substitute another strong cheese, such as Blue cheese or Gorgonzola.

TURKEY SALAD VINAIGRETTE
Margaret Trojan
Beaver Crossing, NE

2 Tbsp. white wine
   vinegar
1 Tbsp. olive oil
2 tsp. lime juice
¼ tsp. salt
¼ tsp. pepper
¼ tsp. ground ginger

¼ c. red onion, chopped
1 jalapeno pepper, seeded
   and chopped
1 lb. turkey breast, cooked
   and cut into ¼ inch
   cubes
4 red leaf lettuce leaves

In medium bowl, whisk vinegar, oil, lime juice, salt, pepper, and ginger. Stir in onion, jalapeno, and turkey. Cover and refrigerate for several hours. To serve, line a plate with lettuce and spoon salad over the top. Serve with bagel chips if desired.

TURKEY WALDORF SANDWICH
Margaret Trojan
Beaver Crossing, NE

1½ c. turkey breast,
   cooked and cut into ½
   inch cubes
½ c. celery, diced
1 small Red Delicious
   apple, cored and cut
   into small cubes

2 Tbsp. walnuts, chopped
1 Tbsp. mayonnaise
1 Tbsp. yogurt
1½ tsp. nutmeg
⅛ tsp. cinnamon
4 lettuce leaves
8 slices raisin bread

In medium size bowl, combine turkey, celery, apple, walnuts, mayonnaise, yogurt, nutmeg, and cinnamon. Cover and refrigerate at least 1 hour or overnight to allow flavors to blend. To serve, arrange a lettuce leaf on bread slice. Spoon ¾ cup turkey mixture over lettuce leaf and top with another bread slice. Repeat with remaining ingredients. Serves 4.

VEGAN ROASTED BABY POTATO SALAD

Pam Schmidt
Edmonton, AB, CAN

2 c. baby red potatoes
1 c. red onion
½ c. tomatoes
3 Tbsp. sunflower or
   canola oil
2½ tsp. balsamic vinegar

1½ tsp. maple syrup
1 tsp. rosemary leaves,
   dried and crumbled
¾ tsp. garlic salt
Sea salt to taste
White pepper to taste

Preheat oven to 400°F. Lightly oil a baking sheet (with edges). Wash and scrub potatoes. Cube. Scatter on baking sheet. Peel onion and thinly slice onion into rounds. Scatter on top of potatoes. Wash and leave tomatoes whole. Place among the potatoes/onions. Place baking sheet in preheated oven. After 5 to 10 minutes, or just until tomatoes start to blacken, remove sheet and use tongs to remove tomatoes. Put potatoes/onions back into the oven and continue to roast for 35 to 45 minutes or until potatoes are fork-tender. While tomatoes are cooling, mix dressing. Combine oil, vinegar, maple syrup, rosemary, and garlic salt in small bowl. Set aside. When tomatoes are cool enough to handle, peel and discard peels. Squeeze out seeds/juice and reserve liquid from another use. Roughly chop tomatoes and place in serving bowl. When potatoes/onions are done, add to tomatoes. Stir the dressing again and pour it over the vegetables. Mix to thoroughly dress the salad. Sprinkle with sea salt and white pepper to taste. Serve hot or cold. Serves 4.

The easiest way to measure vegetables is to place 4 cups of water in an 8 cup measuring cup and drop in the raw, whole vegetables. You can adjust the vinegar and spices to taste, or decrease oil to your preference.

VEGETABLE CASSEROLE

Marjorie Abell
Grinnell, KS

2 (16 oz.) pkg. frozen
   vegetables, thawed and
   drained
2 cans cream of
   mushroom soup
2 c. cheese, shredded
⅔ c. sour cream
1 (8 oz.) pkg. cream
   cheese (room
   temperature)

¼ c. mayonnaise
½ tsp. pepper
1 (6 oz.) can French fried
   onions
1 (small) can water
   chestnuts, drained
1 (small) can mushrooms,
   drained

In large bowl, combine vegetables, soups, 1 cup cheese, sour cream, water chestnuts, mushrooms, cream cheese, mayonnaise, pepper, and about ½ the fried onions. Pour into shallow greased 9x13 inch casserole. Bake in 350°F. oven, covered, about 45 minutes or until vegetables are done. Sprinkle remaining cheese and onions across top and bake, uncovered, 5 minutes more. Freezes well.

VEGETABLE CASSEROLE

Neva Jones
O'Neill, NE

1 (10 oz.) box frozen
   broccoli
1 (10 oz.) box frozen
   cauliflower
1 (8 oz.) can carrots
1 (15 oz.) can French cut
   green beans

¾ c. processed American
   cheese
1 stick margarine
1 can cream of chicken
   soup
½ c. pretzels, crushed
Almonds, slivered

Melt together cheese and margarine; add cream of chicken soup. Pour ½ of the broccoli, cauliflower, carrots, and green beans into a greased casserole and add a layer of slivered almonds and ½ of the pretzels. Add rest of vegetables, a few more almonds, and the rest of the pretzels. Bake at 350°F. for 30 minutes. Serves 6.

VEGETABLE PIE

Kathy Hogue
Topeka, KS

2 Tbsp. vegetable oil
2 cloves garlic, chopped
3 (medium) tomatoes, cored and chopped
2 (small) onions, chopped
1 (small) eggplant, peeled, quartered, and sliced
1 (small) green pepper, seeded and sliced
1 c. corn (fresh or frozen)

Salt and pepper
3 (medium) zucchini, sliced
6 Tbsp. Parmesan cheese, grated
1 (9 inch) pie shell (unbaked)
2 Tbsp. (¼ stick) butter, cut in pieces

Heat oil and garlic in large skillet over medium high heat. Add tomatoes, onion, eggplant, green pepper, corn, and salt and pepper. Saute until vegetables are crisp-tender, about 7 minutes. Stir in zucchini and continue cooking until zucchini is crisp-tender. Sprinkle 2 tablespoon cheese over bottom of pie shell. Add ½ of vegetables using slotted spoon. Sprinkle with 2 tablespoons cheese and dot with 1 tablespoon butter. Add remaining vegetables; sprinkle with butter. Bake at 350°F. until crust is golden brown, about 40 minutes. Serve hot.

This makes a hearty accompaniment to any meal.

VEGETABLE SALAD BARS

Annilee Kniffen
Lorena, TX

2 (8 oz.) tubes refrigerated crescent rolls
¾ c. mayonnaise or salad dressing
½ c. sour cream
2 (8 oz.) pkg. cream cheese, softened
1 pkg. Ranch style dressing mix
¾ c. green peppers, chopped

¾ c. green onion, chopped
¾ c. tomato, diced
¾ c. broccoli, chopped
¾ c. carrots, sliced
¾ c. cauliflower, sliced
¾ c. Cheddar cheese, shredded

Cover the bottom of an 11x17 inch jelly roll pan with sheets of crescent roll dough, patting, sealing, and stretching to fit. Bake 7 to 8 minutes at 350°F. until lightly browned. Combine salad dressing, sour cream, cream cheese, and Ranch dressing mix. Spread over crust when cooled.

Combine the vegetables, tossing to mix and spread over the cheese mixture. Cover with plastic wrap and push veggies into cheese layer. Remove wrap. Top with the Cheddar cheese. Refrigerate, covered, 3 to 4 hours. Cut into bars to serve.

WALDORF PARTY SALAD

Barb Kasel
Adams, MN

3 c. apples, diced
1 c. seedless grapes
1 c. mini marshmallows
½ c. walnut halves

¼ c. salad dressing
½ c. heavy cream, whipped

Combine fruit, marshmallows, and nuts; toss lightly. Combine whipped cream and salad dressing. Fold into fruit salad. Chill. Serves 4 to 6.

YUMMY POTATOES

Coleen Koch
Summerfield, KS

1 (32 oz.) pkg. frozen hash browns
⅔ c. processed American cheese
½ c. margarine
½ c. shredded Cheddar cheese

1 pt. half & half
2 c. crushed Corn Flakes cereal
¼ c. melted butter

Put hash browns in bottom of 9x13 inch baking dish. Cook processed cheese, margarine, Cheddar cheese, and half & half until all cheeses are melted. Pour over hash browns. Melt the margarine and mix with Corn Flakes and place over top of all. Do not stir. Bake at 350°F. for 1 hour.

Notes

Desserts

Desserts
Recipe Contest Winners

First
Mile High Pie
Kelly Larson, Marquette, Kansas
Page 231

Second
Monday Night Delight
Keith Mueller, Halstead, Kansas
Page 234

Third
Grandma's Surprise-Burnt Sugar Bundt Cake
Maxine Mai, Lenora, Kansas
Page 223

DESSERTS

1995 REUNION CAKE

Carol F. Mandrell
Olton, TX

1 box Angel food cake mix
1 can sweetened condensed milk

1 (16 oz.) container frozen strawberries, thawed
1 (16 oz.) container whipped topping

Bake cake according to instructions on box. Cool. Crumble cake into bite-size pieces into a 9x13 inch pan. Pour condensed milk over the top. Pour strawberries over top, then spread whipped topping over all.

ALMOND JOY CAKE

Margaret Trojan
Beaver Crossing, NE

1 box chocolate cake mix (any brand with pudding)
1 c. evaporated milk
1 c. sugar
24 large marshmallows
1 (14 oz.) pkg. coconut

1½ c. sugar
½ c. evaporated milk
½ c. margarine
1½ c. chocolate chips
1 c. English walnuts or pecans, coarsely chopped

Mix cake according to directions on package and put in an 11½ x 17 inch pan. Bake at 350°F. for 20 to 25 minutes. While cake is baking, prepare filling. Heat evaporated milk, sugar, and marshmallows until melted. Add coconut. While cake is hot, pour filling over top. For frosting, heat sugar, evaporated milk, and margarine until it begins to boil. Add chocolate chips, stirring until melted. Add nuts and pour over cake, spreading evenly.

AMBROSIA PIE

Nancy Morey
Edwards, MO

½ c. flour
¾ c. walnuts, finely
  chopped
1 c. coconut
1¼ c. sugar
¼ c. butter
1 (8 oz.) pkg. cream
  cheese

1 tsp. vanilla
1 (20 oz.) can chunked
  pineapple
1 c. sour cream
1 packet unflavored
  gelatin

To make the crust, combine flour, walnuts, ½ cup coconut, ¼ cup sugar, and butter; mix to form coarse crumbs. Press into the bottom and up the sides of a 9 inch pie plate. Bake in a 350°F. oven for 20 minutes. Cool completely. To prepare filling, combine the cream cheese, remaining cup of sugar, and vanilla. Drain the pineapple and reserve the juice. Fold the sour cream and pineapple into the cream cheese mixture and set aside. In another bowl mix the gelatin with the reserved pineapple juice and set aside until thickened. Combine the cream cheese and pineapple mixture with the thickened juice and fill the cooled pie shell. Top with ½ cup coconut and chill for several hours before serving.

ANGEL FOOD CAKE

Maudie Burden
Centerview, MO

1½ c. sugar
1 c. cake flour
12 egg whites (large egg
  whites)
2 tsp. cream of tartar

¼ tsp. salt
1 tsp. vanilla
1 tsp. almond
1 c. sugar

Beat egg whites with salt until fluffy. Add cream of tartar and beat until stiff. Add vanilla, almond, sugar, egg whites, 2 tablespoons at a time. Beat. Sift ½ cup sugar with flour 3 times, then add to egg mixture 1 tablespoon at a time. Put in Angel food tube pan and put in cold oven at 350°F. and bake for 30 to 35 minutes or until done.

APPLE CAKE

Martha Plowman
Douds, IA

2 c. sugar
½ c. shortening
2 eggs
2 c. flour
2 tsp. baking soda
1 tsp. salt

1 tsp. cinnamon
1 tsp. allspice
1 tsp. nutmeg
5 c. apples, diced
½ c. walnuts, chopped

Mix sugar and shortening, add eggs and mix well. Add flour, baking soda, salt, cinnamon, allspice, and nutmeg. Mix in apples and nuts. Pour into a greased 9x13 inch pan. Bake at 325°F. for 1 hour.

APPLE CRUMB PIE

Kim Oborny
Durhan, KS

5 to 7 (6 c.) tart apples
1 (9 inch) unbaked pie
   shell, deep dish
½ c. sugar

2 to 2½ tsp. cinnamon
¾ c. flour
⅓ c. sugar
6 Tbsp. butter

Peel, core, and slice apples into bite-size pieces. Mix apples, sugar, and cinnamon together, then pour into unbaked pie shell. Topping: Combine flour, sugar and cut in butter until crumbly. Sprinkle over the apples. Bake at 400°F. for 35 to 40 minutes or until topping is golden brown. May need to cover pie edges with foil if they brown too quickly.

I like to use Jonathan apples with this recipe.

APPLE DUMPLINGS

Carol F. Mandrell
Olton, TX

2 (8 count) cans crescent
   rolls
2 cooking apples
2 sticks margarine

1 Tbsp. cinnamon
1½ c. sugar
12 oz. Mountain Dew
   (regular, not sugar free)

Peel and core apples. Cut each apple into eight slices. Place 1 slice of apple in center of crescent roll. Roll up from the large to small end. Put all in a 9x13 inch baking dish. Melt margarine. Mix with cinnamon and sugar. Pour over dumplings. Pour Mountain Dew over all. Bake at 350°F. for 45 minutes.

APPLE PIZZA

Margaret Trojan
Beaver Crossing, NE

2 c. flour
¾ tsp. salt
6 oz. milk
2¼ tsp. baking powder
3 oz. vegetable oil
6 large apples, sliced
⅔ c. sugar
¼ c. margarine

½ c. pecans, chopped
½ c. flour
2 tsp. cinnamon
1½ c. powdered sugar
3 Tbsp. milk
1 Tbsp. margarine, softened
1 tsp. vanilla

For crust mix flour, salt, milk, baking powder, and vegetable oil. Dough will be sticky. Oil hands and press into 11x15 inch pan. Place apple slices on crust. Mix sugar, margarine, pecans, flour, and cinnamon. Spread over sliced apples. Bake at 350°F. for 35 to 40 minutes or until apples and crust are done. Mix glaze ingredients of powdered sugar, milk, margarine, and vanilla. Glaze while warm. Freezes well and can be served as breakfast, dessert, or appetizer snacks.

APPLESAUCE

Thelma Maxwell
Dodge City, KS

6 or 8 apples
½ c. water

½ to ¾ c. Red Hot candies

Core apples, slice and cook in water with Red Hots to make red applesauce. Or, just cook without Red Hots for natural applesauce, replacing Red Hots with ½ cup sugar. Put mixture in blender after apples are cooked soft.

Makes a simple no-bake easy dessert.

APPLESAUCE BROWNIES

Alene Fosler
Sublette, KS

1 c. white sugar
½ c. butter
1 egg
2 c. flour
1 c. applesauce
½ tsp. baking powder
½ tsp. baking soda

¼ tsp. cinnamon
1 c. raisins
½ c. sugar
3 Tbsp. butter, melted
¼ c. nuts
½ c. coconut

Mix white sugar, butter, egg, flour, applesauce, baking powder, baking soda, cinnamon, and raisins together and put into a greased 9x13 inch pan. Mix together topping ingredients, ½ cup sugar, butter, nuts, and coconut cover mixture with topping. Bake at 350°F. about ½ hour.

APRICOT ALMOND BARS

Treva Gangwish
Wood River, NE

1 (18.25 oz.) box yellow cake mix
½ c. butter, softened
1 egg
½ c. sugar
¼ c. flour

4 eggs
2½ c. dried apricots, chopped
1½ c. almonds, sliced
¾ c. apricot jam, melted

Heat oven to 350°F. Grease 13x9 inch pan. In large bowl, combine all crust ingredients, cake mix, butter, and egg. Beat at low speed until crumbly. Press mixture firmly in bottom of greased pan. Bake at 350°F. for 10 to 15 minutes or until edges are golden brown. In the same bowl, combine sugar and flour; mix well to make filling. Add 4 eggs and stir with spoon until well blended. Fold in apricots. Gently fold in the almonds. Remove pan from oven and pour apricot mixture evenly over partially baked crust. Return to oven and bake an additional 15 to 20 minutes or until filling is set. Remove from oven and gently brush with melted jam. Cool 45 minutes or until completely cooled before cutting into bars. Make 24 bars.

These bars will keep well if placed in an airtight container and stored in a cool place. They are very pretty on a cookie plate and taste very good. One of our favorites.

APRICOT BARS

Ellen Olivier
Harper, KS

¾ c. margarine
1 c. sugar
1 egg
1⅓ c. coconut
½ tsp. vanilla
2 c. flour

¼ tsp. baking powder
½ c. nuts, chopped
1 (12 oz.) jar apricot preserves
½ c. dried apricots, diced

Cream margarine and sugar. Add egg; mix well. Combine flour and baking powder and add to margarine mixture. Add coconut, nuts, and vanilla; mix well. Press ⅔ of dough into a 9x12 inch pan. Cook apricots in microwave for 4 minutes with ½ cup water added to them. Spread preserves and the dried apricots over dough. Drop remaining dough by teaspoons over the preserves and spread. Bake at 375°F. for 20 to 25 minutes.

A family favorite.

APRICOT POUND CAKE

Marilyn Scott
Van Buren, AR

2 sticks margarine
3 c. sugar
6 eggs
3 c. flour
½ tsp. salt
¼ tsp. baking soda
1 c. cream

½ tsp. rum flavoring
1 c. sour cream
½ tsp. lemon flavoring
½ tsp. orange flavoring
1 tsp. vanilla
½ c. apricot brandy

Cream margarine and sugar. Beat in eggs, one at a time. Combine dry ingredients. Combine sour cream and all flavorings. Add flour mixture to creamed mixture alternately with sour cream mixture. Mix well. Bake 1 hour and 40 minutes at 350°F.

APRICOT-OATMEAL COOKIES

Kimberly D. Heil
Ulysses, KS

2 sticks margarine, melted
2 (large) eggs
2 c. brown sugar
½ tsp. almond extract
2 c. flour
2½ c. oatmeal

½ tsp. baking powder
½ tsp. baking soda
⅛ tsp. salt
½ c. almonds, ground
½ lb. dried apricots, diced

Cream margarine, eggs, sugar, and extract. Add flour, oatmeal, baking soda, and powder, and salt. Mix thoroughly. Add apricots and almonds. Mix. Drop onto cookie sheets and bake at 350°F. for 10 to 12 minutes. Store in tightly sealed container. Makes 4 dozen cookies.

This recipe can be made with dried apples and walnuts instead of dried apricots and almonds. If you do so, replace the almond extract with 1 teaspoon vanilla extract. If you prefer not to use nuts, replace them with an additional ½ cup of oatmeal.

AUNT CLEO'S ICE BOX PECAN WAFERS (1934)

Lucile Fuller
Wichita, KS

1 lb. light brown sugar
1 lb. butter
3 eggs

3¾ c. flour
1 tsp. baking soda
1 c. pecan pieces

Cream together the brown sugar and butter in large mixer bowl. Add eggs and beat. Add flour and baking soda sifted together, then pecans. After mixing, make dough into rolls (2 or 3 about 8 inches long). Wrap rolls in foil and chill. Slice thin and bake on cookie sheet until firm, but not brown. Bake at 350°F. as needed; dough will keep months in refrigerator.

BAKLAVA

Iola Egle
Bella Vista, AR

1 lb. sweet butter, just
   barely melted
1 lb. Phyllo pastry dough
3 to 4 c. nutmeats,
   coarsely chopped
   (walnuts, almonds,
   pecans)
2 Tbsp. sugar

2 tsp. cinnamon
½ tsp. ground cloves
   (optional)
2 c. sugar
½ c. honey
1 c. water
½ tsp. lemon juice

Combine nutmeats, sugar, cinnamon, and cloves. With a pastry brush, brush melted butter on bottom of 15x10x2 inch baking pan. Place 1 sheet of Phyllo dough on buttered pan. Brush with butter. Layer 4 to 5 more sheets, brushing each with butter. Sprinkle ⅓ of the nut mixture on layered-buttered Phyllo. Repeat this procedure 3 times, ending with Phyllo, and brush top with butter. With a very sharp knife, cut Baklava into square or diamond-shaped pieces. Pour remainder of butter over each piece. Bake at 350°F. for 35 minutes. Reduce heat to 300°F. and bake 10 to 15 minutes more. Remove from oven and let set for 5 minutes. Prepare syrup with 2 cups sugar, honey, water, and lemon juice. Bring to a boil and simmer over low heat for 10 to 15 minutes. Pour cooked syrup over Baklava.

Let the Baklava set overnight to soak up any syrup that runs off. Serve in "bake cups" from a pretty plate.

BANANA BRAN MUFFINS

Maudie Burden
Centerview, MO

½ c. margarine, softened
1 c. sugar
2 eggs
3 (medium) ripe bananas,
  mashed
½ c. buttermilk
1½ c. all-purpose flour

1½ tsp. baking soda
½ tsp. salt
4 c. raisin bran
1 c. miniature semi-sweet
  chocolate chips
½ c. pecans, chopped

In a mixing bowl, cream margarine and sugar. Add the eggs, bananas, and buttermilk. Combine the flour, baking soda, and salt. Stir into creamed mixture just until moistened. Fold in the cereal, chocolate chips, and pecans. Fill greased or paper-lined muffin cups ⅔ full. Bake at 350°F. for 23 to 25 minutes or until toothpick comes out clean. Cool for 5 minutes before removing from pans to wire racks. Yields 2 dozen.

BANANA COOKIES

Maudie Burden
Centerview, MO

1¼ c. flour
½ tsp. baking soda
¼ tsp. nutmeg
¼ tsp. cinnamon
½ tsp. salt
½ c. walnuts, chopped

½ c. shortening
1 c. sugar
1 egg
¾ c. bananas, mashed
1¾ c. rolled oats

Sift dry ingredients. Cream shortening; add egg, bananas, walnuts, and oats. Mix. Stir in dry ingredients. Drop on cookie sheet. Bake at 350°F. for 15 minutes.

BANANA SURPRISE

Janet Rauch
Deep River, IA

½ c. sugar
3 Tbsp. cornstarch
¼ tsp. salt
2 c. milk
3 egg yolks, slightly
  beaten
1 Tbsp. margarine,
  softened

1 tsp. vanilla
2 bananas
1¼ c. chocolate graham
  crackers
¼ c. margarine
¼ c. sugar

Mix sugar, cornstarch, and salt in 1½ quart pan. Gradually stir in milk and cook over medium heat, stirring constantly, until mixture thickens and boils. Boil for 1 minute; add margarine and vanilla. Let cool. Add to chocolate crust which has been made in pie pan or 9x13 inch cake dish. Slice bananas and add to pudding as you fill it. To make the crust, mix graham crackers, butter, and sugar; press in dish. Top dessert with whipped topping and refrigerate.

BAVARIAN APPLE TORTE

Julie Klein
St. Peters, MO

½ c. butter
⅓ c. sugar
¼ tsp. vanilla
1 c. flour
1 (8 oz.) pkg. cream
  cheese
¼ c. sugar

1 egg
½ tsp. vanilla
⅓ c. sugar
½ tsp. cinnamon
4 c. apples, peeled and
  sliced
¼ c. almonds, sliced

To make the crust, cream butter, sugar, and vanilla. Blend in flour. Spread dough on bottom and sides of 9 inch pie plate. To make the filling, combine softened cream cheese and sugar. Mix well. Add egg and vanilla; mix well. Pour into pastry-lined pan. To make the topping, combine sugar and cinnamon. Toss apples in sugar mixture. Spoon mixture over cream cheese layer. Sprinkle with almonds.

BETH'S BANANA PUDDING

Velma Twyman
Boise City, OK

1 (large) pkg. vanilla
  pudding
2 c. milk
1 can sweetened
  condensed milk

1 (8 oz.) container
  whipped topping
1 pkg. vanilla wafers,
  crushed
5 or 6 bananas

Mix pudding and 2 cups of milk until thick. Add Eagle Brand milk and whipped topping; continue beating until creamy. Layer pudding, wafers, and bananas. Add crushed cookies to top.

BILL HOGUE'S APPLE GOODIE

Kathy Hogue
Topeka, KS

1½ c. sugar
1½ c. water
¼ tsp. cinnamon
¼ tsp. nutmeg
6 to 10 drops red food
  coloring
3 Tbsp. margarine
2 c. sifted all-purpose
  flour

2 tsp. baking powder
1 tsp. salt
⅔ c. shortening
½ c. milk
6 medium apples, pared,
  cored, sliced

Combine sugar, water, spices, and food coloring; bring to a boil. Remove from heat; add butter. Sift together dry ingredients; cut in shortening till mixture resembles coarse crumbs. Add milk all at once and stir just until flour is moistened. On lightly floured surface, roll into rectangle about ¼ inch thick. Cut solid piece and place in 9x13 inch glass pan. Cut remaining dough into ½ inch strips. Place apples over dough and top with remaining strips in criss cross pattern. Cover with syrup mixture and liberally sprinkle with cinnamon sugar. Bake at 375°F. for 50 to 55 minutes.

Serve with vanilla ice cream. We love the aroma of this baking in our kitchen.

BISCUITS WITH CHOCOLATE KISSES

Carol F. Mandrell
Olton, TX

1 (10 count) can biscuits
10 (plus) chocolate kisses

1 can coconut pecan cake frosting

Scantly spray a casserole dish with cooking spray. Place one kiss in the center of each biscuit, wrapping the biscuit around the chocolate and sealing the edges. Place the biscuits in a casserole dish; scatter a few more kisses on top, then top with the cake frosting. Bake at 375°F. for 15 to 20 minutes or until biscuits are done.

BROWN SUGAR SQUARES

Debbie Hunt
Anthony, KS

½ c. shortening
1½ c. firmly packed
 brown sugar
1 c. all-purpose flour
2 eggs, well beaten
2 Tbsp. all-purpose flour
½ tsp. baking powder

¼ tsp. salt
1 tsp. vanilla
½ c. flaked coconut
1 c. nuts (walnuts,
 pecans, almonds, or
 peanuts), chopped

Cream shortening. Add ½ cup brown sugar gradually, continuing to beat until well blended. Add 1 cup flour, working mixture with wooden spoon until crumbly. Spread in ungreased 8 inch square cake pan, pressing down evenly. Bake at 300°F. about 25 minutes or until light brown. Remove from oven; set aside. Combine remaining 1 cup brown sugar and eggs; beat well. Stir in remaining ingredients; blend well. Spread over the baked layer. Bake at 350°F. for 30 minutes. Cool in pan on cake rack. Cut into squares. Makes 9 to 12 squares.

BROWNIE PIZZA

Flo M. Burtnett
Gage, OK

½ c. all-purpose flour
2 Tbsp. cocoa powder
½ tsp. baking powder
½ c. margarine
1½ c. chocolate chips

½ c. brown sugar, packed
2 (large) eggs
1 tsp. vanilla
1 c. white chocolate chips
½ c. M&M's

Coat a 12 inch pizza pan with nonstick spray. Mix flour, cocoa powder, and baking powder in a medium bowl until well blended. Melt margarine and one cup chocolate chips in medium saucepan over low heat, stirring often. Remove from heat when mixture is well blended. Stir in sugar, then eggs and vanilla, until blended. Pour into flour mixture and stir until smooth. Spread mixture into prepared pizza pan. Sprinkle the remaining ½ cup chocolate chips around the edge. Bake at 350°F. for 15 to 20 minutes until a toothpick inserted in center comes out clean. Remove from oven and immediately sprinkle white chips in the middle. Let stand until soft, then spread to edge of chocolate chip rim. Sprinkle M&M's on the pizza. Cool completely, then cut into 12 wedges.

BROWNIES

Donna J. Walker
Kismet, KS

2 sticks margarine
2 c. flour
1 tsp. vanilla

4 eggs
2 c. sugar
6 Tbsp. cocoa

Melt margarine with cocoa. Bring to a boil; add sugar, one cup at a time. Add egg after each cup of sugar and flour. Add vanilla; bake at 350°F. for 20 to 25 minutes.

BURNT SUGAR PIE

Mrs. Wilbur (Myrna) Booth
Cainsville, MO

¾ c. burnt sugar syrup
1½ c. water (hot)
6 eggs
1½ c. white sugar
3 heaping Tbsp.
   cornstarch
¼ c. margarine
1 tsp. vanilla
1 tsp. butter flavoring

4 c. milk
⅛ tsp. salt
6 egg whites
1 tsp. vanilla
½ tsp. cream of tartar
⅔ c. sugar
2 pie crusts, baked and
   ready

Use heavy saucepan on stove and add ¾ cup white sugar to burn on the stove until golden brown; also have a little heated water on hand to heat sugar. When it is brown enough, pour this in the sugar with a lid so as not to spew out on you. About a cup or more heated. Turn burner down low and let it get like syrup. Add to burnt sugar syrup. Mix all these ingredients in a big mixing bowl. First, beat until foamy egg yolks; save whites for the top. Add this to your egg yolks, white sugar, cornstarch, margarine, vanilla, and butter flavoring. If you use regular margarine, skip the butter flavoring; add whole milk or 2% if you don't want it too rich and ⅛ teaspoon salt. Pour this mixture in the pan on the stove with the burnt sugar; turn your burner up and cook, stirring constantly, until thick. If you think it needs more milk, add (same with cornstarch). For topping, take the egg whites that were set aside; add 1 teaspoon vanilla and teaspoon cream of tartar. Add gradually while whipping sugar. Whip until soft peaks stay firm; add to the top of the pies and brown. This will make two pies.

BUTTER PECAN BUNDT CAKE

Mary Jeans
Blackwell, OK

1 box butter pecan cake
  mix
1 c. water
4 eggs

¾ c. oil
1 can coconut pecan
  frosting mix
1 c. pecans

Combine cake mix, water, eggs, and oil in bowl. Beat for 2 minutes on medium speed. Stir in frosting mix and nuts. Pour in Bundt pan. Bake at 350°F. for 45 to 50 minutes or until done.

BUTTER PECAN ICE CREAM

Margaret Trojan
Beaver Crossing, NE

1 can sweetened
  condensed milk
1½ c. pecans, chopped
  and toasted

3 Tbsp. margarine, melted
1 Tbsp. maple flavoring
2 c. half & half cream
2 c. whipped cream

In a large bowl, combine sweetened condensed milk, pecans, margarine, and maple flavoring; mix well. Stir in half & half and whipped cream. Pour into ice cream freezer container. Freeze according to directions for freezer. Makes 1½ quarts.

BUTTERMILK PINEAPPLE SHERBET

Lucile Fuller
Wichita, KS

3 c. sugar
1 container (equal to 4 eggs) Egg Beaters
1 (10 oz.) can evaporated milk

2 pt. half & half
6 Tbsp. lemon juice
1 (20 oz.) can crushed pineapple in natural juice

In large mixer bowl, beat together the sugar, Egg Beaters, then add milk, half & half, crushed pineapple with juice, and lemon juice. Pour into container for 1 gallon freezer and freeze in usual manner.

This is better if allowed to age for a day before serving. It keeps very well in freezer.

BUTTERSCOTCH CHEESECAKE WITH CHOCOLATE DRIZZLE

Julie Schmidt
Smith Center, KS

1 c. graham cracker crumbs
3 Tbsp. sugar
3 Tbsp. melted butter or margarine
3 (8 oz.) pkg. cream cheese, softened
½ c. sugar

2 Tbsp. all-purpose flour
1⅔ c. (10 oz. pkg.) butterscotch chips
2 Tbsp. milk
4 eggs
½ c. semi-sweet chocolate chips
1 Tbsp. shortening

For crust heat oven to 325°F. Combine first 3 ingredients in a small bowl. Press mixture onto bottom of 9 inch springform pan. Bake 10 minutes. Increase oven to 350°F. Beat cream cheese, sugar, and flour in large bowl on medium speed of mixer until smooth. Place butterscotch chips and milk in small microwave-safe bowl. Microwave at high 1 minute; stir. Stir butterscotch mixture into cream cheese mixture. Add eggs, one at a time, mixing well after each addition. Pour over prepared crust. Bake 40 to 45 minutes or until center is almost set. Remove from oven to wire rack. With knife, immediately loosen cake from side of pan. Cool completely; remove side of pan. To prepare drizzle, melt chocolate chips and 1 tablespoon of shortening in microwave for 30 seconds on high. Drizzle over top of cheesecake. Cover and refrigerate. Makes 12 servings.

If you are in a hurry, instead of making the chocolate drizzle, we have used chocolate syrup over the top of each slice. This was the first cheesecake I had ever made in a springform pan. It was so easy to make, but really looked like you had spent all day on it!!

BUTTERSCOTCH DESSERT

Juanna Beth Lewis
Darlington, ID

½ c. (1 stick) margarine, melted
1 c. flour
¼ c. walnuts, chopped
1 (8 oz.) pkg. cream cheese, softened

1 c. powdered sugar
½ (8 oz.) container whipped topping
2 (3 oz.) pkg. instant butterscotch pudding
3½ c. cold milk

Mix together margarine, flour, and walnuts until crumbly; press into 9x13 inch pan. Bake at 350°F. for 10 minutes. Cool. Beat together cream cheese and powdered sugar until light and fluffy. Fold whipped topping into cream cheese mixture and spread over baked and cooled crust. Mix together instant pudding and milk until starting to thicken, about 2 minutes. Spread over cream cheese mixture. Top with remainder of whipped topping. Sprinkle with chopped walnuts.

This dessert is easy to make and is always a favorite for company dinners.

CAKE THAT DON'T LAST

Pauline Riley
Dodge City, KS

3 c. flour
2 c. sugar
1 tsp. baking soda
1 tsp. salt
1⅓ c. oil
3 eggs, beaten

1 (20 oz.) can crushed pineapple
2 c. ripe bananas
½ c. pecans
1½ tsp. vanilla

Mix flour, sugar, and baking soda. Add eggs and oil. Mix, but don't beat. Fold in pineapple, bananas, pecans, and vanilla. Pour into greased and floured Bundt pan. Bake at 350°F. for 1 hour and 20 minutes. Remove from oven and place a plate over pan before inverting the Bundt pan. Let cool.

CAKEY-PIE

Jennifer Tupps
Galion, OH

1 box cake mix   **1 can pie filling**

Prepare cake as package directs for 9x13 inch pan. Mix and pour into pan. Using tablespoon add spoonfuls of pie filling in dollops over cake batter. Bake cake according to package directions.

Serve warm or cold. This is cobbler-like. Our favorite combinations are devils food/cherry pie filling, spice/apple filling, orange/apricot filling.

CANDY BAR CHEESECAKE

Colleen Jeffery
Burr Oak, KS

1 (8 oz.) pkg. cream cheese
1 (8 oz.) container whipped topping
1 c. chocolate chips

2 Tbsp. water
5 individual Reese's peanut butter cups
1 prepared pie crust

Bake pie crust as directed. Allow to cool. Microwave chocolate chips and water. Stir by hand until smooth. Allow chocolate mixture to cool. Beat cream cheese with electric mixer until softened. Add whipped topping and beat on low speed until smooth. Fold in chocolate mixture and three Reese's peanut butter cups. Pour into prepared pie crust. Top with two crumbled peanut butter cups. Refrigerate. Serves 6 to 8.

For variety, other candy bars can be substituted.

CARAMEL OATMEAL BARS

Linda Pauls
Buhler, KS

1¾ c. quick or old-fashioned oats
1¾ c. all-purpose flour, divided
¾ c. brown sugar, packed
½ tsp. baking soda
¼ tsp. salt

¾ c. butter, melted
1 (12 oz.) pkg. chocolate chips
1 c. nuts, chopped
1 c. caramel ice cream topping

Grease bottom of 13x9 inch baking pan. Combine oats, 1½ cups flour, sugar, baking soda, and salt in large bowl. Stir in butter; mix well. Reserve 1 cup oat mixture; press remaining onto bottom of prepared baking pan. Bake for 12 to 15 minutes in 350°F. oven or until golden brown. Sprinkle with chocolate chips and nuts. Mix caramel topping with remaining flour in small bowl; drizzle over nuts to within ¼ inch of pan edges. Sprinkle with reserved oat mixture. Bake for 18 to 22 minutes or until golden brown. Cool in pan on wire rack. Can be served warm or refrigerated until firm. Servings depend on how large or small bars are cut.

CARNATION KEY LIME PIE

Fern Mishler
Ransom, KS

1 (9 inch) graham cracker pie crust
1 (14 oz.) can sweetened condensed milk
½ c. (about 3 medium limes) fresh lime juice
2 c. whipped topping, frozen

Beat sweetened condensed milk and lime juice in a small mixer bowl until combined. Pour into graham cracker pie crust. Spread thawed whipped topping over the top of this mixture. Refrigerate for 3 hours or until set.

CAROL'S CHRISTMAS COOKIES

Coleen Koch
Summerfield, KS

1 c. shortening
2 c. sugar
3 eggs
1 tsp. salt
1 tsp. vanilla
1 tsp. baking soda
3½ c. flour

Cream shortening, sugar, and eggs. Add other ingredients and mix well. Roll out dough to ¼ inch thickness. Cut with favorite shape cookie cutter on floured surface. Bake at 325°F. for 10 minutes. Cool slightly, then freeze. After the cookies have frozen, remove from freezer and thaw. Frost with your favorite cookie frosting and refreeze. Thaw and enjoy!

We really don't know why all the freezing makes a difference, but they are a favorite with our family.

CARROT BANANA BREAD

Maudie Burden
Centerview, MO

⅓ c. vegetable oil
1 c. sugar
2 eggs
2 c. all-purpose flour
1 tsp. baking soda
½ tsp. salt

½ tsp. ground cinnamon
1 c. ripe bananas, mashed
(2 to 3 medium
bananas)
1 c. carrots, grated
½ c. pecans, chopped

In a mixing bowl, combine oil and sugar. Add eggs; mix well. Combine flour, baking soda, salt, and cinnamon; gradually add to the creamed mixture alternately with bananas. Stir in carrots and pecans. Transfer to a greased 9x5x3 inch loaf pan. Bake at 350°F. for 55 to 65 minutes or until a toothpick inserted near the center comes out clean. Cool for 10 minutes before removing from pan to a wire rack to cool completely. Yields 1 loaf.

CHERRY SQUARES

NanCee Maynard
Box Elder, SD

1 (16 oz.) box Angel food
cake mix

1 (22 oz.) can cherry pie
filling

Combine dry cake mix and cherry pie filling. Pour into an ungreased 9x13 inch baking dish. Bake at 350°F. for 30 to 35 minutes. Cool and cut into squares. Top with whipped topping and fresh cherries.

This smells wonderful baking and is so light.

CHERRY TURNOVERS

Janee Montgomery
Kearney, NE

1 (21 oz.) can cherry pie
filling
1 lb. margarine
6 Tbsp. milk

1 (8 oz.) pkg. cream
cheese
4 c. flour
½ tsp. butter flavoring

Let cream cheese and margarine reach room temperature; put in a bowl. Add the other ingredients; mix, cover, and chill overnight. Take out a piece of dough about the size of a walnut and roll out on a floured board the size of a coffee cup. Put a teaspoon of pie filling on top. Fold over and press with a floured fork to seal. Put on ungreased cookie sheet and bake at 375°F. for 15 minutes or until lightly browned. Glaze with a powdered sugar glaze.

Turnovers can be frozen unbaked. The dough will keep a few days in the refrigerator.

CHOCOLATE CAKE

Connie M. Terry
Ellsworth, KS

2 c. sugar
½ c. shortening
2 eggs
2 c. flour
½ c. cocoa
½ c. buttermilk or sour
  milk

1 tsp. baking soda
1 c. boiling water
1 c. brown sugar, packed
½ c. whipping cream

Cream sugar and shortening; add eggs. Add flour, cocoa, and buttermilk. Mix. Put in baking soda and pour hot water over top. Mix into dry mixture. Put in a 9x13 inch pan and bake at 350°F. for 30 minutes. For caramel frosting, mix together and cook brown sugar and whipping cream over medium heat until soft ball stage. Remove from heat and stir until thick. Spread on cake.

This cake is a family recipe I learned from my mother when I was young. We baked this cake from memory at home and I still do when I make it.

CHOCOLATE CHERRY CAKE

Betty Mead
Paradise, KS

½ c. margarine
1 egg
1½ c. cake flour
¾ tsp. salt
¼ c. maraschino cherries,
  chopped
1 c. sugar

2 (1 oz.) sq. chocolate,
  melted
1 tsp. baking soda
1 c. milk
2 Tbsp. cherry juice
½ c. nuts

Soften shortening. Add sugar; cream well. Add egg; beat well. Stir in chocolate. Sift flour, salt, and baking soda. Add to creamed ingredients with milk alternately. Beat smooth. Add cherries, juice, and nuts. Bake in 8x8x2 inch pan at 350°F. for 40 minutes.

CHOCOLATE CHIP CHEESECAKE

Stacy Menges
Watsontown, PA

1¾ c. graham crackers, finely crushed
¼ c. sugar
6 Tbsp. butter, melted
3 (8 oz.) pkg. cream cheese

3 eggs
2 tsp. vanilla
1 c. sour cream
1 c. white sugar
1 bag mini chocolate chips

Prepare graham cracker crust in a 9 inch springform pan. Mix graham cracker crumbs, sugar, and butter; mix. Press onto bottom and part way up sides of pan. Beat cream cheese, sugar, and vanilla until creamy. Beat in 1 egg at a time. Blend in sour cream. Pour in mini chocolate chips; mix. Bake at 350°F. for 60 to 70 minutes until center is set and firm. Turn off oven, leaving door slightly ajar. Leave in oven 1 hour. Remove, cool in pan, then chill. Keep refrigerated. Before removing springform pan after cool, use butter knife to go around inside of pan to help remove.

If you like cheesecake, you'll love this recipe!

CHOCOLATE CHIP COOKIES

Arlene Bontrager
Hutchinson, KS

1¼ c. sugar
1 c. shortening (butter flavor)
½ c. vegetable oil
1 c. brown sugar
3 tsp. vanilla
3 eggs

4 c. flour
1 tsp. salt
1½ tsp. baking soda
1 c. semi-sweet chocolate chips
1 c. peanut butter chips
1 c. pecans, chopped

Cream well sugars, shortening, and oil. Add vanilla and eggs; beat well. Mix flour, baking soda, and salt together, then add a spoonful at a time as mixer is going on very lowest speed until all flour mixture has been added. Stir in chips and nuts. Drop by tablespoon on ungreased cookie sheets. Bake 8 to 10 minutes at 350°F. Makes about 6 dozen cookies.

CHOCOLATE CHIP POUND CAKE

Marilyn Scott
Van Buren, AR

1 box yellow cake mix
1 regular box instant
  chocolate pudding
1 oz. sour cream
¼ c. water

1 c. oil
4 eggs
1 tsp. vanilla
6 oz. chocolate chips

Mix all ingredients and pour into greased and floured Bundt cake pan. Bake 1 hour at 350°F.

CHOCOLATE CHIP SENSATION

Julie Klein
St. Peters, MO

1 (18 oz.) pkg. refrigerated
  chocolate chip cookie
  dough
1 (8 oz.) pkg. cream
  cheese, softened

⅓ c. sugar
1 pt. half & half
1 (3.4 oz.) box chocolate
  instant pudding
¼ c. nuts, chopped

Shape cookie dough into a 12 inch circle, about ¼ inch thick, on a pizza pan. Bake in 350°F. oven for 12 to 15 minutes. Cool completely. Mix cream cheese and sugar and spread over cooled cookie. Mix half & half with pudding for two minutes. Let stand for five minutes until thickened. Spread pudding over cream cheese mixture. Sprinkle with nuts. Serve immediately or refrigerate.

You may top with M&M's, mini chocolate chips, sprinkles, or whatever you like instead of nuts.

CHOCOLATE CHIP TREASURE COOKIES

Pat Stutz
Utica, KS

1½ c. graham cracker
  crumbs
½ c. flour
2 tsp. baking powder
1 (14 oz.) can sweetened
  condensed milk

½ c. butter, softened
1 (12 oz.) pkg. semi-sweet
  chocolate chips
1 c. walnuts or pecans,
  chopped
1 c. coconut

Mix crumbs, flour, and baking powder. In another bowl, beat condensed milk and butter until smooth. Add graham cracker mixture; mix well. Stir in chocolate, chips, and nuts. Drop by tablespoon onto ungreased cookie sheet. Bake 9 to 10 minutes at 350°F. Let set on cookie sheet a minute before removing.

Store in loosely covered container at room temperature.

CHOCOLATE ICE CREAM DESSERT

Lisa Petzold
Elmer, OK

1 stick margarine
1 c. flour
1 c. pecans
1 (8 oz.) pkg. cream cheese, softened
1 c. whipped topping

1 c. powdered sugar
1 qt. chocolate ice cream, softened
2 c. milk
2 (small) boxes instant chocolate pudding

For the first layer, melt margarine in microwave in a 9x13 inch dish. Stir in flour and pecans. Pat evenly in dish. Microwave for 5 minutes. Cool crust. For the second layer, beat cream cheese, Cool Whip, and powdered sugar until creamy. Spread over cooled crust. For the third layer, mix milk, ice cream, and pudding until it thickens. Pour pudding over cream cheese mixture. Top pudding with whipped topping. May be frozen.

CHOCOLATE LOVER'S OATMEAL DELIGHTS

Pat Habiger
Spearville, KS

1¼ c. flour
⅓ c. unsweetened cocoa
½ tsp. baking soda
½ tsp. salt
1 c. butter, softened
1½ c. sugar
1 egg

¼ c. water
1½ tsp. vanilla
3 c. quick-cooking oats
1 c. semi-sweet chocolate chips
1 c. peanut butter flavored chips

In a medium mixing bowl, combine flour, cocoa powder, baking soda, and salt. Set aside. In very large mixing bowl, beat butter for about 30 seconds. Add the sugar and beat until combined. Beat in egg, water, and vanilla till mixed well. Beat in as much flour as you can. Using

200

wooden spoon, stir in remaining flour and the oats. Stir in chocolate pieces and peanut butter flavored pieces. Drop dough by rounded spoonfuls 2 inches apart on ungreased cookie sheet. I like to use parchment paper. Bake in 350°F. oven for 10 to 12 minutes. Makes about 4 dozen cookies.

CHOCOLATE MACAROON BARS

Jenny Pachta
Belleville, KS

1 pkg. devil's food cake mix
1 egg
1 can sweetened condensed milk
1 c. coconut
1 (12 oz.) pkg. chocolate chips
1 Tbsp. margarine

Combine cake mix with melted margarine. Mix with fork until crumbly. Pat in greased 9x13 inch pan. Mix sweetened condensed milk, egg, and ¾ cup coconut and chocolate chips. Pour on top of crust. Sprinkle reserved coconut on top. Bake 20 to 25 minutes at 350°F.

CHOCOLATE MACAROON CAKE

Brigit Gasper
Tipton, KS

1 (18.25 oz.) pkg. chocolate cake mix
1 box instant chocolate pudding
¾ c. oil
¾ c. water
4 eggs
1 egg white
½ c. sugar
1 c. coconut
1 stick butter
4 Tbsp. cocoa
6 Tbsp. milk
3½ c. powdered sugar
1 c. nuts, chopped
1 c. coconut

Beat cake mix, pudding, oil, water, 4 eggs, and vanilla with electric mixer on medium speed for 5 minutes. Set aside. Beat egg white on high speed of mixer. Gradually beat in ½ cup sugar, beating well until stiff peaks form. Fold coconut into egg white mixture carefully with spoon. Grease and flour Bundt or Angel Food cake pan. Pour in half of chocolate cake batter. Spoon egg white mixture onto batter, being careful to keep it away from the sides of the pan. Carefully pour remaining batter on top. Bake for 45 minutes to 1 hour at 325°F. or until toothpick inserted is clean. Cool in pan for 15 minutes. Invert onto serving plate. Bring 1 stick butter, cocoa, and 6 tablespoons milk to boil in saucepan.

Remove from heat. Add powdered sugar, nuts, and coconut. Mix and frost cake while it is still warm.

This cake is an old recipe from an old television program in the 70's. It is very good and people who like coconut love it.

CHOCOLATE MOCHA UPSIDE-DOWN CAKE

*Robert Wolfe
McCracken, KS*

¾ c. white sugar
1 c. sifted flour
2 tsp. baking powder
⅛ tsp. salt
1 sq. Baker's chocolate
2 Tbsp. butter
½ c. milk

1 tsp. vanilla
½ c. brown sugar
½ c. white sugar
3 Tbsp. cocoa
8 oz. (liquid) cold, black coffee

Mix the ¾ cup white sugar, flour, baking powder, and salt together. Melt the chocolate and butter together and stir into the mix. Add your milk and vanilla and mix to the consistency of a good cake batter. Place the batter into an 8x8 or 9x9 inch greased baking pan dusted with cocoa. The remaining ingredients and for the topping. Mix the brown sugar, the ½ cup white sugar, and 3 teaspoons cocoa together well and sprinkle evenly over the batter. Take the cold coffee and slowly pour it over the topping. The liquid will be on the top when you put it in the oven. Bake in a 350°F. oven for about 45 minutes. Cool, cut into squares, and serve upside down so the chocolate sauce is on top.

This is an old family recipe handed down to me from my mother and her mother before her. When I left home to strike out on my own, it was one of the things I just couldn't leave without. It is absolutely wonderful when served with a topping of real whipped cream or ice cream.

CHOCOLATE SHEET CAKE

Juanita K. Parker
Ness City, KS

2 c. granulated sugar
2 c. all-purpose flour
4 Tbsp. cocoa powder
1 tsp. baking soda
1 tsp. cinnamon
1 c. water
½ c. buttermilk or sour milk
2 eggs

1 tsp. vanilla
1 c. butter or margarine
4 c. powdered sugar
1 c. walnuts, chopped
1 tsp. vanilla
½ c. margarine
¼ c. unsweetened cocoa powder
6 Tbsp. milk

Heat oven to 400°F. Grease and flour 15x10 inch jellyroll pan. In large bowl, combine sugar, flour, cocoa, baking soda, and cinnamon. In small saucepan, bring butter and water to a boil; stir into sugar mixture. Whisk in buttermilk (sour milk), eggs, and vanilla until thoroughly blended. Pour batter into prepared pan (batter will be thin). Bake 20 minutes or until toothpick inserted in center comes out clean. Prepare frosting in a large bowl; combine sugar and walnuts. In small saucepan, bring butter, cocoa, and milk to a boil. Stir into sugar mixture; blend thoroughly. Stir in vanilla. Spread on warm cake. Let cool, then cut into 24 pieces. Makes 24 servings.

CHOCOLATE WALNUT BISCOTTI

Natasha Bruning
Ellsworth, KS

½ c. (1 stick) margarine or butter
¾ c. sugar
2 eggs
1 tsp. vanilla
2 c. flour

1½ tsp. baking powder
¼ tsp. salt
4 sq. semi-sweet chocolate, chopped
1 c. walnuts, chopped

Heat oven to 325°F. Beat margarine and sugar until light and fluffy. Beat in eggs and vanilla. Mix flour, baking powder, and salt. Stir in chocolate and walnuts. Shape dough into 2 (14½ inch) slightly flattened logs. Place 2 inches apart on greased and floured cookie sheet. Bake 25 minutes or until lightly browned. Place on cutting board; cool 5 minutes. Cut each log into diagonal slices about ¾ inch thick. Place slices upright on cookie sheet ½ inch apart. Bake 10 minutes or until slightly dry. Cool on wire racks. Makes about 3 dozen.

I am 11 years old. My Aunt Connie helped me make this cookie, as I am just learning.

CHOCOLATE-TOFFEE FLAN CAKES

Coleen Koch
Summerfield, KS

2 flan pan layers
  chocolate cake
1½ c. marshmallow creme
2 Tbsp. milk

4 c. whipped topping
1 oz. Baker's chocolate
1 c. English toffee bars

Make cake layers according to cake mix directions. Invert layers on large round plate after baking. Cool. Mix marshmallow creme and milk together over low heat. Melt Baker's chocolate and mix into heated mixture. Cool slightly. Fold in whipped toping and ¾ cup chopped candy bar. Spread filling evenly in well of each flan layer. Garnish with extra chopped candy bar.

I use 6 Heath bars and mash them with a hammer before opening. Filling freezes well if you wish to make only one layer. This is a very rich dessert.

CINNAMON BARS

Debbie Hinman
Carter, SD

1¼ c. sugar
¾ c. brown sugar
2 c. sifted flour
½ c. butter
½ c. pecans, chopped
½ c. flaked coconut

1 egg
1 c. buttermilk
1 tsp. vanilla
¾ tsp. salt
1 tsp. cinnamon
1 tsp. baking soda

Mix together the sugar, brown sugar, and flour. Cut in the butter. To 2 cups of this, add the chopped pecans and coconut and press it into a 9x13 inch pan. Beat together the remaining ingredients and add the remaining flour mixture. Spread over the first layer and bake at 350°F. for 35 to 40 minutes. When cool, drizzle with powdered sugar icing.

CINNAMON ICE CREAM

Gwenda Batterman
Amarillo, TX

3 pt. half & half
½ pt. whipping cream
5 whole eggs
2 c. sugar

⅛ tsp. salt
1 Tbsp. vanilla
1 (9 oz.) pkg. cinnamon
  Red Hots candies

Beat eggs well. Mix remainder of ingredients with eggs. Store in refrigerator overnight. Re-stir. Pour into one gallon ice cream freezer and fill with milk to fill line. Freeze.

CLOUD NINE COOKIES

Juanita Gross
Clearwater, KS

1½ lb. white almond bark
1 c. peanut butter
  (chunky)

4 c. mini marshmallows
2 c. crisp rice cereal
1 c. pecans, chopped

In microwave, melt bark; stir in peanut butter. Add cereal, pecans, and marshmallows. Stir well to coat thoroughly. Drop by teaspoonfuls onto wax paper. Remove when cool.

CLUB CRACKER BARS

Rita Schiefelbein
Clear Lake, SD

⅔ c. white sugar
¼ c. brown sugar
1 stick butter
¼ c. milk
1 c. graham cracker
  crumbs

⅔ c. peanut butter
½ c. semi-sweet
  chocolate chips
½ c. butterscotch chips

Lightly butter bottom of 9x13 inch pan and line with layer of cracker crumbs. Using a heavy saucepan, bring filling to boil and boil for 5 minutes, stirring constantly so it does not burn. Pour over crackers, then top with another layer of crackers. To prepare frosting, melt ⅔ cup peanut butter, ½ cup semi-sweet chocolate chips, and ½ cup butterscotch chips. Spread on top of crackers. Cool in refrigerator and cut into cracker-size bars. Store in refrigerator, or these bars also freeze well.

COCONUT CARAMEL OAT COOKIES

Nanette Conger
Fairfield, IA

½ c. butter or margarine
½ c. milk
1 c. white sugar
1 tsp. vanilla extract

½ tsp. salt
25 caramels
3 c. quick-cooking oats
1 c. flaked coconut

In a heavy saucepan, bring butter or margarine and milk to a boil; add sugar, vanilla, and salt. Cook for 1 minute. Add caramels and stir until melted, about 4 minutes. Stir in oats and coconut. Drop by heaping tablespoonfuls onto waxed paper. Let stand until set. Makes 4 dozen cookies.

COCONUT CRANBERRY BARS

Arlyss Alexander
Clay Center, KS

1½ c. graham cracker
    crumbs (about 24)
½ c. margarine, melted
1½ c. vanilla or white
    chips

1½ c. cranberries, dried
1 can sweetened
    condensed milk
1 c. coconut, flaked
1 c. pecans, chopped

Combine cracker crumbs and margarine; press into a greased 13x9 inch baking pan. In a bowl, combine the remaining ingredients and mix well. Gently spread over the crust. Bake at 350°F. for 25 to 28 minutes or until edges are golden brown. Cool on a wire rack and cut into bars. Yields 3 dozen.

These are very delicious and easy to make.

COCONUT CREAM MERINGUE PIE

Maudie Burden
Centerview, MO

⅔ c. sugar
¼ c. cornstarch
¼ tsp. salt
2 c. milk
3 egg yolks, lightly beaten
1 c. flaked coconut, finely chopped
2 Tbsp. margarine
½ tsp. vanilla
3 egg whites
¼ tsp. cream of tartar
6 Tbsp. sugar
1 (9 inch) pastry shell, baked
½ c. coconut

In a saucepan, combine the sugar, cornstarch, and salt. Gradually stir in milk until smooth. Bring to a boil; cook and stir for 2 minutes or until thickened. Gradually stir 1 cup hot filling into egg yolks; return all to the pan, stirring constantly. Bring to a gentle boil; cook and stir for 2 minutes. Remove from the heat; stir in chopped coconut, margarine, and vanilla until margarine is melted. To prepare the meringue, in a mixing bowl, beat the egg whites on medium speed until foamy. Add cream of tartar; beat until soft peaks form. Gradually beat in sugar, 1 tablespoon at a time, on high until stiff peaks form. Pour hot filling into crust. Spread with meringue, sealing edges to crust. Sprinkle with flaked coconut. Bake at 350°F. for 13 to 15 minutes or until golden brown. Cool on a wire rack for 1 hour; chill for 1 to 2 hours before serving. Refrigerate leftovers. Yields 6 to 8 servings.

COCONUT CREAM PIE

Arlene Bontrager
Hutchinson, KS

3 c. milk
⅔ c. sugar
2 Tbsp. flour, rounded
2 Tbsp. cornstarch
3 eggs, separated
⅛ tsp. salt
1 Tbsp. butter
1 tsp. vanilla
½ tsp. coconut flavoring
¾ c. coconut
1 (9 inch) baked pie shell
1 Tbsp. cornstarch
½ c. water
3 egg whites
6 Tbsp. sugar
1 tsp. white vanilla
⅛ tsp. salt

Combine sugar, flour, cornstarch, and salt in medium size saucepan. Add milk slowly and stir. Stir in slightly beaten egg yolks. Cook over medium to low heat, stirring all the time until thickened. Cook for 2 minutes and remove from heat. Add butter and vanilla and stir in coconut. Pour into baked pie shell. Combine cornstarch and water. Cook until clear. Cool slightly. Beat egg whites and salt to soft rounded peaks. Add sugar gradually and continue beating at high speed until fairly stiff; add vanilla and salt. Add slightly warm cornstarch mixture to meringue and beat on high speed until very stiff; spoon into crust and seal edges. Garnish with a sprinkle of coconut over the top. Bake in oven at 375°F. until meringue is lightly browned. Let cool. Refrigerate pie.

COFFEE CAKE

Jacob Fangman
Hereford, TX

1 c. margarine
1¾ c. sugar
4 eggs
3 c. flour
2 tsp. baking powder

½ tsp. vanilla
1 (21 oz.) can cherry pie filling (or blueberry or apple)

Cream margarine and sugar. Add eggs, one at a time. Still using mixer, add flour, baking powder, and vanilla. Spread 1¼ cups batter in a greased 8x8 inch pan. Spread 1 cup of pie filling over batter; cover with 1¼ cups batter. Have oven preheated to 350°F; bake about 45 minutes. Makes two 8x8 inch coffee cakes.

COFFEE CHIP COOKIES

Janell Papke
Cortland, NE

1 c. shortening
2 c. brown sugar, packed
2 eggs
1 c. water (boiling)
2 Tbsp. instant coffee granules

4 c. all-purpose flour
2 tsp. baking powder
1 tsp. baking soda
3 c. (24 oz.) semi-sweet chocolate chips

In a mixing bowl, cream shortening and brown sugar. Add eggs, one at a time, beating well after each addition. Combine water and coffee; set aside. Combine flour, baking powder, and baking soda; add to creamed mixture alternately with coffee. Stir in chocolate chips. Refrigerate for 1 hour. Drop dough by rounded tablespoonful 2 inches apart onto greased baking sheet. Bake at 350°F. for 10 to 12 minutes or until golden around the edges. Remove to wire racks. Makes 3½ dozen.

CONNIE'S RICE PUDDING

NanCee Maynard
Box Elder, SD

½ c. sugar
1 Tbsp. cornstarch
2 large eggs, separated
2½ c. milk

1 Tbsp. lemon juice
½ c. raisins
1 c. instant rice
1 c. boiling water

Add 1 cup instant rice to 1 cup boiling water and let stand for 5 minutes. Heat oven to 350°F. Mix ½ cup sugar, cornstarch, and salt. Lightly beat the egg whites. Stir egg yolks into milk and add to the cornstarch mixture. Beat with mixer 1 minute. Fold in egg whites. Stir in rice, lemon juice, and raisins. Place ungreased 1½ quart baking dish into an empty cake pan. Pour rice mixture into baking dish and fill cake pan with boiling water 1 inch deep. Bake 90 minutes (stirring every 30 minutes) until pudding is creaming and most of liquid is absorbed. Add more water to cake pan as needed.

This is the creamiest rice pudding and so easy to make.

CRANBERRY DATE BARS

Charlotte Schmidt
Clintonville, WI

1 (12 oz.) bag cranberries
   (fresh or frozen)
1 (8 oz.) pkg. dates,
   chopped
5 Tbsp. water
1 tsp. vanilla extract
2 c. all-purpose flour

2 c. old-fashioned oats
1½ c. brown sugar,
   packed
½ tsp. baking soda
½ tsp. salt
1 c. butter, melted

In a covered saucepan over low heat, simmer cranberries, dates, and water for about 15 minutes, stirring often, until the cranberries have popped. Remove from the heat; stir in vanilla and set aside. In a large bowl, combine the flour, oats, brown sugar, baking soda, and salt. Stir in butter until well blended. Pat ½ into an ungreased 13x9 inch baking pan. Bake at 350°F. for 8 minutes. Spoon cranberry mixture over crust. Sprinkle with the remaining oat mixture. Pat gently. Bake at 350°F. for 25 to 30 minutes or until browned. Do not overbake.

This is one of my most requested recipes to make for family parties.

CRANBERRY PIE

Lynda Bozarth
Liberal, KS

1 (20 oz.) pkg. cranberries
2 c. water

2 c. sugar
2 pkg. unflavored gelatin

Cook cranberries in water until skins pop. Strain mixture in colander or food mill. Put strained juice in a saucepan and add sugar. Cook over medium heat about ten minutes, stirring constantly. Add gelatin that has been softened in ¼ cup cold water. Pour in a baked pie shell. Serve with sweetened whipped cream. This makes a 10 inch deep pie pan full.

CREAM PIE

Marilyn Barner
Belle Plaine, KS

1½ c. sugar (scant)
4 rounded Tbsp.
  cornstarch
3 egg yolks

3 Tbsp. margarine
3 c. milk (2% or whole)
1½ tsp. vanilla
⅛ tsp. salt

Mix sugar and cornstarch together in saucepan; add slightly beaten egg yolks and milk, vanilla, and salt. Cook over medium heat until boiling and thickened. Remove from heat and add margarine and stir until melted. Pour pie mixture into a 9 inch baked pie crust. Use egg whites to make meringue.

You can use this cream pie recipe to make banana pie and pineapple pie.

CREAM PUFF DESSERT

Glennys Bruning
Ellsworth, KS

1 c. water
1 c. flour, sifted
4 eggs
½ c. butter
¼ tsp. salt
2 (3 oz.) pkg. instant
  vanilla pudding

3½ c. milk
1 (8 oz.) pkg. cream
  cheese
1 (8 oz.) container
  whipped topping

Heat water and shortening in saucepan until boiling. Pour the flour and salt into hot mixture. Beat thoroughly; stir and cook over low heat until mixture forms a stiff ball. Remove from heat; add unbeaten eggs, one at a time, beating thoroughly after each egg is added (by hand). Spread on 11x15 inch cookie sheet, greased. Bake at 400°F. for 20 to 30 minutes until lightly browned. To prepare filling, mix together instant pudding, milk, and cream cheese. Spread on cream puff. Top with 8 ounces whipped topping. Refrigerate till set.

This is so easy and the cream puff base can be made ahead of time. You can drizzle chocolate syrup over the whipped topping. Makes an elegant looking dessert.

CREAMY COCONUT CAKE

Marilyn Scott
Van Buren, AR

1 box white cake mix
1 can sweetened
   condensed milk

1 can cream of coconut
1 pkg. whipped topping
1 pkg. coconut

Bake cake according to directions on box and allow to cool. Poke holes into cake with wooden spoon handle. Mix sweetened condensed milk and cream of coconut together, then pour into holes. Put whipped topping on cake and sprinkle with coconut. Keep refrigerated.

CREAMY FROSTING

Joshua Jecha
Timken, KS

1½ c. heavy cream
1½ c. sugar

1 tsp. vanilla

Mix cream and sugar together and cook to a soft ball stage at 240°F. Remove from heat and stir in vanilla. Stir until it becomes thick. Frost cake.

This takes some practice to get it just right.

DAD'S FAVORITE CARROT CAKE

Amy Edwards
Tulsa, OK

2 c. sugar
1 c. vegetable oil
4 eggs
2 c. flour
2 tsp. baking powder
2 tsp. baking soda
2 tsp. cinnamon
1 tsp. salt

3 c. grated carrots, packed
8 oz. cream cheese, softened
½ stick butter
1 lb. powdered sugar
1 tsp. vanilla
1 c. chopped pecans

Mix sugar and oil. Add eggs and beat well. Sift dry ingredients together and add to this mixture. Add carrots and mix well. Bake in two 7x11 inch round pans or one 13x9 inch (grease and flour pans). Bake for 35 minutes at 350°F. or until cake tests done. To make the icing, cream butter and cream cheese together. Mix in powdered sugar and vanilla and beat until fluffy. Stir in pecans and mix well. Frost cake when completely cooled.

Father's Day always comes during the wheat harvest season. We always make this cake to take to the field for my dad. It is his favorite!

DATE LOGS

Nanette Conger
Fairfield, IA

½ c. butter or margarine
1 c. white sugar
1 (large) egg
1 (8 oz.) pkg. dates, chopped

2½ c. Rice Krispies cereal
½ c. pecans, finely chopped
1 tsp. vanilla extract
Coconut

Melt butter or margarine; beat in sugar, egg, and dates. Cook, stirring constantly, 10 minutes or until dates are melted. Remove from heat; add Rice Krispies, nuts, and vanilla. Cool slightly. Using buttered hands, shape into 2 inch logs and roll in coconut. Cool completely. Makes 4 to 5 dozen cookies.

DELICIOUS APPLE CAKE

Donna L. Thorp
Kismet, KS

2 c. flour
2 c. sugar
1 tsp. baking soda
½ tsp. salt
1 tsp. vanilla
2 tsp. cinnamon
2 eggs
1 c. oil

1 c. pecans
4 c. apples, thinly sliced
2 (small) pkg. cream cheese
3 Tbsp. butter, melted
1 tsp. vanilla
1½ c. powdered sugar

Mix together flour, sugar, baking soda, salt, vanilla, cinnamon, eggs, oil, pecans, and apples with spoon. Do not use mixer. Batter will be stiff. Spread into floured and greased Bundt cake pan. Bake at 350°F. for 45 minutes. To prepare frosting, mix cream cheese, butter, vanilla, and powdered sugar. Spoon generously over top part of cake.

DEVIL'S FOOD PUDDING (SLOW-COOK)

Betty Mead
Paradise, KS

⅓ c. sugar
2 Tbsp. shortening
1 egg
1 (1 oz.) sq. unsweetened chocolate

1¼ c. flour
1 tsp. baking soda
½ c. buttermilk
½ tsp. vanilla

Cream sugar and shortening. Add egg; mix well. Beat in chocolate; stir together flour, baking soda, and pinch of salt. Add to creamed mixture alternately with buttermilk and vanilla; beat well. Divide into two well greased 16 ounce vegetable cans. Cover tightly with foil. Place in slow-cooker; pour ½ cup of warm water around cans. Cover; cook on high heat for 1½ hours. Remove cans; cool 10 minutes. Unmold. Yields two small round cakes to be sliced and served with a dip of ice cream or sauce.

DOODLE CAKE

Elizabeth Brattin Keever
Pierce City

2 c. flour
2 c. sugar
1½ c. crushed pineapple
(not drained)
2 eggs
1 tsp. baking soda

1 tsp. salt
1 c. sugar
⅔ c. evaporated milk
1½ c. coconut
½ to 1 c. nuts
1 stick butter

Combine flour, sugar, pineapple, eggs, and baking soda and mix well. Pour in greased and floured 9x13 inch pan. Bake at 350°F. for 30 minutes or until done. To prepare icing, mix remaining ingredients; bring to boil. Set aside until cake is baked. Pour over cake while cake is hot.

Better the second day if it lasts that long!

EASY CHERRY-PEACH DESSERT

Martha Ritter
Marquette, KS

1 (21 oz.) can cherry pie
filling
1 (29 oz.) can sliced
peaches, cut into
chunks

1 stick margarine
1 pkg. yellow cake mix
Cinnamon

Put cherry pie filling and peaches with half of peach juice in a 9x13 inch pan. Sprinkle cinnamon, to your liking, over all of fruit. Mix cake mix and margarine together until crumbly. Cover cherries and peaches with crumbly mixture. Bake at 350°F. for 30 to 45 minutes.

Serve with vanilla ice cream.

EASY FUDGE

Coleen Koch
Summerfield, KS

1 lb. processed American
cheese
1 lb. stick margarine
4 lb. powdered sugar

1 c. cocoa
1 lb. pecans
1 tsp. vanilla

Melt cheese and margarine together. Sift powdered sugar and cocoa together and gradually add to cheese-margarine mixture. Stir in vanilla and nuts. Spread in lightly buttered 9x13 inch pan to cool.

This makes a very smooth fudge with no cheesy taste.

ERMA'S COOKIES

Neva Jones
O'Neill, NE

36 vanilla caramels
3 Tbsp. half & half or
   cream
1 c. Corn Flakes, crushed
   slightly with your hands

1 c. crisp rice cereal
1 c. coconut
1 c. nuts

Melt the caramels in the half & half over very low heat. Remove from heat and add the Corn Flakes, crisp rice cereal, coconut, and nuts. Mix together and form in small balls, a little smaller than a walnut; cool and enjoy.

FAIR BROWNIES

Jenny Pachta
Belleville, KS

1½ c. oil
3 c. sugar
6 eggs
1½ tsp. vanilla

2¼ c. flour
¾ c. cocoa
1½ tsp. salt
½ c. nuts (optional)

Mix oil, sugar, eggs, and vanilla together. Add flour, cocoa, salt, and nuts. Combine well. Pour into a greased 10x15 inch pan. Bake at 350°F. for 20 minutes. Let cool and frost if desired.

FAVORITE CHOCOLATE CAKE

Glenda Adcock
Miami, TX

1 box German chocolate
   cake mix
¾ c. margarine, melted

1 (14 oz.) bag caramels
1 c. pecans
¼ c. evaporated milk

Mix cake according to directions on box. Pour ½ of the batter into a 9x13 inch coated cake pan. Bake 15 minutes at 350°F. While baking, melt caramels in the margarine and evaporated milk. Pour on the cake, sprinkle with the pecans, and pour the rest of the cake batter over the top. Bake another 20 minutes.

To please the chocoholic, add chocolate chips with the pecans, or frost the cake with chocolate icing.

FOUR LAYER PUDDING DESSERT

Christy Kleffner
Brinktown, MO

1 c. flour
1 stick butter, melted
2 c. chopped pecans
1 (8 oz.) pkg. cream
cheese
1 c. powdered sugar
2 (8 oz.) containers
whipped topping

1 pkg. chocolate instant
pudding
1 pkg. butterscotch
instant pudding
2½ to 3 c. milk
1 tsp. vanilla

Melt butter in a 9x12 inch pan. Mix in flour and ½ of the pecans and pat into the bottom. Bake for 15 minutes at 325°F. Let cool. Second layer: Beat cream cheese, powdered sugar, and 1 package of whipped topping together. Spread over first layer and let cool. Third layer: While second layer is cooling, mix puddings, milk, and vanilla. Spread over second layer and refrigerate. Fourth layer: Spread second package of whipped topping over top and sprinkle with the rest of the pecans. Refrigerate.

FREEZER PIE CRUST

Carol Price
Cordell, OK

5 lb. all-purpose flour
1 Tbsp. salt
3 lb. shortening

1 c. white corn syrup
2¾ c. water

In large bowl, blend flour and salt. Cut in shortening. Add corn syrup and water. Knead lightly to mix well. Divide into 20 equal sized balls (about 8 ounces each) and place each in a sandwich bag. Store in larger freezer bag in freezer until ready to use. Take out as needed, thaw in microwave for 30 seconds, and roll out a single pie crust.

FRUITY CONFETTI CAKE

Shana Lambert
Palco, KS

1 box vanilla cake mix   **1 c. Trix cereal**

Mix cake mix as directed. Add crushed Trix cereal into mix; blend well. Bake as directed on box. Frost if desired. Can also be baked into cupcakes.

Quick and easy cake for kids.

FUDGE BARS

Karen Sysel
Dorchester, NE

1 (18 oz.) pkg. white cake mix (dry)
2 eggs
⅓ c. oil
1 (14 oz.) can sweetened condensed milk

1 c. semi-sweet chocolate chips
¼ c. margarine, cut into small pieces

Preheat oven to 350°F. Combine dry cake mix, eggs, and oil. With floured hands, press ⅔ of cake mixture into greased 13x9 inch baking pan. In microwave-safe bowl, microwave sweetened condensed milk, chocolate chips, and butter 45 seconds; stir. Microwave another 45 seconds longer; stir until chips are completely melted and mixture is smooth. Pour over top of chocolate layer. Bake at 350°F. for 20 to 25 minutes or until lightly browned. Cool. Cut into bars.

GEORGIA BOZARTH'S BANANA ICE CREAM

Lucille Fuller
Wichita, KS

2½ c. sugar
1 ctn. (equal to 4 eggs) Egg Beaters
2 pt. half & half
1 (12 oz.) can evaporated milk

6 Tbsp. lemon juice
3 ripe bananas
Orange juice

In large mixer bowl, beat together the sugar and Egg Beaters; add half & half and milk, then lemon juice. Pour into the container for 1 gallon ice cream freezer. Add bananas, sliced thin. Fill to freezing level with orange juice and freeze in usual manner.

GERDIE TAMTOM'S OATMEAL COOKIES
Glennys Bruning
Ellsworth, KS

1 c. shortening	1 tsp. salt
1 c. brown sugar	2 tsp. baking soda
1 c. white sugar	1 tsp. cinnamon
2 eggs	2 c. oatmeal
1 tsp. vanilla	1 c. raisins, soaked 1 hour
2½ c. flour	1 c. nuts (optional)

Cream shortening and sugars; add eggs. Sift flour, baking soda, salt, and cinnamon together and add to creamed mixture. Add oatmeal and raisins (nuts if desired). Bake in 350°F. oven for 8 to 10 minutes. Cookies will be soft.

GINGER COOKIES
Julie Schmidt
Smith Center, KS

¾ c. shortening	2 tsp. baking soda
1 c. white sugar	1 tsp. cinnamon
4 Tbsp. molasses	¾ tsp. ground cloves
1 egg	¾ tsp. ginger
2 c. flour	⅛ tsp. salt

Cream shortening and sugar; add molasses and egg. In a separate bowl mix remaining ingredients and gradually add to cream mixture, beating well. Roll in small balls and roll in sugar. Bake at 375° for 7 to 8 minutes. Makes 2 dozen cookies.

These are so soft and yummy! I had only eaten ginger cookies from the store and they don't even compare to these.

GINGERSNAP PUMPKIN PIE

Jean Lorenz
Sanford, CO

1 (9 inch) graham cracker crust
1½ c. half & half
1 (3.4 oz.) pkg. instant butterscotch pudding
1 (8 oz.) container whipped topping, thawed
1 c. pecans or walnuts, chopped
1 c. gingersnap cookies, crumbled
2 tsp. pumpkin pie spice

Beat half & half and pudding mix in large mixing bowl with wire whisk for 1 minute. Let stand 5 minutes. Fold in whipped topping and remaining ingredients. Spoon into graham cracker crust. Freeze until firm. Let stand at room temperature 10 minutes before serving. Store in freezer.

GLAZED APPLE COOKIES

Charlene Fry
Burlingame, KS

½ c. margarine
1⅓ c. brown sugar
1 egg (unbeaten)
1 tsp. vanilla
¼ c. milk
2½ c. flour
1 Tbsp. cinnamon
1 tsp. baking soda
½ tsp. salt
1 tsp. cloves
½ tsp. nutmeg
1 c. raisins
1 c. apples, peeled and chopped
1 c. nuts, chopped
1½ c. powdered sugar
1 Tbsp. vanilla
2 Tbsp. margarine
2½ Tbsp. milk

To prepare cookie dough, cream margarine and sugar. Add egg and vanilla. Sift flour, cinnamon, baking soda, salt, cloves, and nutmeg together. Add alternately with milk. Stir in nuts, apples, and raisins. Drop by teaspoonful on greased cookie sheet. Bake 8 to 10 minute at 375°F. To prepare glaze, mix together powdered sugar, vanilla, margarine, and milk. Brush this glaze on cookies.

These cookies are very tasty and moist.

GRAHAM CRACKER CAKE

Marjorie Abell
Grinnell, Ks

½ c. shortening
1 c. sugar
3 eggs, separated
1 c. (scant) milk
23 graham crackers

2 tsp. baking powder
1 c. nuts (any kind you
 prefer)
½ tsp. salt

Cream shortening and sugar together; beat the yolks until light and add to sugar mixture. Add the milk. Roll the crackers fine. Mix baking powder with cracker crumbs and add this to the other mixture together with salt and chopped nuts. Last, fold in the beaten egg whites. Bake in 2 layers in 375° to 400°F. oven. For extra large 3 layer cake, double recipe.

GRAHAM CRACKER COOKIES

Ruthye DeWald
Bazine, KS

Graham crackers (whole)
½ to ¾ c. pecans or
 walnuts, chopped

1 stick margarine
½ c. sugar

Line a 10x15 inch cookie sheet with foil. Place whole graham crackers on foil. Sprinkle chopped pecans on graham crackers. Put margarine and sugar in saucepan; bring to a boil on medium heat. Boil for 3 minutes. Stir occasionally. Pour over nuts and graham crackers. Bake 10 minutes at 350°F. Cool and break into pieces.

GRANDKIDS CHOICE
THANKSGIVING CAKE

Euda Switcher
Oklahoma City, OK

2 c. graham crackers,
 crushed
1 c. pecans, chopped
¼ c. butter, softened
2 c. sugar
1 (16 oz.) can pumpkin
1 c. vegetable oil
3 (large) eggs
2½ c. flour
1 tsp. salt

2 tsp. baking soda
2 tsp. baking powder
2 tsp. cinnamon
3 c. powdered sugar
½ c. butter, softened
1 (3 oz.) pkg. cream
 cheese
1 tsp. vanilla
½ c. caramel ice cream
 topping

In large mixer bowl, combine graham cracker crumbs, pecans, and butter. Beat at medium speed until crumbly. Grease and flour 3 round 8 inch cake pans. Press mixture evenly on bottom of pans. In same bowl, combine sugar, pumpkin, oil, and eggs. Beat 1 minute at medium speed. Combine flour, salt, baking powder, baking soda, and cinnamon. Add to pumpkin mixture. Beat at medium speed for 3 minutes. Spread batter over crumb mixture in pans. Bake at 350°F. for 30 to 35 minutes or until wooden pick inserted in center comes out clean. Invert on wire rack and cool. Spread with caramel icing. To prepare icing, mix powdered sugar, butter, cream cheese, and vanilla. Place 1 layer of cake, nut side down, on serving plate; spread with ½ cup of icing. Place next layer on top of first layer, using another ½ cup of icing, then third layer. With the remaining icing, frost sides of cake. Drizzle caramel topping over top of cake and let some run down side of cake.

My grandchildren voted this their favorite dessert at Thanksgiving.

GRANDMA BOZARTH'S MAHOGANY CAKE

Lynda Bozarth
Liberal, KS

⅔ c. shortening
2 c. sugar
3 eggs
1 c. buttermilk, plus 3 Tbsp. buttermilk, divided
1 Tbsp. baking soda
1 tsp. vanilla

1¾ c. flour
½ c. hot coffee
½ c. cocoa
⅓ c. butter
⅔ c. brown sugar
3 Tbsp. milk
1 c. powdered sugar

Dissolve cocoa in hot coffee and set aside to cool. Mix baking soda in the 3 tablespoons of buttermilk; set aside. Cream shortening and sugar. Add beaten eggs. Add flour and the 1 cup buttermilk alternately. Mix in the soda with buttermilk, then add the chocolate coffee mixture and vanilla. Bake in a 9x12 inch pan at 350°F. for about 30 minutes or until tests done. To prepare the caramel frosting, mix ⅓ cup butter, ⅔ cup brown sugar, 3 tablespoons milk, and 1 cup powdered sugar. Melt butter in saucepan. Stir in brown sugar. Boil and stir over low heat 2 minutes. Stir in milk; bring to a boil, stirring constantly. Cool to lukewarm.

GRANDMA BOZARTH'S RAW APPLE CAKE

Diane Davis Reed
Parkville, MO

1 c. sugar
1 large egg
⅓ c. shortening
1 c. flour
1 tsp. cinnamon
1 tsp. baking soda

¼ tsp. nutmeg
¼ tsp. cloves
1 tsp. salt (optional)
2 c. apples (raw), peeled
  and diced

Cream together sugar, egg, and shortening. Sift together flour, cinnamon, baking soda, nutmeg, cloves, and salt. Add apples. Gradually add apple mixture to first mixture. Bake in greased, floured pan at 350°F. for 45 minutes. Serve plain or with whipped cream or ice cream. Baking time varies according to how much moisture there is in the apples. Cake is done when it has an even glaze over the top.

GRANDMA'S BROWNIE SHEET CAKE

Kim Oborny
Durham, KS

2 c. flour
2 c. sugar
1 c. margarine
4 Tbsp. cocoa
1 c. water
½ c. milk
2 eggs
1 tsp. baking soda
½ tsp. cinnamon

1 tsp. vinegar
1 tsp. vanilla
½ c. margarine
4 Tbsp. cocoa
6 Tbsp. milk
1 lb. powdered sugar
1 tsp. vanilla
1 c. pecans or walnuts
  (optional)

In a bowl, combine flour and sugar. Bring to a boil margarine, cocoa, and water and pour this over the sugar and flour mixture. Add milk, eggs, baking soda, cinnamon, vinegar, and vanilla; mix well and pour into greased pan (makes a large sheet cake). Bake at 350°F. for 30 minutes. To prepare the icing, start 5 minutes before the cake is done. Melt and bring to a boil margarine, cocoa, and milk. Remove from heat and add powdered sugar and vanilla; beat well. Add nuts, if you desire, and spread over cake while still hot.

Icing can be a little thick.

GRANDMA'S BUTTERMILK COOKIES

Arlene Bontragler
Hutchinson, KS

1¾ c. sugar
¾ c. lard
3 eggs
¼ tsp. salt
1 tsp. vanilla
¾ c. cream

1 tsp. baking soda, dissolved in 1 Tbsp. hot water
¾ c. buttermilk
5 c. flour (approx.)
3 tsp. baking powder

Cream together in large bowl the sugar and lard; add eggs, salt, and vanilla. Combine flour and baking powder in bowl; set aside. Combine cream and buttermilk with baking soda and water; add alternately with flour mixture. Roll out and cut with cookie cutter and place on greased cookie sheet. Sprinkle cookies with sugar before baking. Bake about 8 minutes in 375°F. oven.

I have also dropped the dough by tablespoon and press with glass dipped in sugar. Grandma Wiens would always have these cookies for us when we would go to see them.

GRANDMA'S SURPRISE-BURNT SUGAR BUNDT CAKE

Maxine Mai
Lenora, KS

⅓ c. granulated sugar
¼ c. warm water
2 sticks margarine
2⅔ c. granulated sugar
1 (8 oz.) pkg. cream cheese (room temperature)
1 egg

⅛ tsp. salt
⅓ c. granulated sugar
½ c. English toffee bits
5 (large) eggs
¼ tsp. salt
1 tsp. vanilla
3 c. flour
¾ c. cola soft drink

Place ⅓ cup sugar in small pan and heat, stirring constantly, until it is dark golden brown. Take off burner; keep stirring for 2 minutes. Add warm water; heat again, stirring until you have a burnt sugar syrup. Set aside and let cool. Place butter and 2⅔ cups sugar in a mixing bowl; cream until white. While this is creaming, place cream cheese, egg, salt, and ⅓ cup sugar in a separate bowl and beat together. Add toffee bits; stir again. Set aside. Add to the creamed butter and sugar mixture the following ingredients, beating after each ingredient is added: Eggs (one at a time), salt, burnt sugar syrup, vanilla, flour, and cola. Place ⅔ of the batter into a well greased and floured 12 cup Bundt pan. Place the cream cheese toffee bit mixture by the teaspoonful into the middle of the batter in a complete circle. Finish placing the rest of the cake batter evenly over the filling. Bake 1 hour and 15 minutes at 325°F. Let stand in pan for 5 minutes before inverting onto serving platter. Sprinkle powdered sugar over the cake.

The filling is the surprise when the cake is cut. This recipe has never failed while burnt sugar layer cakes many times fall frequently. It was grandmother's favorite cake flavor.

GRAPE TAPIOCA

Thelma Maxwell
Dodge City, KS

¼ c. quick tapioca
¼ c. sugar
⅛ tsp. salt
2½ c. grape juice, frozen
  and diluted, or canned
  grape juice

1 Tbsp. lemon juice

Combine tapioca, sugar, and salt in saucepan; add juice and cook to a boil. Add lemon juice and cool. Serve plain or with ice cream or whipped topping.

Delicious and very quick. Other fruit juices may be used. I usually double this recipe as it keeps well in refrigerator to use later.

HAWAIIAN PIE

Ruthe Zimmerman
Tunas, MO

1 (20 oz.) can crushed
  pineapple
1 c. cold water
1 c. coconut
½ c. sugar

⅛ tsp. salt
3 Tbsp. cornstarch
2 eggs
¾ tsp. coconut flavor
  (optional)

In a 3 quart saucepan, mix pineapple, water, coconut, sugar, salt, and cornstarch, then carefully separate the eggs. Add the yolks to the ingredients in the saucepan. Beat the egg whites until stiff or peaks form; set aside. Cook the mixture in the saucepan until thick, stirring constantly. Fold the egg whites into the hot mixture, then add the coconut flavoring and mix well. Pour into a prepared pie crust and sprinkle with extra coconut. This will fill a 9 inch pie pan, nicely rounded.

The original name is Hawaii Food Pie.

HERSHEY CAKE

Rochelle Fangman
Hereford, TX

8 (1.55 oz.) plain
  Hershey's candy bars
2 c. sugar
2 sticks margarine
4 eggs
1 c. buttermilk

2 tsp. vanilla
¼ tsp. salt
2½ c. flour
⅛ tsp. baking soda
1 c. pecans (optional)

Melt candy. Cream margarine and sugar. Add eggs, one at a time, and cream well after each. Add candy and vanilla. Add buttermilk and soda alternately with flour and salt. Do not overbeat. Bake in tube pan or loaf pans at 300°F. for approximately 1 hour and 25 minutes.

One cup of pecans may be added if desired. Cake is moist.

HONEY COOKIES

Gladys Wilkerson
Tuttle, OK

½ c. shortening
1 c. sugar
2 Tbsp. honey
2 eggs

2 c. flour
1 tsp. baking soda
1 tsp. vanilla
Pecan halves or pieces

Cream shortening, sugar, honey, and eggs. Add flour, baking soda, and vanilla. Top with pecans. Bake 10 to 12 minutes in 350°F. oven. Take from oven while still soft; overcooking is not good.

HONEY PUMPKIN CAKE

Ann V. Gallentine
Clayton, KS

1⅔ c. flour
½ c. honey
2 pkg. artificial sweetener
1 tsp. baking soda
½ tsp. salt
½ c. water

⅓ c. cooking oil
1 tsp. vinegar
½ tsp. allspice
½ tsp. cinnamon
½ c. canned pumpkin

Mix all together. Bake in a greased 8x8 inch pan at 325°F. for 40 minutes or until done.

This is nice for people who can't have sugar.

JAPANESE FRUIT PIE

Marilyn Scott
Van Buren, AR

½ c. raisins
½ c. coconut
½ c. pecans
1 c. sugar

2 eggs
1 stick margarine
1 tsp. vanilla
1 pie crust

Cream together margarine and sugar. Mix well. Add other ingredients and blend together. Pour into unbaked pie crust. Bake 30 minutes at 350°F.

KARSYNN'S CRAZY CARROT CAKE

Kim Robinson
Dexter, NM

2 c. sugar
¾ c. buttermilk
¾ c. cooking oil
3 eggs
2 tsp. vanilla
2 c. all-purpose flour
2 tsp. baking soda
½ tsp. salt
2 tsp. cinnamon
2 c. carrots, grated

1 c. pecans, chopped
1 (8 oz.) can crushed
  pineapple
1 (3 oz.) can flaked
  coconut
1 pkg. cream cheese
1¼ c. butter
1½ c. powdered sugar
½ tsp. vanilla

Mix together the sugar, buttermilk, oil, eggs, and vanilla. Add and mix well flour, baking soda, salt, and cinnamon. Next, add grated carrots, chopped pecans, drained pineapple, and coconut until mixed thoroughly. Using a 9x13 inch pan, lightly spray with vegetable spray and flour. Bake in a 350°F. preheated oven for 45 to 50 minutes. Let cool completely. To prepare frosting, Mix together thoroughly the room temperature cream cheese, butter, powdered sugar, and vanilla. Spread evenly over cooled cake and keep refrigerated.

LEMON BARS

Pat Stutz
Utica, KS

1 box Angel food cake
  mix

1 (24 oz.) can lemon pie
  filling

Prepare cake mix according to directions. Mix gently by hand the pie filling and cake mix. Pour into 10½ x 15½ inch pan. Bake at 350°F. for 20 to 25 minutes.

Very simple, but very good.

LEMON CHESS BUTTERMILK PIE

Sandra Hicks Chrane
Abilene, TX

3 c. sugar
2½ Tbsp. flour
6 eggs
1 stick margarine or
  butter

1⅓ c. buttermilk
⅛ tsp. salt
1 tsp. lemon flavoring

Mix melted margarine, sugar, eggs, flour, and salt. Add buttermilk and lemon flavoring. Pour into unbaked pie shells. Bake at 350°F. for 45 minutes. Yields two 9 inch pies.

I have won 4 blue ribbons with this pie.

LEMON LUSH

Beth Zucker
Bucyrus, OH

2 sticks butter
2 c. flour
1 c. nuts
2 (8 oz.) pkg. cream
  cheese, softened

2 c. powdered sugar
2 c. whipped topping
2 (small) pkg. instant
  lemon pudding
3 c. milk

First layer: Mix together butter, flour, and nuts and pat in the bottom of 9x13 inch buttered pan. Bake at 400°F. for 15 to 20 minutes. Second layer: Blend together cream cheese and powdered sugar. Fold into cheese and sugar mixture. Third layer: Mix together lemon pudding and milk. Top with whipped topping and nuts; refrigerate until cool.

Can vary pudding flavor.

LEMON SHEET CAKE

Julie Schmidt
Smith Center, KS

1 (18¼ oz.) pkg. lemon
 cake mix
4 eggs
1 (15¾ oz.) can lemon pie
 filling
1 (3 oz.) pkg. cream
 cheese, softened

½ c. butter or margarine,
 softened
2 c. confectioners sugar
1½ tsp. vanilla extract

In a large mixing bowl, beat the cake mix and eggs until well blended. Fold in pie filling. Spread into a greased 15x10x1 inch baking pan. Bake at 350°F. for 18 to 20 minutes or until a toothpick inserted near the center comes out clean. Cool on a wire rack. In a small mixing bowl, beat cream cheese, butter, and confectioners sugar until smooth. Stir in vanilla. Spread over cake. Store in the refrigerator. Yield: 30 to 35 servings.

LIGHT AND CREAMY CHEESECAKE

Kay Willoughby
Houston, TX

2 (8 oz.) pkg. cream
 cheese
¾ c. sugar, divided
 between egg whites
 and cream cheese
 mixture

4 eggs, separated
¼ c. sour cream
½ tsp. lemon zest
 (optional)
1 tsp. vanilla

Start water boiling for water bath baking. Soften cream cheese in microwave at low power for 1 minute. Separate eggs. Whip egg whites and add ¼ cup sugar, one tablespoon at a time. Mix together cream cheese, egg yolks, sugar, and sour cream. When it is smooth and well blended, add egg white mixture. Mix until blended. Add vanilla. Pour into foil covered pan and put this pan in larger pan for water bath. Bake at 500°F. for 12 minutes and then at 200°F. for 50 minutes.

LITTLE CRISPIE COOKIES

Barbara Koelling
Paradise, KS

1 box cake mix (if
   chocolate, add 3 Tbsp.
   water)

1 stick margarine
1 egg
1 c. Rice Krispies cereal

Melt margarine. Beat egg. Mix everything and roll in balls. Place on ungreased cookie sheet and bake at 350°F. for 9 to 12 minutes or till edges are golden brown.

MAKES ITS OWN CRUST COCONUT PIE

Beverly Long
Lowry City, MO

4 eggs
1½ c. sugar
½ c. flour
¼ c. butter, melted

2 c. milk
1½ c. coconut
1 tsp. vanilla

Combine ingredients in order given and mix well. Pour in greased pie pan and bake at 350°F. for 45 minutes or until golden brown. This will be soft in the middle.

MARSHMALLOW ICE CREAM

Julie Schmidt
Smith Center, KS

6 eggs
2 c. sugar
1 pt. jar marshmallow
   creme
1½ Tbsp. vanilla

1 pt. whipping cream
1 pt. half & half
1 to 2 drops lemon
   flavoring (optional)

Beat eggs with sugar, marshmallow creme, vanilla, and lemon flavorings. Add whipping cream and half & half. Pour into 1 gallon ice cream freezer and freeze as directed.

This is our family's favorite homemade ice cream. My son who is 10 especially loves it and wonders why we ever have to buy ice cream at the store again!

MAYONNAISE CAKE AND FROSTING

Alice P. Boehme
Mullinville, KS

2 c. flour
1 c. sugar
⅓ c. cocoa
⅛ tsp. salt
2 tsp. baking soda
1 c. mayonnaise
1 c. lukewarm water

1 tsp. vanilla
1 box powdered sugar
¼ c. butter
½ c. cocoa
1 tsp. vanilla
2 Tbsp. milk
2 Tbsp. coffee

Sift dry ingredients. Add mayonnaise and water. Stir well. Add vanilla. Pour batter into a greased and floured 9x13 inch cake pan. Bake at 350°F. for 25 minutes. Prepare frosting by mixing together powdered sugar, butter, cocoa, vanilla, milk, and coffee. Spread on cake when cool.

MELT-IN-YOUR-MOUTH PEANUT BUTTER COOKIES

Barb Kasel
Adams, MN

2½ c. flour
1 tsp. baking soda
1 tsp. salt
1 c. shortening (½ c. shortening and ½ c. softened butter or margarine)

1 c. brown sugar
1 c. white sugar
1 c. peanut butter
2 eggs, beaten
2 Tbsp. water
1 tsp. vanilla

Mix flour, baking soda, and salt. Set aside. Cream shortening and sugars. Add peanut butter. Add eggs, water, and vanilla. Add flour mixture; mix well. Make into balls and press with fork. Bake at 350°F. for 10 to 12 minutes.

Everybody loves these delicious peanut butter cookies.

MICROWAVE PEANUT PATTIES

Almeta Stowe
Blair, OK

2½ c. sugar
1 c. Milnot brand milk
2½ to 3 c. raw peanuts
⅔ c. white syrup
⅛ tsp. salt

4 Tbsp. butter
Few drops of red food
  coloring
½ tsp. vanilla
1½ c. powdered sugar

Microwave sugar, Milnot, peanuts, white syrup, and salt on high 18½ minutes, stirring every 3 to 4 minutes. Add butter, few drops of red food color, vanilla, and powdered sugar. Drop by tablespoon on wax paper or greased cookie sheet.

This is a family tradition during peanut harvest.

MILE HIGH PIE

Kelly Larson
Marquette, KS

1¼ c. flour
⅓ c. brown sugar
½ c. butter, melted
½ c. nuts, chopped
  (optional)
1 (10 oz.) pkg.
  strawberries, partly
  thawed, sliced

1¼ c. sugar
2 egg whites
1 (9 oz.) container
  whipped topping

Mix together flour, brown sugar, and butter; bake in an 8x8 inch shallow pan. Bake 20 minutes. Stir twice while baking. When baked, pack into 9x13 inch pan. While it is warm, save some crumbs for topping (approximately ¼ cup). Let cool after packing into pan. To prepare filling, beat egg whites and sugar at high speed for 5 minutes. Add strawberries and continue to beat at high speed for another 10 minutes. Add whipped topping and stir in very well. Pour strawberry mixture on top of packed crumbs and top with remaining crumbs, then freeze it for 1 hour or until ready to serve.

Keeps in freezer nicely for a week. My family thinks this dessert tastes like strawberry ice cream.

MILK CHOCOLATE BROWNIES

Tracy Vonderschmidt
Leona, KS

½ c. margarine
2 c. sugar
1½ c. flour
½ c. cocoa

¼ tsp. salt
4 eggs
2 tsp. vanilla

Melt margarine in a saucepan. Pour into a mixing bowl. Add sugar, flour, cocoa, salt, eggs, and vanilla. Mix on low to medium speed until well blended. Pour into a greased 13x9 inch baking pan. Bake at 350°F. for 25 minutes or until a toothpick comes out clean.

I have been making this dessert ever since I was old enough to bake. It mixes up quickly and works great for potlucks on last minute notice.

MILK CHOCOLATE BROWNIES

Barbara Koelling
Paradise, KS

½ c. margarine
2 c. sugar
1½ c. sifted flour
½ c. cocoa

¼ tsp. salt
4 eggs
2 tsp. vanilla
1 c. nuts, chopped

Melt butter in saucepan. Add sugar, flour, cocoa, salt, eggs, and vanilla. Mix well. Stir in nuts. Bake in greased 13x9x2 inch pan. Bake at 350°F. for 25 minutes.

MISTAKE PIE

Ashley Sippel
Ellsworth, KS

1 (small) can crushed
  pineapple
1 (8 oz.) container
  whipped topping

1 (3 oz.) pkg. instant
  vanilla pudding
Graham cracker crust
Nuts (optional)

Fold ingredients together and pour into pie crust. Chill and serve.

My aunt made this pie and goofed on one of the ingredients, but we couldn't remember what it was. I liked it the way she made it, and I always ask for it on my birthday.

MOCK GERMAN CHOCOLATE CAKE

Thelma Baldock
Delphos, KS

1 (18.25 oz.) box white cake mix
1 pkg. instant chocolate pudding (dry)
1 Tbsp. oil
2 eggs
2 c. milk
1 tsp. vanilla
1 c. evaporated milk
3 egg yolks, beaten
1 tsp. vanilla
1 c. pecans, chopped
1 c. sugar
½ c. butter
1⅓ c. coconut

Combine ingredients; beat well for 3 minutes. Pour into oiled 9x13 inch pan. Bake at 350°F. for 40 to 50 minutes. To prepare frosting, combine evaporated milk, egg yolks, 1 teaspoon vanilla, sugar, and butter. In saucepan cook until thick, stirring constantly. Remove from heat. Stir in coconut and nuts. Beat and spread on cake.

MOM'S OATMEAL CAKE

Phylis Carlson
Clarinda, IA

1 c. oatmeal (quick)
1 stick margarine
1¼ c. boiling water
1⅓ c. flour
1 tsp. baking soda
1 tsp. cinnamon
1 tsp. nutmeg
1 c. brown sugar
1 c. white sugar
2 eggs
6 Tbsp. melted butter
¼ c. cream
½ c. sugar
½ tsp. vanilla
1 c. coconut
1 c. nuts, chopped

Pour boiling water over the oatmeal; let stand while mixing other ingredients. Mix margarine, boiling water, flour, baking soda, cinnamon, nutmeg, brown sugar, white sugar, and eggs; add oatmeal last. Bake at 350°F. for 25 minutes in 9x13 inch pan. To prepare the frosting, boil butter, cream, sugar, and vanilla and add 1 cup coconut and 1 cup chopped nutmeats. Spread over cake and put under broiler.

Evaporated milk may be used instead of cream.

MONDAY NIGHT DELIGHT

Keith Mueller
Halstead, KS

2 c. Oreo chocolate
   sandwich cookies,
   crushed
¼ c. sugar
½ c. margarine, melted
1 (8 oz.) pkg. cream
   cheese, softened
¼ c. sugar

1 (12 oz.) container
   whipped topping,
   divided in half
4 Skor candy bars,
   crushed and divided
2 (small) boxes instant
   chocolate pudding
3 c. milk

Mix crushed Oreos, ¼ cup sugar, and ½ cup melted margarine. Press into ungreased 13x9 inch pan for crust. Mix cream cheese, ¼ cup sugar, and ½ of whipped topping with an electric mixer until smooth. Place this mixture on top of Oreo crust. On top of the cream cheese mixture, spread 2 crushed Skor candy bars. (These crush better if cold.) Mix instant chocolate pudding with 3 cups of milk. Stir and spread on top of crushed candy bars. Add the remaining 6 ounces of whipped topping on top of pudding. Spread the 2 remaining crushed candy bars on top of whipped topping. Refrigerate until set.

MOTHER'S PINEAPPLE HONEYMOON CAKE

Sandra Chrane
Abilene, TX

2 c. flour
1¼ c. sugar
3¼ tsp. baking powder
½ c. shortening
¾ c. plus 2 Tbsp. milk
1½ tsp. vanilla
3 eggs

1 (large) can crushed
   pineapple filling
   (undrained)
1 (heaping) c. sugar
4 Tbsp. butter
1 Tbsp. cornstarch
¼ c. water

Sift together flour, sugar, and baking powder; add shortening, milk, and vanilla. Beat 2 minutes. Add eggs and beat 2 minutes. Bake at 350°F. for 25 minutes in three 9 inch layer cake pans. To make the pineapple filling, heat pineapple, sugar, and butter in a saucepan. Combine cornstarch and water; stir into other ingredients. Cook until it turns clear. Frost between layers and top of cake.

This recipe is over 100 years old.

MRS. STOVER'S FUDGE

Glennys Bruning
Ellsworth, KS

4 c. sugar
1 can Carnation milk
½ lb. butter
2 (12 oz.) pkg. chocolate
   bits

1 pt. marshmallow creme
1 c. nuts
1 tsp. vanilla

Boil sugar, milk, and butter to a firm ball. Stir constantly. Remove and stir in chocolate bits, marshmallow creme, nuts, and vanilla. Pour into dish. Cool.

NANNY'S BUTTERMILK POUND CAKE

Cindy Woody
Blooming Grove, TX

6 egg whites
3 c. sugar
1 c. shortening
6 egg yolks
3 c. flour

¼ tsp. baking soda
¼ tsp. salt
1 c. buttermilk
2 Tbsp. vanilla or lemon
   extract

Preheat oven to 350°F. Beat egg whites stiff, but not dry. Set aside. Cream sugar and shortening. Add egg yolks gradually. Sift together flour, salt, and baking soda. Add these dry ingredients alternately with buttermilk and vanilla or lemon. Fold egg whites in thoroughly, but do not beat. Pour into a greased and floured tube pan. Bake about 1 hour or until a toothpick inserted in the middle comes out clean.

This is a heavy, moist pound cake like your grandmother used to bake. We eat it hot with butter or strawberries and whipped cream.

NEVER FAIL PIE CRUST

Arlene Bontrager
Hutchinson, KS

3 c. flour
1 tsp. salt
1¼ c. shortening (or 1 c.
   lard)

1 egg, well beaten
5 Tbsp. cold water
1 Tbsp. white vinegar

Cut shortening into flour and salt until well blended. Combine egg, vinegar, and water in small bowl. Pour liquid into flour mixture all at once. Mix until all flour is moistened and forms a ball. Handle lightly. Roll out; makes 2 to 3 single crusts for pie.

Makes a flakier crust if lard is used. Will keep in refrigerator for several days. I like to fill several pie plates and store in freezer until needed.

NO BAKE CHIPS AHOY PIE
Bobbi Higgs
Ulysses, KS

1 prepared graham
  cracker crust
1 can sweetened
  condensed milk

1 pkg. Chips Ahoy
  chocolate chip cookies
1 (small) container
  whipped topping

In blender mix 1 can sweetened condensed milk, 1 carton whipped topping, and 10 broken Chips Ahoy cookies. Mix in blender till mixed and the cookies are broken small. Scoop into prepared graham cracker crust. With remaining cookies, crush with rolling pin and sprinkle on top of pie. Let refrigerate 2 hours and enjoy.

OATMEAL CHOCOLATE CHIP COOKIES
Donna L. Thorp
Kismet, KS

1 c. real butter
1 c. sugar
1 c. brown sugar
2 eggs
½ tsp. vanilla

1¾ c. flour
1 tsp. baking soda
1 tsp. cinnamon
3 c. old-fashioned oats
1 bag chocolate chips

Cream sugar and butter together; add egg and vanilla. Mix flour, baking soda, cinnamon, and oats. Add chocolate chips. Bake at 350°F. for 10 to 12 minutes.

Use the real butter and old-fashioned oats; that makes them taste like the cookies Grandma used to make.

OATMEAL PIE (POOR MAN PECAN PIE)

Betty Mead
Paradise, KS

1 unbaked 9 inch pie shell
¾ c. sugar
¾ c. corn syrup
¾ c. oatmeal

½ c. coconut, shredded
¼ lb. margarine, melted
2 eggs, well beaten

Preheat oven to 350°F. Mix all ingredients together. Pour into unbaked pie shell. Bake for 40 to 50 minutes.

OLD-FASHIONED CUSTARD PIE

Lois Mills
Lake City, KS

1 (9 inch) pastry shell,
    baked 5 minutes and
    cooled
4 eggs, slightly beaten
½ c. sugar

¼ tsp. salt
1 to 1½ tsp. vanilla
1 tsp. almond extract
2½ c. scalded milk
½ tsp.+ nutmeg

Blend eggs, sugar, salt, vanilla, and almond extract. Add ½ teaspoon nutmeg. Using wire whip, whisk lightly. Blend in milk, whisking as you pour. Sprinkle in a little nutmeg as you whisk. Pour into pie shell. Bake in 400°F. oven 25 to 30 minutes or until knife comes out clean. Cool.

This pie has been a favorite in our family for years.

ON CLOUD NINE LEMON PIE

Iola Egle
Bella Vista, AR

1 c. sifted flour
½ tsp. salt
⅓ c. lard or shortening
1 egg, slightly beaten
1 tsp. lemon rind, finely
    grated
1 Tbsp. lemon juice
1 Tbsp. water
¾ c. granulated sugar
¼ c. cornstarch
1 c. water

½ c. lemon juice, freshly
    squeezed
2 egg yolks, slightly
    beaten
4 oz. cream cheese
3 egg whites
⅛ tsp. salt
½ tsp. cream of tartar
4 Tbsp. confectioners
    sugar
1 tsp. vanilla

Sift flour and salt into mixing bowl. Cut in shortening until particles are the size of small peas. Combine slightly beaten egg, lemon rind, and lemon juice. Sprinkle over flour mixture while tossing and stirring lightly with a fork. If necessary, add 1 or 2 more tablespoons water. Form dough into ball, then flatten to ½ inch thickness; smooth edges. Roll out on floured surface to make circle 1½ inches larger than inverted 9 inch pan. Fit dough loosely into pan. Trim pastry from edge of pan. Fold edge of pie pastry to make generous rim before fluting. Bake shell in 400°F. oven for 12 minutes. Cool. Combine sugar and cornstarch with water, lemon juice, and slightly beaten egg yolks in saucepan. Cook over medium heat, stirring constantly, until thick. Add cream cheese and blend well. Cool. Beat egg whites with salt and cream of tartar until stiff, but not dry. Slowly add confectioners sugar and vanilla. Spread over lemon pie filling and delicately make stiff peaks for pie decoration. Bake in 400°F. oven for about 3 minutes; watch closely so it doesn't burn. Chill at least 2 hours before slicing.

This recipe is over 50 years old and my mother could make it taste gourmet. It is still a favorite of everyone today.

ORANGE DELIGHT

Lynda Bozarth
Liberal, KS

2 pkg. orange gelatin
2 c. vanilla ice cream
1 (small) can mandarin
    oranges

1 banana

Drain oranges, reserving juice. Add enough water to juice to make 1¾ cups. Heat liquid until boiling. Stir into gelatin until dissolved. Add ice cream by spoonfuls and stir until melted. The mixture should start to thicken. Add drained oranges and then bananas. Pour in a mold and chill several hours.

This is a dish that my children always looked forward to at Grandma's house.

OREO COOKIE DESSERT

Brigit Gasper
Tipton, KS

36 Oreo chocolate
  sandwich cookies,
  crushed
½ c. butter
2 (1 oz.) sq. unsweetened
  chocolate

2 c. powdered sugar
3 egg yolks, beaten
3 egg whites
½ gal. vanilla ice cream,
  softened

Line 13x9 inch pan with 1 cup crushed Oreos. Melt butter and chocolate. Stir in powdered sugar and beaten egg yolks. Stir quickly. Mix in egg whites and cook over medium-low heat until bubbly. Cool slightly. Spread over crumbs in pan. Spread softened ice cream over the 2 layers and sprinkle remaining Oreo crumbs on top. Freeze. Set out about 15 to 20 minutes before serving to make serving easier.

This is a very rich dessert, but everyone who tries it loves it. You may substitute your favorite flavor of ice cream for the vanilla.

OUR FAVORITE COOKIES

Diane Meisinger
Hillsboro, KS

1 c. shortening
1 c. sugar
1 c. light brown sugar
2 eggs, beaten
1 tsp. baking powder
⅓ tsp. salt
1 (6 oz.) pkg. semi-sweet
  chocolate chips

1 (6 oz.) pkg. butterscotch
  chips
1¼ tsp. baking soda,
  dissolved in 2 Tbsp.
  cold water
3 c. flour
1 tsp. vanilla
½ c. pecans, chopped

Cream shortening, sugars, egg, and vanilla. Dissolve baking soda in cold water; add to mixture. Blend sifted dry ingredients. Add pecans, chocolate, and butterscotch chips. Drop by teaspoonfuls onto ungreased baking sheet. Bake at 375°F. for 8 to 9 minutes. Do not overbake.

PEACH DELIGHT

Alice James
Ellis, KS

1 c. flour
1 stick margarine
¼ c. brown sugar
½ c. pecans, chopped
1 c. powdered sugar
1 (8 oz.) pkg. cream
cheese

1 (8 oz.) container
whipped topping
2 pkg. peach gelatin
2 c. boiling water
2 c. frozen peaches, sliced

To prepare crust, mix flour, margarine, brown sugar, and nuts. Pat into a 9x13 inch greased pan. Bake 18 to 20 minutes at 325°F. Let cool. To make filling, beat powdered sugar and cream cheese, then fold in whipped topping. Refrigerate. Boil the water and add gelatin for the topping. Have your peaches slightly thawed. Add to gelatin. When it just starts to thicken, pour over filling. You may use 5 fresh peaches, sliced, but add one cup of ice water to gelatin.

When you cut into squares to serve, it looks very pretty if you put a spoonful of whipped topping on each square.

PEACH PIE

Kim Oborny
Durham, KS

⅔ c. sugar
⅓ c. all-purpose flour
¼ tsp. ground cinnamon
6 c. fresh peaches, sliced
(6 to 8 medium)
1 tsp. lemon juice

1 (9 inch) unbaked pie
shell
¾ c. flour
⅓ c. sugar
6 Tbsp. margarine

In a large bowl, mix sugar, flour, and cinnamon. Stir in peaches and lemon juice. Mix well. Pour into unbaked pie shell. Combine flour and sugar; cut in margarine until crumbly. Sprinkle over peaches. Preheat oven to 425°F. and bake 35 to 40 minutes or until topping is golden brown and juices begin to bubble around edges.

May need to cover edges with foil if they brown too quickly.

PEANUT BUTTER BROWNIES

Julie Haverland
Deepwater, MO

1 c. peanut butter
(crunchy)
⅓ c. butter
2½ c. sugar
1¼ c. brown sugar
5 eggs
2 tsp. vanilla
4 c. flour

5 tsp. baking powder
2 tsp. salt
½ c. peanuts, chopped
⅔ c. peanut butter
1 lb. powdered sugar
¼ c. milk
⅛ tsp. salt
1 tsp. vanilla

Cream butters and sugars together; add eggs and vanilla and mix. Add dry ingredients slowly while mixing. Mixture will be very stiff. Spread in jelly roll cookie sheet, 18x15 inches; sprinkle with chopped nuts and bake 35 minutes at 350°F. To make the frosting, beat ⅔ cup peanut butter, powdered sugar, milk, salt, and vanilla together until smooth. May need to add more liquid to make spreadable. Ice and cut while warm.

PEANUT BUTTER CEREAL SNACKS

Donna L. Thorp
Kismet, KS

1 c. light corn syrup
1 c. sugar
1 c. peanut butter

2 c. Cheerios cereal
1½ c. Rice Krispies cereal
1½ c. Corn Flakes cereal

Bring corn syrup and sugar to a boil. Remove from heat. Stir in peanut butter. Pour over cereal and stir to cover evenly. Scoop out with table-spoon or ice cream scoop onto wax paper. Makes about 35 treats.

Other corn and rice cereals can be substituted.

PEANUT BUTTER PIE

Margaret Trojan
Beaver Crossing, NE

⅓ c. peanut butter
1 (3 oz.) pkg. cream
cheese
2 Tbsp. butter, softened
1 c. powdered sugar

¼ c. milk
1 (8 oz.) container
whipped topping
1 chocolate crumb crust

944-07

241

Mix peanut butter, cream cheese, and butter until smooth. Add sugar and milk. Fold in whipped topping. Pour over crust. Cover and freeze for at least 4 hours. Garnish with crushed peanuts, chocolate curls, or chocolate crumbs.

This can also be doubled and put in 11x7 inch pan. Could be layered in parfait dishes also.

PEANUT BUTTER YO YO'S

Euda Witzer
Oklahoma City, OK

½ c. shortening
½ c. peanut butter
½ c. sugar
½ c. brown sugar
1 egg

1¼ c. flour
¾ tsp. baking soda
½ tsp. baking powder
½ tsp. salt
½ c. fruit jam

Beat together shortening, peanut butter, sugars, and egg. Add flour, baking soda, baking powder, and salt. Cover and chill. Preheat oven to 350°F. Roll dough into ¾ inch balls; place about 2 inches apart on greased cookie sheet. Bake about 8 to 10 minutes. When cool, put cookies together with one teaspoon of fruit jam.

PECAN PIE

Debbie Hunt
Anthony, KS

3 eggs, well beaten
1 c. Karo corn syrup
½ c. sugar

1 c. pecan halves
1 tsp. vanilla
½ tsp. salt

Mix all ingredients in order given. Pour into an unbaked pie shell and bake for 45 to 50 minutes at 325°F.

This has become a tradition at Thanksgiving and Christmas dinners and it is very easy to make!

PECAN PIE

Arlene Bontrager
Hutchinson, KS

3 eggs, well beaten
⅛ tsp. salt
¾ c. light brown sugar
1 c. light corn syrup
1 tsp. vanilla

2 Tbsp. butter, melted
1½ c. pecans
1 (9 inch) unbaked pie
   shell

In medium bowl, beat eggs, salt, and brown sugar together. Add corn syrup and mix well. Add vanilla and butter and mix well. Stir in pecans. Either whole or chopped pecans can be used. Pour into 9 inch unbaked pie shell. Bake 10 minutes at 400°F., then bake at 350°F. for 35 to 40 minutes until done.

I shield the edges of the pie with aluminum foil so it doesn't brown too much.

PECAN SQUARES

Belinda Nichols
Edmond, OK

3 c. flour
½ c. sugar
1 c. butter, softened
½ tsp. salt
4 eggs

1½ c. light syrup
1½ c. sugar
3 Tbsp. melted butter
1½ tsp. vanilla
2 c. chopped pecans

Mix flour, sugar, butter, and salt to resemble coarse crumbs. Press into 15x10 inch baking pan. Bake at 350°F. for 20 minutes. In another bowl, combine remaining ingredients and stir in pecans. Spread evenly over hot crust. Bake at 350°F. for 25 minutes. Cool on wire rack. Makes 4 dozen.

PECAN TARTS

Lois Mills
Lake City, KS

1 (3 oz.) pkg. cream
   cheese, softened
½ c. margarine, softened
1 c. all-purpose flour
¼ tsp. salt

1 egg
¾ Tbsp. margarine,
   melted
1 tsp. vanilla
⅔ c. pecans, chopped

In a mixing bowl, beat cream cheese and margarine. Blend in flour and salt. Chill for 1 hour. Shape into 1 inch balls. Press into the bottom and up sides of greased mini muffin cups. To prepare filling, beat egg in a small mixing bowl. Add brown sugar, margarine, and vanilla; mix well. Stir in pecans. Spoon into unbaked shells. Bake at 325°F. for 25 to 30 minutes. Cool in pan. Yields about 20.

PEPPERMINT CREAM FUDGE
Margaret Trojan
Beaver Crossing, NE

2½ c. sugar
⅔ c. evaporated milk
½ c. margarine
1½ c. semi-sweet
   chocolate chips
1 (7 oz.) jar marshmallow
   creme

1 tsp. vanilla
¼ tsp. peppermint extract
¼ c. plus 1 Tbsp.
   peppermint candies,
   finely crushed

Bring sugar, milk, and margarine to a boil, stirring constantly. Boil 6 minutes or until candy thermometer reaches 238°F.; remove from heat. Stir in chocolate chips. Stir in marshmallow creme, vanilla, peppermint, extracts, and ¼ cup crushed peppermint candy until blended. Pour into a greased 9 inch square pan. Sprinkle with 1 tablespoon crushed peppermint candy. Cool and cut into squares.

Especially good at Christmas. Can use crushed peppermint candy canes.

PINEAPPLE AND BANANA SALAD
Marilyn Scott
Van Buren, AR

1 Tbsp. margarine
½ c. sugar
1 heaping Tbsp. flour
1 (large) can crushed
   pineapple

5 whole bananas
1 egg

Put sugar and flour in large pan. Mix ½ cup pineapple juice with egg. Combine with sugar and flour mix; cook on low heat. Stir until thick; add margarine. Stir in sliced bananas and pineapple.

PINEAPPLE CAKE

Eleanor Odle
Prairie View, KS

2 c. flour
2 c. sugar
1 tsp. baking soda
2 eggs
½ c. cooking oil
⅛ tsp. salt

2½ c. crushed pineapple
⅔ c. evaporated milk
1 c. sugar
1 stick butter
1 c. nuts
1 c. coconut

Combine flour, sugar, baking soda, eggs, oil, and salt. Mix by hand; add undrained pineapple. Mix well. Bake in sprayed sheet cake pan in 400°F. oven for 20 minutes. While cake is baking, prepare frosting. Combine milk, butter, and sugar. Boil 10 minutes; add nuts and coconut. Put on cake while warm.

PINEAPPLE CHEESECAKE SQUARES

Theresa Fangman
Hereford, TX

2 c. flour
⅔ c. margarine, softened
½ c. almonds, finely chopped and toasted
½ c. powdered sugar
2 (8 oz.) pkg. cream cheese, softened
½ c. sugar
2 eggs

⅔ c. unsweetened pineapple juice
¼ c. flour
¼ c. sugar
1 (20 oz.) can crushed pineapple, well drained (reserve 1 c. juice)
½ c. whipping cream

Heat oven to 350°F. To prepare crust, mix flour, margarine, almonds, and powdered sugar in medium bowl with a fork until crumbly. Press firmly and evenly in bottom of ungreased rectangular pan, 13x9x2 inches. Bake crust until set, 15 to 20 minutes. Beat cream cheese in medium bowl until smooth and fluffy; beat in ½ cup sugar and eggs. Stir in ⅔ cup pineapple juice. Pour cream cheese mixture over hot crust. Bake just until center is set, about 20 minutes. Cool completely. Mix flour and ¼ cup sugar in 2 quart saucepan. Stir in 1 cup reserved pineapple juice. Heat to boiling over medium heat, stirring constantly. Boil and stir 1 minute. Remove from heat; fold in pineapple. Cool completely. Beat whipping cream in chilled bowl until stiff. Fold into pineapple mixture. Spread carefully over dessert. Cover loosely and refrigerate until firm, about 4 hours. Cut into about 3 inch squares. Makes 12 squares.

PINEAPPLE COOKIES

Mervin Schmidt
Montezuma, KS

4 c. white sugar
4 eggs, beaten
2 c. corn oil
2 c. crushed pineapple
  with juice

2 tsp. vanilla
4 tsp. baking powder
1 tsp. salt
9 c. sifted flour
1 tsp. baking soda

Cream sugar and oil. Add beaten eggs and mix thoroughly. Add pineapple and vanilla. Add baking powder, salt, flour, and soda; mix well. Drop from teaspoon onto lightly greased cookie sheet. Bake at 350°F. for 10 minutes.

These cookies freeze well, and have better flavor if put in freezer overnight.

PINEAPPLE PUDDING

Sue Love
Chillicothe, TX

2 (small) pkg. instant
  vanilla pudding
1 c. milk
16 oz. sour cream
1 (16 oz.) container
  whipped topping

1 (15 oz.) can crushed
  pineapple, drained
⅓ box graham crackers,
  crushed

Mix together with mixer pudding, milk, sour cream, and whipped topping; fold in drained pineapple. In a 13x9 inch pan, spread the crushed graham crackers; put pudding mixture on top. Can decorate with a few more crushed graham crackers.

This is so good, and very easy, very elegant in a fancy dessert dish.

PINEAPPLE-APRICOT PIE

Janet Rauch
Deep River, IA

1 (large) can crushed
  pineapple
2 heaping Tbsp. flour
1 (3 oz.) box apricot
  gelatin

1 c. sugar
2 c. flour
2 sticks margarine
½ tsp. salt
½ c. water

Mix pineapple, flour, gelatin, and sugar together and put in 2 crust pie shell made from flour, margarine, salt, and water. Bake at 350°F. for 45 minutes.

POPPY SEED CAKE

Brigit Gasper
Tipton, KS

1 (18.25 oz.) box white
   cake mix
4 eggs
¼ c. poppy seeds
½ c. oil
1 c. hot water

1 box instant coconut
   pudding
1 tsp. almond extract
1 c. powdered sugar
3 tsp. water
½ tsp. almond extract

Mix cake mix, eggs, poppy seeds, oil, hot water, pudding, and 1 teaspoon almond extract in mixing bowl and beat on medium speed for 4 minutes. Pour into greased and floured Bundt pan. Bake 40 to 50 minutes at 350°F. Let cake cool in pan for 10 minutes. Invert onto plate. To prepare topping, combine powdered sugar, water, and ½ teaspoon almond extract. Drizzle over cake.

This is a very old recipe. It freezes very well if you want to make it ahead of time. I have also substituted lemon extract and lemon cake mix and it is great that way, too.

PRALINE DROPS

Merrill Powers
Spearville, KS

½ c. margarine
⅔ c. brown sugar
1 egg
½ tsp. vanilla
½ tsp. maple flavoring
1⅔ c. flour, sifted
½ tsp. baking soda
¼ tsp. salt

½ c. brown sugar
1 Tbsp. corn syrup
1 Tbsp. water
1 c. powdered sugar,
   sifted
1 Tbsp. (or more) water
Pecan halves

Cream margarine; add brown sugar and beat. Add egg, vanilla, and maple flavoring; beat well. Add flour, baking soda, and salt; mix until smooth. Drop by teaspoonfuls onto prepared cookie sheet and top with a pecan half. Bake at 350°F. for 8 to 10 minutes. Frost while warm. To make frosting, boil ½ cup brown sugar, 1 tablespoon corn syrup, 1 tablespoon water, stirring constantly. Remove from heat and beat in 1 cup powdered sugar and 1 tablespoon or more of water.

If you like brown sugar, you will find these yummy! They are not as sugary sweet as a true Louisiana praline cookie.

PRALINE-BOTTOM PUMPKIN PIE

Margaret Trojan
Beaver Crossing, NE

¼ c. butter
½ c. toasted pecans, chopped
½ c. brown sugar, packed
1 (9 inch) baked pie shell
1 (2¼ to 3 oz.) pkg. custard mix

⅓ c. sugar
2 tsp. pumpkin pie spice
⅔ c. milk
⅔ c. evaporated milk (not sweetened condensed)
1 (16 oz.) can pumpkin

In saucepan, melt butter. Stir in the pecans and brown sugar. Cook and stir until mixture bubbles, then spread over bottom of baked pie shell. Cool. In 2 quart saucepan, combine custard mix, granulated sugar, and spice. Stir in milk and evaporated milk and pumpkin. Cook and stir until mixture bubbles. Cover and cool 10 minutes. Pour into pie shell. Chill until firm.

Garnish with whipped cream.

PRIDE OF IOWA COOKIES

Jacob Fangman
Hereford, TX

1 c. brown sugar
1 c. white sugar
1 c. shortening
2 eggs
2 c. flour
1 tsp. baking soda

1 c. applesauce
3 c. rolled oats
½ c. nuts (if desired)
½ tsp. salt
1 tsp. baking soda
1 tsp. vanilla

Blend sugar and shortening. Add eggs. Sift dry ingredients together and add to first mixture. Stir in vanilla, applesauce, oats, and nuts. Mix well and drop by teaspoonfuls on greased cookie sheet. Flatten with sugared glass. Bake in 375°F. oven until light brown, about 8 minutes. Makes 5 dozen.

PRUNE CAKE

Dana K. Reese
Fyffe, AL

2 c. flour
1 tsp. baking soda
¼ tsp. salt
1 Tbsp. cinnamon
1 Tbsp. nutmeg
1 Tbsp. allspice
1 c. corn oil
1½ c. sugar
3 eggs
1 Tbsp. vanilla
1 c. buttermilk

1½ c. prunes, coarsely
  cut, cooked, and
  drained
2 c. walnuts or pecans
1 c. sugar
½ c. buttermilk
¼ c. butter
¼ c. light corn syrup
1 tsp. baking soda
1 tsp. vanilla

Sift flour, baking soda, salt, cinnamon, nutmeg, and allspice together and set aside. Cream oil and sugar; add eggs and vanilla, beating after each is added. Add dry ingredients alternately with buttermilk; stir in prunes and walnuts. Bake in a 9 inch tube pan, ungreased, at 350°F. for 1 hour. To make the topping, boil sugar, buttermilk, butter, syrup, baking soda, and vanilla in saucepan for 10 minutes. Pour over the cake immediately from oven.

PUDDING PIE DELIGHT

Shana Lambert
Palco, KS

1 box vanilla pudding
1 box chocolate pudding
1 graham cracker crust

1 banana, sliced
10 strawberries, sliced

Prepare each pudding as directed. Pour chocolate pudding into graham cracker crust. Place sliced banana on chocolate pudding. Pour vanilla pudding on top of banana. Top with sliced strawberries. Chill for 1 hour before serving.

249

PUMPKIN APPLE PIE

Karmen Krug
Waldo, KS

⅓ c. packed brown sugar
1 Tbsp. cornstarch
½ tsp. ground cinnamon
¼ tsp. salt
⅓ c. water
2 Tbsp. butter
3 c. tart apples, peeled

1 (9 inch) pie crust pastry
¾ c. pumpkin (canned)
¾ c. evaporated milk
⅓ c. sugar
1 egg
Whipped cream (optional)

In a saucepan, combine brown sugar, cornstarch, cinnamon, and salt. Add water and butter; bring to a boil. Add apples. Cook and stir for 4 minutes. Can also be done in the microwave in a microwave-safe bowl. Place pastry in 9 inch pie pan; add apple mixture. In a bowl, whisk pumpkin, milk, sugar, egg, cinnamon, and salt until smooth; pour over apple layer. Flute edges of pastry. Bake at 375°F. for 50 to 55 minutes or until knife inserted in middle comes out clean. If necessary, cover edges with foil to prevent overbrowning. Cool completely. Garnish with whip cream if desired. Store in refrigerator. Yields 6 to 8 servings.

PUMPKIN COOKIES WITH PENUCHE FROSTING

Jacalyn Nichols
Copeland, KS

½ c. sugar
½ c. brown sugar
1 c. margarine, softened
1 c. pumpkin (canned)
1 tsp. vanilla
1 egg
2 c. flour
1 tsp. baking powder
1 tsp. baking soda

1 tsp. cinnamon
¼ tsp. salt
¾ c. nuts, chopped
3 Tbsp. margarine
½ c. brown sugar
¼ c. milk
1½ to 2 c. powdered
   sugar

Cream sugars and margarine; blend in egg, vanilla, and pumpkin. Sift flour, baking powder, baking soda, cinnamon, and salt together and add to pumpkin mixture; mix well. Stir in nuts. Drop onto greased cookie sheet. Bake at 350°F. for 10 to 12 minutes. Cool. Prepare frosting: Bring margarine and brown sugar to a boil, stirring constantly, for 1 minute or until slightly thickened. Cool 10 minutes. Stir in milk; beat in powdered sugar until smooth. Spread on cooled cookies.

These are really moist, soft cookies.

PUMPKIN SUPREME

Amber Uhlenhake
Ossian, IA

1 (15 oz.) can pumpkin
1 (12 oz.) can evaporated
  milk
3 eggs
1 c. sugar

4 tsp. pumpkin pie spice
1 pkg. yellow cake mix
1½ c. pecans, chopped
¾ c. melted margarine

Mix the first five ingredients and pour into a greased 9x13 inch pan. Sprinkle with dry cake mix. Generously sprinkle nuts over top of the cake mix layer. Pour melted margarine over top. Bake at 350°F. for 50 to 60 minutes.

QUICK AND EASY FRUIT COBBLER

Jeanette Neibling
Highland, KS

1 (¼ lb.) stick butter
1 c. sugar
1 c. flour
1½ tsp. baking powder
¾ c. milk

1¾ c. peaches, rhubarb, or
  blackberries, sliced and
  fresh or frozen
1 c. sugar

Melt butter in 9x13 inch cake pan in oven. Combine 1 cup sugar, flour, baking powder, and milk. Pour mixture over melted butter in cake pan. Do not stir. Add fruit over flour mixture, then cover with 1 cup sugar. Bake for 30 minutes at 350°F.

Delicious served with ice cream, whipped cream, or milk. This is a great way to enjoy your home-grown fruits.

QUICK AND EASY PECAN PIE

Annilee Kniffen
Lorena, TX

3 egg whites
1 c. sugar
1 tsp. vanilla
1 c. pecans, chopped

20 round snack crackers,
  finely crushed
1 small container whipped
  topping

Beat egg whites, gradually adding sugar until stiff. Mix in vanilla, cracker crumbs, and pecans. Bake in pie plate sprayed with cooking spray in a 350°F. oven about 35 minutes. When cool, top with whipped topping.

RED HOT CANDY FLUFF

Juanita Gross
Clearwater, KS

1 (20 oz.) can crushed
   pineapple, drained
¼ c. Red Hot candies
2 c. miniature
   marshmallows

1 (8 oz.) container
   whipped topping,
   thawed

Combine pineapple and Red Hots. Refrigerate 8 hours or overnight. Stir in marshmallows and topping. Cover and refrigerate until served. Makes 6 to 8 servings.

REESE'S CAKE

Lori Mercer
Kellerton, IA

1 yellow cake mix
1½ c. water
⅓ c. oil

2 eggs
1 c. peanut butter
1 c. chocolate chips

Mix all ingredients and bake at 350°F. for 25 to 30 minutes. Frost with chocolate frosting.

This is a heavy cake, but very good. Consistency is like that of a brownie.

ROLLED OAT CHOCOLATE DROPS

Thelma Maxwell
Dodge City, KS

½ c. butter
1 c. quick-cooking rolled
   oats
¼ c. nuts (pecans or
   walnuts), chopped
2¾ c. powdered sugar
⅔ c. peanut butter

¾ c. coconut
¼ lb. dates, finely
   chopped
1 tsp. vanilla
⅓ stick paraffin
1 c. chocolate bits (semi-
   sweet)

Melt butter. Add remaining ingredients. Mix well by hand. Shape into small balls and dip in chocolate glaze. To prepare glaze, melt paraffin and chocolate bits. Stir until melted.

Grandkids love these chocolate drops for either cookies or as candy.

ROOT BEER FLOAT CAKE

Beverly Feit
Eaton, CO

1 pkg. yellow cake mix
1¼ c. root beef soft drink
2 eggs
¼ c. vegetable oil

2 containers whipped
   topping
Butter flavor cooking
   spray

Place small bowl and beaters in the refrigerator to keep cold before mixing the frosting. Place a 13x9x2 inch pan on a piece of wax paper. Using a pen, trace around the pan to make a pattern. Cut around the marking. Spray the pan, place the wax paper in the pan, and spray it. Combine cake mix, root beer, eggs, and oil. Mix well. Pour cake mix in the pan and bake at 350°F., for 35 to 40 minutes. Leave cake in the pan for about 5 minutes. Go around the cake with a knife. Use a large piece of cardboard covered with foil. Place it over the cake and turn the pan upside down. Remove the wax paper and let it cool. To prepare frosting, mix 1 cup of root beer into the whipped topping. Beat at high speed until peaks form. Continue until light and fluffy, about 2 minutes. Cover and refrigerate until cake is cool.

It's an easy and fun cake to make.

RUST HAVEN CAKE

Charlotte Schmidt
Clintonville, WI

1 (8 oz.) c. dates, cut up
   small
1½ c. hot water
1¼ tsp. baking soda
½ c. canola oil
1 c. sugar

2 eggs
⅓ c. cocoa
¼ tsp. salt
2 c. all-purpose flour
½ c. chocolate chips
1 c. nuts

Soak dates in hot water and baking soda. In mixer bowl, mix oil and sugar; add eggs and blend. Add cocoa, salt, flour, and the liquid from the dates; blend in slowly. Mix for 1 to 2 minutes. When mixed, add the dates slowly and blend. Before baking, put about ½ cup chocolate chips and cup of nuts on top. Bake in 9x13 inch pan in 350°F. oven 28 to 30 minutes.

S'MORES PIZZA

Margaret Trojan
Beaver Crossing, NE

1 pizza crust (unbaked)
½ c. sugar
2 Tbsp. flour
½ c. milk
1 egg
1 egg yolk
1½ lb. margarine
1 tsp. vanilla

1 c. mini marshmallows
1 c. chocolate chips (mini)
   or a combo of semi-
   sweet and sweet chips
3 Tbsp. flour
3 Tbsp. sugar
2 Tbsp. margarine,
   softened

Combine sugar and flour with wire whip; add milk. Cook, stirring over low heat, to a boil. Beat egg and yolk together. Add a small portion of hot mixture to eggs, then gradually all of it. Heat again to boiling, stirring. Cook one minute or until thick. Top pizza crust with this and bake at 375°F. for 15 minutes or until brown on edges. For crumb topping, crumble flour, sugar, and margarine together; sprinkle over top. Sprinkle topping, then sprinkle marshmallows and chips. Place under broiler to soften marshmallow to light brown. Best if served warm.

SAUCY APPLE SWIRL

Brigit Gasper
Tipton, KS

¼ c. sugar
2 tsp. cinnamon
1 (18.25 oz.) box yellow
   cake mix

1⅔ c. applesauce
3 eggs

Blend sugar and cinnamon. Grease 10 inch Bundt or tube pan and dust with 1 tablespoon of cinnamon-sugar mixture. Blend cake mix, applesauce, and eggs until moistened. Beat as directed on cake mix package. Reserve 1½ cups batter. Pour remaining batter in pan. Sprinkle with remaining cinnamon-sugar mixture, then top with reserved batter. Bake at 350°F. for 35 to 45 minutes or until toothpick inserted in center is clean. Cool cake in pan for 15 minutes, then invert onto serving plate. May drizzle with confectioners icing glaze if desired.

My mother made this cake for my dad, and it was one of his favorites. It is a favorite of my family and quick and easy to make.

SKY HIGH STRAWBERRY PIE

Dorothy Bozarth
Liberal, KS

1½ c. flour
½ c. vegetable oil
1½ tsp. sugar
⅛ tsp. salt
2 Tbsp. milk
2 egg whites

1 c. sugar
1 (10 oz.) pkg. frozen
  strawberries
1 tsp. vanilla
2 Tbsp. lemon juice
1 c. whipping cream

Mix flour, oil, sugar, salt, and milk in 9 inch pie pan. Divide dough and press with fingers into two 9 inch pie pans. Bake at 425°F. for 10 minutes or until slightly golden. In large mixer bowl, beat the egg whites until stiff. Add 1 cup sugar, strawberries (thawed), vanilla, and lemon juice. Beat 15 minutes. Fold in the whipping cream. Fill pie shells and freeze 4 to 6 hours. If using fresh strawberries, mash 1 pint with ⅓ cup of sugar. Garnish with whole strawberries with hulls attached split lengthwise.

SNOWFLAKE COOKIES

Tammy Bell
Osawatomie, KS

1 pkg. chocolate or lemon
  cake mix
1 (8 oz.) container
  whipped topping

1 egg
Powdered sugar

Mix cake mix, whipped topping, and egg; roll into balls. Roll balls in powdered sugar. Bake at 350°F. for 8 to 10 minutes. Makes about 2 dozen cookies.

These are great to make for bake sales or if you need to make something quick.

SOFT SUGAR COOKIE

Maxine Brattin
Wheaton, MO

4½ c. flour
1 tsp. baking soda
1 tsp. salt
2 tsp. baking powder
1 tsp. cream of tartar
2 eggs
1 c. vegetable oil
1 c. powdered sugar

1 c. granulated sugar
2 tsp. vanilla
2 sticks softened
  margarine
3 c. powdered sugar
2 tsp. vanilla
¼ c. milk
2 Tbsp. butter

In a large bowl, blend flour, baking soda, salt, baking powder, and cream of tartar. In another large bowl, mix the next 6 ingredients. Beat on high speed until smooth and creamy. Add the first dry mixture to this and mix well. Roll into small balls and place on an ungreased cookie sheet 2 inches apart. Lightly flatten with a greased glass dipped in sugar. Bake at 350°F. for 7 to 10 minutes. Makes 6 to 7 dozen. Icing: Mix remaining 4 ingredients; beat until creamy. Add food coloring if desired.

SOUR CREAM COFFEE CAKE

Glennys Bruning
Ellsworth, KS

½ c. butter
1 c. sugar
2 eggs
1 container sour cream
2 c. flour
½ tsp. baking soda
1½ tsp. baking powder

½ tsp. salt
½ tsp. vanilla
⅔ c. brown sugar
½ c. white sugar
2 tsp. cinnamon
1 c. nuts

Cream butter and sugar thoroughly. Add eggs, one at a time, beating after each addition. Sift dry ingredients together and add alternately with cream and creamed mixture, beginning and ending with flour mixture. Add vanilla. Prepare a topping with brown sugar, white sugar, cinnamon, and nuts. Put ½ the batter into greased 7x12 inch pan and sprinkle the topping over it. Add rest of batter and remaining topping. Bake in 325°F. oven for 40 minutes.

This recipe was put together by my mother-in-law.

SOUR CREAM PIE

Betty Mead
Paradise, KS

1 c. sour cream
2 egg yolks
1 c. sugar
1 c. raisins

1 Tbsp. flour
1/4 tsp. cinnamon
1/4 tsp. cloves
1/8 tsp. salt

Mix well and pour into unbaked pie shell. Bake at 350°F. for 35 to 40 minutes. If using sweet cream, add 1 teaspoon of vinegar.

SPECIAL K COOKIES

Rochelle Fangman
Hereford, TX

1 stick margarine
1 1/2 c. sugar
1 1/2 c. Karo corn syrup

2 c. peanut butter
2 tsp. vanilla
8 c. Special K cereal

Boil butter, sugar, and Karo syrup for 2 minutes and 15 seconds; remove from heat. Add peanut butter and vanilla; stir and mix well. Add cereal and stir well. Drop by teaspoonfuls on wax paper. Cool and eat.

SPICE CAKE

Melanie Sippel
Ellsworth, KS

1 c. sugar
1/2 c. shortening
2 eggs
1 c. buttermilk
1 1/2 c. flour
1/2 c. raisins

1 tsp. baking soda
1 tsp. cinnamon
1/4 tsp. salt
1/4 tsp. cloves
1/4 tsp. nutmeg
Nuts (optional)

Mix in order given. Mix spices, baking soda, and salt with the flour. Add raisins. Pour into a 7x12 inch pan. Bake 30 minutes in 350°F. oven.

I am 13 years old. My great-grandma used to make this cake from memory. We frost it with peanut butter frosting, but any frosting will do.

SPICY WALNUT COOKIES

Marjorie Abel
Grinnell, KS

2 c. walnut pieces
½ c. sugar
1½ Tbsp. cinnamon

1 tsp. vanilla
2 egg whites, whisked
   until frothy

Grind nuts, sugar, and cinnamon in food processor or blender. Combine with egg whites and vanilla. Drop by teaspoon on oiled cookie sheet. Bake at 350°F. for 15 minutes. Cookies will be soft; do not overbake. Makes 15 cookies.

Heart healthy recipe as no flour, no salt, no shortening. I usually double or triple recipe, as there is always someone to give them to.

STRAWBERRY CHIFFON

Rita Schiefelbein
Clear Lake, SD

2 c. flour
1 c. butter
½ c. brown sugar
1 c. slivered almonds or
   chopped walnuts
1 (10 oz.) pkg. frozen
   strawberries, thawed

2 egg whites
1 c. sugar
1 Tbsp. lemon juice
1 tsp. vanilla
1 c. whipping cream

Mix flour, butter, brown sugar, and nuts. Put in 9x13 inch pan and bake at 325°F. for 20 minutes, stirring every 5 minutes while baking. Press ½ of this mixture into pan while warm. Combine strawberries (do not drain), egg whites, sugar, lemon juice, and vanilla in large mixing bowl. Beat 20 to 25 minutes until almost over top of bowl. (I use a large electric mixer, and it's important to beat the entire 20 to 25 minutes). Beat whipping cream and fold in strawberry mixture. Pour over crust and top with remaining crumbs. Freeze overnight. Remove from freezer and let stand a few minutes before cutting and serving.

This is a great dessert to serve for showers or after a dinner because it's light, not heavy and rich.

STRAWBERRY CHIFFON PIE

Barbara Koelling
Paradise, KS

⅔ c. sugar
1 pkg. unflavored gelatin
1 c. strawberries, crushed
3 egg whites

¼ tsp. cream of tartar
⅓ c. sugar
1 c. whipped topping
1 (9 inch) pie shell

Blend ⅔ cup sugar, gelatin, and strawberries in a saucepan and cook to a full rolling boil, stirring constantly. Place pan in cold water; cool until mixture mounds slightly when dropped from spoon, then fold into a meringue made from egg whites, cream of tartar, and ⅓ cup sugar; carefully blend in whipped topping. Pile into baked pie shell. Chill several hours until set. Serve cold; garnish with whipped topping and strawberry halves.

One 10 ounce package of frozen strawberries may be used in place of fresh berries; use ¼ cup sugar.

STRAWBERRY DELIGHT

Charlene Fry
Burlingame, KS

1 c. sifted flour
½ c. margarine
¼ c. brown sugar
½ c. nuts, chopped
2 egg whites
2 Tbsp. lemon juice

1 c. sugar
1 (10 oz.) pkg. frozen strawberries
1 regular size container whipped topping

To prepare crust and topping, combine flour, margarine, sugar, and nuts. Mix until crumbly. Press into 8 inch square pan. Bake 20 to 25 minutes at 350°F. until crisp. Cool and break into crumbs. To prepare filling, combine egg whites, lemon juice, sugar, and berries in bowl. Beat with mixer 15 to 20 minutes. Fold in whipped topping. Place ½ of crumb mixture in bottom of 9 inch square pan. Pour in filling. Sprinkle other crumbs over top and freeze. Cut into squares to serve.

STRAWBERRY ICE CREAM

Barbara Long
Montezuma, IA

6 eggs
1 c. sugar
2 (14 oz.) sweetened
   condensed milk
1 qt. half & half

20 oz. frozen strawberries
2 (12 oz.) bottles
   strawberry pop
1 Tbsp. vanilla

Beat the eggs sugar, and half & half until well blended. Cook over medium heat until the mixture coats the spoon or until 160°. Cool and add sweetened condensed milk, pop, strawberries, and vanilla. Place in a 1½ gallon freezer and freeze using manufacturer's directions.

This is very smooth and freezes and stores without becoming hard.

SURPRISE CUPCAKES

Brigit Gasper
Tipton, KS

1 (8 oz.) pkg. cream
   cheese, softened
1 (6 oz.) pkg. chocolate
   chips
1 egg
⅓ c. sugar
½ tsp. salt
3 c. flour

2 c. sugar
½ c. cocoa
1 tsp. salt
2 tsp. baking soda
⅔ c. oil
2 c. water
2 Tbsp. vinegar
1 tsp. vanilla

Combine cream cheese, egg, ⅓ cup sugar, and ½ teaspoon salt. Add chocolate chips and set aside. Sift together the flour, 2 cups sugar, cocoa, 1 teaspoon salt, and baking soda. Add the oil, water, and vinegar. Mix until smooth. Fill paper lined cupcake pans ⅔ full with chocolate batter and top with a heaping teaspoonful of cream cheese filling. Bake at 350°F. for 25 minutes. Makes 30 cupcakes.

This was one of my favorites that my mother made when I was young. It is my daughter's favorite now.

TOASTED PECAN PUDDING

Kim Due
Friend, NE

½ c. margarine, melted
1½ c. coconut
1 c. flour
1 c. pecans, chopped
¼ c. brown sugar

2 (3.4 oz.) pkg. instant
vanilla pudding
3 c. cold milk
1 (8 oz.) container
whipped topping

Combine margarine, coconut, flour, pecans, and brown sugar. Spread onto an ungreased cookie sheet. Bake at 325°F. for 25 to 30 minutes, stirring occasionally. Cool. Meanwhile, beat pudding mix and milk together on low speed for 2 minutes. Chill for 5 minutes. Fold in whipped topping. Place ½ of the pecan mixture in 9x13 inch pan. Spread pudding mixture over this and top with remaining pecan mixture. Chill.

This is best served the same day it is made.

VAL'S CARAMEL PECAN PIE

Mona Redinger
Hale Center, TX

½ lb. caramels
½ c. water
½ c. margarine
2 eggs

¾ c. sugar
¼ tsp. vanilla
1 c. pecans
1 pie shell

Place caramels, water, and margarine in a microwave safe bowl; heat on high until melted and smooth. Check frequently, stirring each time. Combine slightly beaten eggs, sugar, salt, and vanilla. Gradually add caramel sauce, mixing well. Add pecans, either chopping or leaving in halves. Pour into prepared pie crust. Bake at 400°F. for 10 minutes, then reduce oven to 350°F. and bake an additional 20 minutes. The filling will be soft at first, but will thicken as it cools.

VANILLA ICE CREAM

Carla Jecha
Timken, KS

2 (3 oz.) boxes vanilla
instant pudding
8 eggs
2 c. sugar

2 Tbsp. vanilla
1 qt. heavy whipping
cream

Beat eggs and sugar together until smooth. Mix pudding according to directions on the box, then mix everything together and put in a 1½ gallon ice cream freezer. Add whole milk to the fill line. Churn the ice cream as you normally would using salt and ice. If made early in the day, it can sit in the freezer bucket (with the ice and salt), covered with a blanket, until ready to serve. This sit time will harden the ice cream.

WACKY CAKE

Kim Oborny
Durham, KS

3 c. flour
3 heaping Tbsp. cocoa
2 c. sugar
2 tsp. baking soda
1 tsp. salt
3 Tbsp. vinegar
¾ c. oil
2 c. water (warm)
3 tsp. vanilla

¼ c. butter or margarine
1 (3 oz.) pkg. cream cheese
1 box powdered sugar
1 tsp. vanilla
Small amount of milk (to desired spreading consistency)

In a 9x13 inch cake pan, mix flour, cocoa, sugar, baking soda, and salt. Make 3 large holes in flour mixture and pour vinegar in 1 hole, oil and vanilla in 1 hole, and the water in the third hole. Mix well. Bake at 375°F. for 30 minutes. Don't overbake. For frosting, cream together margarine, cream cheese, and powdered sugar. Add vanilla and milk. Mix well. Frost when cake is completely cool.

WHITE COCONUT CAKE

Ilene Jessup
Paragon, IN

1 box white cake mix
1 pkg. coconut, shredded
1 c. milk
4½ Tbsp. flour

¾ c. margarine
4½ Tbsp. shortening
1½ c. sugar
2 tsp. vanilla

Prepare cake mix as directed on box. For frosting, mix milk and flour together and cook on medium heat until thick. Cool mixture well. Cream margarine, shortening, and sugar together. Add cooled paste mixture. Add vanilla and beat with mixer until it whips up like whipped cream. Spread frosting on bottom layer of cake; add shredded coconut. Place top layer on bottom layer; ice top side. Add coconut as needed to top and side of cake.

ZIPPY PIE

Amber Uhlenhake
Ossian, IA

1 frozen pie crust
1 pkg. cream cheese
1 (8 oz.) container
   whipped topping

4 Butterfinger candy bars,
   crushed

Bake the pie crust until golden brown; cool. Mix together the cream cheese, whipped topping, and 3½ of the Butterfingers. Fluff into the pie crust. Garnish the top with the remaining candy bar. Chill.

For a different twist, try using a graham cracker crust. This dessert is amazing!

ZUCCHINI SQUARES

Martha Mink
Dodge City, KS

4 eggs
2 c. sugar
2 c. oil
1 tsp. salt
1 tsp. baking soda
2 tsp. cinnamon
2 c. flour
2 c. zucchini, grated

1 tsp. vanilla
1 c. nuts, chopped
2 Tbsp. margarine
2 tsp. vanilla
2 (3 oz.) pkg. cream
   cheese
2 c. powdered sugar

Mix together eggs, sugar, and oil. Add salt, baking soda, cinnamon, flour, zucchini, vanilla, and nuts. Pour into a greased sheet cake pan. Bake in 350°F. oven for 30 to 40 minutes. To prepare frosting, beat together margarine, vanilla, cream cheese, and powdered sugar. Spread on cooled cake, then cut into squares.

This freezes well.

Notes

Quick & Easy

Quick & Easy
Recipe Contest Winners

First
Taquito Casserole
Sandra Chrane, Abilene, Texas
Page 280

Second
Alfredo Chicken Broccoli Pizza
Sandi Loiseau, Frankfort, Kansas
Page 265

Third
Bacon Corn Chowder
Karmen Krug, Waldo, Kansas
Page 265

QUICK AND EASY

❖ ❖ ❖

ALFREDO CHICKEN BROCCOLI PIZZA

Sandi Loiseau
Frankfort, KS

1 (12 inch) prepared pizza crust
¾ c. roasted garlic Parmesan Alfredo sauce
1½ c. broccoli (frozen or fresh), chopped and cooked

2 boneless chicken breasts, cooked and chopped
1 (8 oz.) pkg. four cheese mix or Mozzarella cheese, shredded

Brush crust with olive oil. Spread Alfredo sauce over crust. Next, sprinkle on the cooked chicken and broccoli over the sauce. Sprinkle the shredded cheese on top. Bake at 425°F. for 10 to 15 minutes until light brown. Slice and serve.

This is a nice alternative to the traditional pizza.

BACON CORN CHOWDER

Karmen Krug
Waldo, KS

6 bacon strips, diced
¾ c. celery, diced
1 (small) onion
1 c. potatoes (uncooked), diced
1 c. water

1 can cream-style corn
1 c. milk
½ tsp. seasoned salt
½ tsp. salt
¼ tsp. garlic powder
⅛ tsp. pepper

In a saucepan, cook the bacon, celery, and onion over medium heat for 10 to 15 minutes or until the bacon is cooked; drain. Add the potatoes and water. Cover and simmer for 20 minutes or until the potatoes are tender. Stir in corn, milk, seasoned salt, salt, garlic powder, and pepper; heat through (do not boil). Refrigerate or freeze leftovers. Yields 4 servings.

BAR-B-QUE SAUCE

Donna Fisk
Montezuma, IA

1 onion, sliced and
  browned
2 Tbsp. vinegar
1 tsp. chili powder

2 Tbsp. brown sugar
1 c. ketchup
1 tsp. liquid smoke

Mix all ingredients together and let simmer for 20 minutes.

Tastes like store bought. Put on chopped leftover roast beef or pork.

BARBECUED WIENERS

Alice P. Boehme
Mullinville, KS

2 Tbsp. instant onions,
  chopped
1 Tbsp. sugar
½ tsp. salt
½ tsp. dry mustard
2 tsp. Worcestershire
  sauce

⅛ tsp. pepper
¾ c. ketchup
¼ c. water
¼ c. lemon juice
½ tsp. liquid smoke
½ tsp. garlic salt
1 lb. wieners

Add all ingredients, except the wieners, in a pan and simmer for 5 minutes. Cut wieners into small pieces and put into sauce and simmer for 15 minutes longer.

My grandchildren love them!

BREAKFAST IN A MUFFIN

6 eggs
¼ c. applesauce
1 c. flour
⅓ c. rolled oats oatmeal
  (quick is fine)
1 Tbsp. baking powder
½ tsp. salt
¼ tsp. ground cinnamon
¼ tsp. pepper

½ c. Cheddar cheese,
  shredded
¼ c. fresh parsley,
  chopped or 1 Tbsp. plus
  1 tsp. dried parsley
  flakes
2 Tbsp. imitation bacon
  bits

Evenly coat 12 muffin cups with cooking spray. In large bowl, beat together eggs and applesauce until blended. Add flour, rolled oats, baking powder, salt, cinnamon, and pepper. Beat until well combined. Stir in cheese, parsley, and bacon bits. Divide batter evenly among the 12 cups. Bake at 375°F. for 15 to 20 minutes or until lightly browned and springs back when lightly touched with finger. Cool in pan 5 minutes. Remove and cool on wire rack or serve.

BROCCOLI AND HAM ROLLS

Barb Kasel
Adams, MN

2 heads broccoli
16 slices ham
2 Tbsp. butter
1 c. milk
2 Tbsp. flour

½ tsp. salt
⅛ tsp. pepper
⅛ tsp. paprika
1 c. Cheddar or processed cheese, grated

Steam fresh broccoli. Cut broccoli into 16 sections. Roll up each piece of broccoli in a thin slice of ham. Place broccoli/ham roll in a casserole dish. To prepare cheese sauce, place butter in 2 cup measuring cup and microwave for 30 to 45 seconds or until melted. Stir in flour and seasonings until smooth. Slowly stir in milk. Microwave 3 to 4 minutes until thickened. Stir in cheese until melted. If cheese has not melted, microwave for 30 seconds to 1 minute. Pour cheese sauce over ham rolls and bake at 350°F. for 15 to 20 minutes or until good and warm.

I serve with hash browns and coleslaw along with dinner rolls for a quick and easy meal.

CABBAGE, HAM AND POTATO SOUP

Judy Hall
McCook, NE

½ c. cabbage, thinly sliced
½ c. ham, diced
2 c. low fat chicken broth

1 potato, cooked and diced
Salt and pepper to taste

Warm all ingredients until cabbage is cooked and the rest of the ingredients are blended. If desired, top with a little shredded cheese.

This soup is quick to make and is really good.

CALLIE'S SUNDAY BRUNCH

Callie Conrad
Flagler, CO

1 doz. eggs, beaten
1 (medium) onion,
  chopped
1 green bell pepper,
  chopped
1 (11 oz.) can corn
  Niblets, drained
1 (7 oz.) can mushrooms,
  drained and chopped

1½ c. milk
½ lb. sausage, browned
  and drained
¼ tsp. Mrs. Dash
  seasoning
½ tsp. salt
Sharp Cheddar cheese,
  shredded (optional)

Saute onion, bell pepper, and mushrooms until translucent; drain excess oil and set aside. Brown sausage; drain excess oil and set aside. Add milk, salt, and Mrs. Dash to eggs; beat until well mixed. Pour eggs into skillet and cook to about ¾ done, then add all of the above ingredients. Finish cooking. Drain off excess liquid. This may be doubled; add sharp Cheddar cheese if desired. Makes 6 servings.

I thought up this recipe with my Grandpa one Sunday morning while my Mom and Dad were doing chores.

CHEESEBURGER SOUP

Roxie Berning
Marienthal, KS

6 to 8 potatoes
2 Tbsp. butter
¼ c. onion, chopped
2 Tbsp. flour
1 qt. milk
½ c. processed cheese
2 Tbsp. parsley

½ tsp. salt
½ tsp. season salt
¼ tsp. monosodium
  glutamate
¼ tsp. red pepper
2 Tbsp. beef bouillon
1 lb. ground beef

Saute onion in butter. Brown ground beef and drain off grease. Cook potatoes until tender. Blend flour and milk together. Add all of this plus cheese, parsley, salt, seasoning salt, monosodium glutamate, red pepper, and beef bouillon. Simmer until warm.

CHILI PIE

Dianne Heil
Ulysses, KS

1 lb. ground beef
1 (15 oz.) can chili without
  beans (hot or mild,
  depending on your
  taste)
½ can water
1 (15 oz.) can kidney
  beans, drained and
  rinsed

1 c. Cheddar or Colby-
  Monterey Jack cheese,
  shredded
1 pkg. cornbread mix
2 to 4 Tbsp. milk

Brown ground beef in a 10 inch ovenproof skillet; add chili, water, and kidney beans. Simmer for 10 minutes. Remove from heat and spread cheese over meat mixture. Top with cornbread mix, prepared according to directions; thin with milk. Bake 20 to 25 minutes at 400°F. or until cornbread is lightly browned. Serves 4.

This quick and delicious dish can be made with leftover chili. It is very easy to make for larger groups, or can be stretched by using 2 cans of beans.

CHOCOLATE SHEET CAKE

Gail Brattin
Monett, MO

2 c. sugar
2 c. flour
1 tsp. baking soda
2 sticks oleo or margarine
4 Tbsp. cocoa
1 c. water
½ c. buttermilk

2 eggs
1 tsp. vanilla
1 stick margarine
4 Tbsp. cocoa
6 Tbsp. buttermilk
1 to 1½ boxes powdered
  sugar

Mix sugar, flour, and baking soda. Melt 2 sticks of margarine, 4 table-spoons cocoa, and water; bring to a rapid boil, then pour over dry ingredients and mix. Add mixture of ½ cup buttermilk, eggs, and vanilla. Beat well. Bake in 11x15 inch greased and floured pan at 350°F. for 20 minutes. Ice cake while hot. For icing, melt 1 stick margarine. Add 4 tablespoons cocoa and 6 tablespoons buttermilk. Bring to boil, then add 1 to 1½ boxes of powdered sugar and vanilla. Beat until smooth. Spread while hot.

Cake batter will be thin before baking.

CHUNKY TOMATO BASIL SOUP

Carolyn Dunn
St. John, KS

1 (10¾ oz.) can condensed tomato soup
1 (5 oz.) can evaporated milk

1 (large) fresh tomato, diced
2 tsp. dried basil

Combine all 4 ingredients in saucepan and heat over medium heat for 5 minutes. Serves 2.

This is my effort to copy a recipe that I enjoyed at a restaurant in Washington, D.C., and it has become one of my mainstays. It doesn't get any easier than this for a light supper. This recipe could easily be doubled or tripled for a large quantity.

COTTAGE CHEESE SALAD

Clara Hinman
Flagler, CO

1 (3 oz.) pkg. lime gelatin
1⅓ c. boiling water
1 c. low fat cottage cheese
½ c. light salad dressing

2 Tbsp. horseradish (makes it tart, perhaps some might prefer less)
1 c. pineapple, drained

Mix gelatin in boiling water; let stand until it begins to set. Add cottage cheese, salad dressing, horseradish, and pineapple; mix and place in a pretty serving dish. Set in the refrigerator.

This salad is fast and easy. Everyone will be asking what that special ingredient is in this delicious salad.

EASY ENCHILADA CASSEROLE

Johnna Lambert
Palco, KS

1½ lb. ground beef
1 can enchilada sauce
½ c. onions, chopped
1 small can corn, drained
1 tsp. minced garlic

3 c. tortilla chips, crushed
2 c. Cheddar cheese
1 can refried beans (optional)

Brown ground beef, onions, and garlic; drain well and mix in corn and enchilada sauce. Layer in the bottom of a baking dish ½ the crushed chips; top with ½ of the meat mixture and then ½ of the Cheddar cheese. Repeat layers. Bake for 30 minutes at 350°F.

You can add a layer of refried beans after the first layer of meat if you want.

EASY FRUIT SALAD

Barb Korth
Randolph, NE

1 can fruit cocktail,
  drained
1 or 2 bananas, cut up

¼ c. mayonnaise
1½ c. whipped topping

Mix all together and serve. You can add more fruit or coconut or marshmallows to your liking.

You would not expect this to taste this good using mayo, but it is truly delicious and so quick.

EASY MEXICAN CASSEROLE

Danielle Crouch
Estancia, NM

1 lb. ground beef,
  browned
1 (medium) onion, diced
1 (14.5 oz.) cans Mexican
  style beans
1 can Ro-Tel diced
  tomatoes and green
  chiles
1 can cream of mushroom
  soup

6 whole corn or flour
  tortillas, torn in bits
  (can substitute Mexican
  chips)
1 to 2 c. Colby-Monterey
  Jack cheese (or any
  cheese)

Brown ground beef slightly; add diced onion and finish cooking meat. Drain most of grease, but leave a small amount in with the meat. Drain beans and Ro-Tel; add to meat, then add soup. Stir and cook over medium heat until soup has melted and ingredients look smooth. Add torn tortillas or crushed chips plus 1½ cups cheese to mixture and stir to mix. Season with salt, pepper, and chili powder or peppers. Top with crushed chips, then cook in a 375° to 425°F. oven until bubbly, about 20 to 30 minutes. Sprinkle top with remaining cheese and serve.

This is a great one-dish meal.

EASY QUICHE DINNER

Cindy Lou Elmore
Cleveland, GA

2 frozen deep dish pie
   shells
1 sq. pkg. broccoli
   (frozen), chopped
1 c. ham, cubed
1 (12 oz.) pkg. Cheddar
   cheese, shredded

8 (large) eggs
1 c. milk
8 medium potatoes
1 pkg. ready-made dinner
   rolls

Wash potatoes and place on cookie sheet; put in the oven on bottom rack. In a large bowl, mix together thawed broccoli, ham, and cheese. Pour ½ of the mixture in each of the pie shells. Using the same bowl, break the eggs into the bowl and add the milk. Mix vigorously with a wire whisk and pour ½ the egg mixture into each of the pie shells. Put the quiches on a large cookie sheet and place in the oven on the top rack. Bake at 375°F. for 45 minutes. Remove the quiches when done and allow them to stand for a few minutes while you warm up the ready-made dinner rolls.

EVERYTHING PIE

Margaret Goss
Carmen, OK

1 prebaked pie shell
3 egg yolks
¾ c. sugar
¼ tsp. salt
3 Tbsp. cornstarch
2 c. milk

1 lb. butter
1 tsp. vanilla
3 egg whites
¼ tsp. cream of tartar
6 Tbsp. sugar
⅔ tsp. vanilla

In a microwave-safe dish, combine egg yolks, sugar, salt, and cornstarch. Add milk and stir. Cover with waxed paper and microwave on high 4 minutes. Stir mixture. Continue to stir at 30 second intervals until the mixture is thick. Add butter and vanilla. Pour in pie shell. To prepare meringue, in a very clean bowl, beat egg whites and cream of tartar until soft peaks form. Slowly add sugar, one tablespoon at a time. When mixture is shiny, add vanilla and put on cream pie and seal to the edge. Bake at 350°F. until lightly brown. Permit it to cool slowly. Store pie in the refrigerator.

This recipe is used to make most cream pies, and is also used for puddings. For coconut pie, add ½ to ¾ cup coconut. For peanut butter pie, add ½ cup peanut butter. For banana pie, add 2 thinly sliced bananas. For pineapple pie, add 1 small can well drained pineapple.

GROUND BEEF SKILLET

Tammy Bell
Osawatomie, KS

1 lb. ground beef
¼ c. onion, chopped
  (optional)
1 c. cooked macaroni
½ c. ketchup
2 (small) cans tomato
  sauce

1 (small) can mushroom
  pieces, drained
1 Tbsp. Worcestershire
  sauce

Brown ground beef and onion; drain off grease. Add rest of ingredients and stir. Cover and simmer 30 minutes.

This recipe reminds me of goulash but has a zesty flavor.

MAGIC MUFFINS

Charlene Fry
Burlingame, KS

10 eggs
1½ c. milk
½ tsp. salt
½ tsp. dry mustard

6 slices bread (no crust)
6 slices ham
6 slices cheese (American
  or Swiss)

Beat eggs and add milk, salt, and dry mustard. Butter 9x13 inch baking dish generously. Butter bread and place ham and cheese on top. Pour egg mixture over and set overnight. Bake at 350°F. for 30 minutes.

MOUNTAIN MAN FRENCH TOAST

Juanna Beth Lewis
Darlington, ID

1 c. flour
2 tsp. baking powder
½ tsp. salt
1 Tbsp. sugar

1 egg
1½ c. milk
¼ c. cooking oil

Mix all ingredients together. Dip slices of white or wheat bread into batter, coating both sides. Brown in hot oil for 1 to 1½ minutes per side. Serve with warm maple syrup.

My husband says it's his favorite breakfast, along with bacon and eggs.

PAULA'S FAVORITE CHICKEN ENCHILADAS

Paula Ford
Arapaho, OK

1 pkg. flour tortillas
1 pkg. cooked chicken
  breast strips
  (southwestern
  seasoned)
1 can cream of mushroom
  soup
1 pkg. four cheese
  Mexican style cheese

1 (5 oz.) can green chilies,
  chopped
½ c. green onions,
  chopped (reserve some
  for garnish on top)
Sliced ripe olives
  (optional)

Heat together in pan chicken strips, mushroom soup, 1 cup cheese, onions, and green chilies. Divide equally between tortillas. Roll tortillas, placing seam on bottom. Place in greased 9x13 inch pan. Cover with foil and bake at 350°F. for 20 minutes. Uncover the last 5 minutes. Preparation time is 15 minutes.

PEACH COBBLER

Beth Zucker
Bucyrus, OH

1 c. sugar
1 c. self-rising flour
1 c. milk

½ c. butter
1 (large) can peaches

Mix sugar, flour, and milk together until smooth. Melt ½ cup butter in 13x9x2 inch pan. Pour milk mixture into center of pan. Pour 1 large can of sliced peaches and juice into center of milk mixture. Bake at 350°F. for 30 to 35 minutes or until crispy brown on top.

PORK LOIN WITH MUSTARD SAUCE

Pauline Riley
Dodge City, KS

1 c. corn syrup (light or
  dark)
⅓ c. brown sugar

¼ c. brown mustard
Pork loin

In small bowl, combine glaze ingredients above. Slice loin; flour and brown in skillet. Cook till done. Pour glaze over and cook for about 1½ minutes.

QUICK AND EASY CHILI

Sharon Harper
Freedom, OK

2 lb. ground beef
1 (large) onion
2 (8 oz.) cans tomato
  soup
1 (14 oz.) can stewed
  tomatoes

1 (14 oz.) can chili beans
1 packet chili seasoning
  mix
1 can cream of mushroom
  soup
½ soup can water

Brown ground beef and onions, then drain and return to pan. Add the rest of the ingredients and cook on medium heat until heated through.

We prefer chili seasoning mix. Beans may be omitted if you wish and if you prefer thicker chili, the water may be omitted.

QUICK CHOCOLATE PIE

Barb Korth
Randolph, NE

1 (8 or 9 inch) pie crust,
  baked
1 (3 or 4 oz.) pkg.
  chocolate pudding
  (instant)
¼ c. milk

1½ c. vanilla ice cream
1 (8 oz.) container
  whipped topping
Chopped peanuts
  (optional)

Mix pudding and milk together. Add ice cream and mix well. Add 1 cup or so of whipped topping. Pour into baked shell. Refrigerate until serving. Top each slice with whipped topping if desired. Sprinkle with chopped peanuts.

SALAD PIZZA

Ruthe Zimmerman
Tunas, MO

2 pkg. crescent rolls
1 pkg. cream cheese
¾ c. salad dressing
2 c. ham, chopped
2 c. lettuce, chopped
1 c. tomatoes, chopped
4 c. cheese, shredded
1 c. cauliflower
1 c. sour cream
2 Tbsp. Ranch dressing
   mix, powdered (or 1
   pkg.)

1 c. broccoli
1 c. carrots, shredded
2 hard-boiled eggs,
   chopped
½ c. bacon bits
½ c. green pepper,
   chopped

Unroll the crescent rolls and pat onto two pizza pans and bake at 375°F. for 12 minutes. Cool. Beat the cream cheese, then add the salad dressing and also the sour cream. Gradually add the powdered Ranch dressing mix. Now spread this mixture over the cooled crescent roll crust. Layer the chopped meat and veggies in the desired order. Top with cheese, eggs, and bacon bits.

I like to mix the dressing the day or evening before for much better flavor. I came up with this recipe by combining three or four various recipes.

SANTA FE SOUP

Euda Switzer
Oklahoma City, OK

1 lb. ground sirloin
1 (large) onion, diced
1 (15 oz.) can corn,
   undrained
1 (15 oz.) can pinto beans,
   undrained
2 (16 oz.) cans diced
   tomatoes, undrained

1 (4 oz.) can diced green
   chilies
1 lb. Mexican style
   processed American
   cheese

Brown meat with onion; drain any fat. In large pot, combine meat mixture, corn, beans, tomatoes, and chilies. Cube cheese and add to soup, stirring over low heat until melted. Makes 5 servings.

SAUCY BURRITOS

Juanna Beth Lewis
Darlington, ID

2 lb. ground beef
1 (15 oz.) can refried
  beans
1 pkg. taco seasoning mix
1 pkg. flour tortillas
1 (16 oz.) container sour
  cream

1 (10 oz.) can mushroom
  soup
8 oz. Cheddar cheese,
  shredded

Brown ground beef; add beans and taco seasoning. Warm tortillas; put spoonful of filling in center; fold sides in, fold top and bottom, and place in greased 9x13 inch pan, seam side down. Mix together sour cream and mushroom soup and pour over burritos, spreading sauce to edges. Sprinkle shredded cheese over sauce. Bake in 400°F. oven until cheese melts, about 10 minutes.

SAUSAGE BURRITOS

Thelma Baldock
Delphos, KS

1 lb. ground pork sausage
1 (medium) onion,
  chopped
½ green pepper, chopped
1 (small) can mushroom
  stems and pieces,
  drained

8 flour tortillas, warmed
6 eggs, beaten
1 c. Cheddar cheese,
  shredded
Salsa (optional)

Brown sausage; drain, leaving 2 tablespoons drippings. Add pepper, onions, and mushrooms. Saute until tender. Spoon into bowl and set aside. In same pan, scramble egg mix with sausage mixture. Spoon equal amounts in each tortilla. Sprinkle 2 tablespoons shredded cheese on each. Fold tortillas; serve with salsa. Makes 8 servings.

-07

277

SAVE THE DAY SAUSAGE
SKILLET

Delora Clubb
Balko, OK

2 to 3 Tbsp. olive oil
4 c. potatoes, thinly sliced
  with skins
1½ c. onions, sliced thin
2 c. red, yellow, and green
  bell peppers, cut in thin
  strips

1 Tbsp. garlic, chopped
1 (15½ oz.) can whole
  kernel corn
Salt and pepper to taste

In large skillet, fry potatoes in olive oil until brown and crispy. In a second skillet, saute onion, peppers, and garlic until tender. Add sausage and corn and cook an additional 3 to 4 minutes, then add to potatoes and fry another 3 to 4 minutes.

My guys really like this filling meal. I serve it with a garden salad and homemade biscuits.

SLOPPY JOES

Donna J. Walker
Kismet, KS

1 lb. ground beef
¼ tsp. salt
¼ tsp. pepper
3 Tbsp. onion
1 can tomato sauce
1 c. ketchup

1 c. water
1 Tbsp. mustard
6 Tbsp. flour
1 Tbsp. sugar
1 tsp. vinegar

Brown ground beef and onion; drain off fat. Add salt, pepper, tomato sauce, ketchup, water, mustard, flour, sugar, and vinegar; simmer 20 to 30 minutes. Serve on buns.

SPANISH RICE, PANTRY STYLE

Linda M. Bolling
Cowgill, MO

1 (46 oz.) can tomato juice
1 c. uncooked rice
2 cubes beef flavored
   bouillon cubes
1 tsp. garlic powder
1 Tbsp. onion flakes

½ lb. ground beef
   (uncooked)
1 Tbsp. sugar
¼ lb. cheese, grated
   (cook's choice)

Put tomato juice, rice, bouillon, garlic, and onion in a four quart pan. Bring to a slow boil and simmer for 15 or 20 minutes until the rice is tender. While this is cooking, you can cook and drain the ground beef. After the rice is tender, add the ground beef and sugar. Top individual bowls with the grated cheese. Add cornbread, bread, or crackers and your meal is ready in less than 30 minutes.

An alternative is to cook 1½ cups of macaroni in the tomato juice instead of the rice, then add 1 tablespoon of oregano. You have a totally different meal.

SPICY POTATO SOUP

Cynthia Ann Mitchell
Fall River, KS

1½ lb. ground beef
1 clove garlic
4 c. potatoes
3 cans tomato sauce

4 c. water
1½ tsp. black pepper
1 tsp. Tabasco sauce
2 tsp. salt

Brown ground beef in skillet with 1 clove of garlic, peeled and diced. Peel potatoes and cut into bite-size chunks. In a Dutch oven or stockpot, combine all ingredients. Simmer on stove top, medium heat, for about an hour or until potatoes are fork-tender.

This is a wonderful quick meal served with either grilled cheese sandwiches or crackers. I usually have cut up veggies and dip to accompany this quicky and satisfying meal.

STIR-FRY CABBAGE

Juanita Gross
Clear Water, KS

1 (small) head cabbage
1 Tbsp. soy sauce
½ Tbsp. sugar
2 Tbsp. water

½ Tbsp. cornstarch
2 Tbsp. water
1 Tbsp. olive oil

Shred cabbage. Combine soy sauce, sugar, and 2 tablespoons water to form a sauce. Set aside. Combine cornstarch and other two tablespoons water. Set aside. Heat oil in wok over high heat until hazy. Add the cabbage; stir-fry for 2 minutes. Stir in the sauce; continue stir-fry until only ½ the sauce is remaining. Slowly add the cornstarch cooking mixture until it thickens. Yield: 4 servings.

TACO BAKE

Barb Korth
Randolph, NE

4 to 6 (8 inch) flour
   tortillas
1 lb. ground beef,
   browned
½ onion, chopped
Salt and pepper to taste

1 pkg. taco seasoning
3 c. Cheddar cheese,
   shredded and divided
2 c. salsa
1 c. sour cream (optional)

Brown ground beef with onion, salt, and pepper; add taco seasoning. Layer 2 to 3 tortillas in bottom of 9x13 inch greased pan. Put ground beef mixture on top. Sprinkle ½ the cheese on top of mixture; add salsa and sour cream. Put remaining tortillas on top and sprinkle with remaining cheese. Bake 30 minutes in 350°F. oven or until cheese is melted and nicely browned.

I brown ground beef in bulk and freeze in smaller containers. It makes this recipe quicker.

TAQUITO CASSEROLE

Sandra Chrane
Abilene, TX

16 taquitos, slightly
   thawed
1 can cream of mushroom
   soup (undiluted)

1 can green chili enchilada
   sauce
1 can Ro-Tel tomatoes

Mix mushroom soup, green enchilada sauce, and tomatoes. Place ta-quitos in 9x13 inch pan sprayed with cooking spray and cover with mixture. Bake 40 minutes at 325°F.

TAVERN IN A BUN

Neva Jones
O'Neill, NE

1 lb. ground beef
1 (small) onion
½ c. water

½ c. ketchup
1 tsp. mustard
Salt and pepper

Dice onion and saute until light brown; brown ground beef until cooked. Add water, ketchup, mustard, salt, and pepper; bring to a boil. Boil three minutes. Serve on buns. Yield: 4 or 5 servings.

TURKEY, HAM AND CHEESE EGG BAKE

Margaret Trojan
Beaver Crossing, NE

1 (16 oz.) loaf French
   bread, cubed
1 (8 oz.) pkg. cream
   cheese, cubed
1 c. turkey ham or plain
   ham
7 slices turkey bacon or
   plain bacon, crisp
   cooked

1 (4 oz.) can green chilies,
   drained and chopped
1 c. Cheddar cheese,
   shredded
1 c. Monterey Jack
   cheese, shredded
10 eggs
2½ c. milk
1 tsp. mustard

Layer French bread in 13x9x2 inch pan. Layer cream cheese, ham and/ or bacon, shredded cheeses, and chilies. Beat together eggs, milk, and dry mustard. Pour over the layers. Chill for 2 to 24 hours. Bake at 325°F. for 40 to 45 minutes. Let stand for 5 to 8 minutes; cut and serve.

Notes

INDEX OF RECIPES

MAIN DISHES

286

QUICK AND EASY

288

This Cookbook is a perfect gift for Holidays, Weddings, Anniversaries & Birthdays.

To order extra copies as gifts for your friends, please use Order Forms on reverse side of this page.

* * * * * * * * * *

Cookbook Publishers, Inc. has published millions of personalized cookbooks for every kind of organization from every state in the union. We are pleased to have the privilege of publishing this fine cookbook.

ORDER FORM

Use the order forms below for obtaining
additional copies of this cookbook.

Fill in Order Forms Below - Cut Out and Mail

You may order as many copies of our Cookbook as you wish for the regular price, plus $2.00 postage and packing per book ordered. Mail to:

High Plains Publishers, Inc.
P.O. Box 760
Dodge City, KS 67801

Please mail _____ copies of your Cookbook @ $12.95 each, plus $2.00 postage and packing per book ordered.

Mail books to:

Name _____

Address _____

City, State, Zip _____

You may order as many copies of our Cookbook as you wish for the regular price, plus $2.00 postage and packing per book ordered. Mail to:

High Plains Publishers, Inc.
P.O. Box 760
Dodge City, KS 67801

Please mail _____ copies of your Cookbook @ $12.95 each, plus $2.00 postage and packing per book ordered.

Mail books to:

Name _____

Address _____

City, State, Zip _____

944-07

Cook Up A Fundraising Success With Cookbook Publishers, Inc.!

Order your own **FREE** no-obligation Cookbook Instruction Kit today!

FAST: Fill out and mail the postage-paid card below.

FASTER: Fax a copy of your completed postage-paid card to 913-492-5947. *Any time of the day.*

FASTEST: Call our Toll-Free Number **800-227-7282.** *Any time of the day.*

Why is a personalized cookbook the right fundraiser for you?

It's as easy as pie!
You collect the recipes, we do the rest!

Selling personalized cookbooks is a piece of cake!
The professional quality of your cookbook—with the prized recipes from your organization—are sure to make it a best-seller!

It's profitable!
It's the easiest way for your organization to add $500, $1000 or MUCH MORE to its treasury.

The Step-by-Step Kit is FREE!
Call or send for your FREE Step-by-Step Cookbook Instruction Kit today. See for yourself just how easy it is to create your own one-of-a-kind cookbook.

Together we can really make those recipes cook!

1-800-227-7282
www.cookbookpublishers.com

▼ *Drop the card in the mail today!* ▼